The Top Shelf Man

(The Unplugged Alpha Volume 2)

*How The Top 5% Of Men Build Wealth,
Live Life On Their Terms, & Keep
High-Value Women*

Written by
Richard Cooper

Additional Chapters by
Steve From Accounting

Edited by
Steve From Accounting

Copyright © 2025 by *Richard Cooper* and *Steve From Accounting*

All rights reserved. No part of this publication may be reproduced, distributed, or transmitted in any form or by any means, including photocopying, recording, or other electronic or mechanical methods, without the prior written permission of the publisher, except in the case of brief quotations embodied in reviews or critical articles.

The events and conversations in this book have been set down to the best of the authors' ability, although some names and identifying details have been changed to protect the privacy of individuals.

Although the authors and publisher have made every effort to ensure that the information in this book was correct at the time of publication, the authors and publisher disclaim any liability for errors, omissions, or any outcomes related to the application of the contents. This material is provided "as is," without warranties of any kind, express or implied.

No part of this book constitutes professional medical, psychological, legal, or financial advice. Readers should seek qualified professional guidance regarding health, relationships, legal, or financial decisions.

I dedicate this book to all the men around the world that never had a strong, masculine role model growing up to teach them about the cold, hard truth of modern women and the world we live in.

Contents

Introduction 14

Important Terms and Concepts 17

Resource Links Compilation 22

PART ONE

Six Wealth Creation Methods 24

    High Ticket Sales 26

    Licensed Professionals 27

    STEM (Science, Technology, Engineering, Math) 29

    C-Suite Jobs (CEO, CTO, COO, etc.) 31

    Commanding an Audience 31

    Entrepreneurship 33

    The Sad Truth About Most Businesses 34

    The Problem 35

    Not Generating Recurring Revenue 36

    Competing on Price 37

    Employing Too Many People 38

    Being Location Dependent 39

    Not Billing in US Dollars 40

    Selling a Physical Product 40

    Vitamins vs Painkillers 41

    Exchanging Time for Money 42

    Business Idea Generation 43

- Problem Solving 44
- Box, What Box? 46
- Invest in Yourself 47
- You Can't Save Your Way to Wealth 48
- In Conclusion 48
- The Cold, Hard Truth 49

The Four Quadrants 50
- The Plugged-In Beta (70% of Men) 52
- The Plugged-In Alpha (15% of Men) 54
- The Unplugged Beta (10% of Men) 55
- The Unplugged Alpha (Top 5% of Men) 57
- In Conclusion 63
- The Cold, Hard Truth 64

Acceptance and Understanding 65
- Learn to Let Go 66
- Stop Being a Hypocrite 67
- My Approach: Letting Go With Grace 67
- Where Anger Catches Hold of You 68
- Flipping the Script 69
- The Shift 70
- The Payoff: Inner Peace and Magnetism 70
- Ways to Break Free 71
- Why it Matters 72
- Hold Yourself Accountable 72
- In Conclusion 73
- The Cold, Hard Truth 74

The Manoswamp 75

The Obsession With all the Different Colored Pills 77

If it's not Drama, it's "Red Meat" 78

Why I Played in the Sandbox in the First Place 79

Why These Underground Groups Stay Underground 81

Sirens (Women) of the Manoswamp 83

The Manoswamp's Obsession With Notch Counts 86

Posers 87

Advice is a Form of Nostalgia 89

No Honor Among Thieves 90

Pen Names 91

My Golden Rule 92

In Conclusion 93

The Cold, Hard Truth 94

Finding Your Tribe 95

How I Found My Tribe 96

Cautionary Note 97

Fight Gyms 98

Motorsports 98

Libertarians 98

Other Groups 99

What Makes a Man Unplugged? 100

How I Solved My Own Problem 100

In Conclusion 104

The Cold, Hard Truth 105

Becky, Today's Modern Woman 107

The Rise of "Becky" 107

Time Waits for No One 110

Becky Is Delusional 110

The Painful Truth 111

When Becky Settles 111

The Six Sixes 113

Top-Shelf Men 114

Are Women Really "Strong and Independent?" 115

Raising a Daughter to Avoid the Becky Trap 116

In Conclusion 118

The Cold, Hard Truth 119

PART TWO

Green Flags 122

Clarity 123

Emotional Maturity 123

Stability 123

Neuroticism 124

Conscientiousness 124

Agreeableness 124

The Other Green Flags 125

In Conclusion 133

The Cold, Hard Truth 134

His Game, Her Game 136

An Epiphany Moment 137

Pre-Selection 138

It's a Feature, Not a Bug 139

Being "Nice" to Women (and Expecting the Same in Return) 140

People Pleasers: The Kings of the "Covert Contract" 141

The Importance of Building Value 142

Men: The Gatekeepers of Commitment 144

When Women "Settle" 147

Most Women Would Rather Be the King's Mistress, Than the Peasants Wife 148

What's Good for the Goose, Isn't Good for the Gander 150

Women: The Gatekeepers of Sex 153

Their Biological Clock Is Always Ticking 155

In Conclusion 157

The Cold, Hard Truth... 158

The Truth About Long-Term Relationships (LTRs) 159

Don't Be a Nice Guy 160

Anger 162

Caging the Wild Animal 164

Abandoning Sexual Options 165

Jealousy vs Managing Risk 171

The Importance of Having Her Respect 172

Setting Healthy Boundaries 173

Never - Ever - Be Her Second Choice 177

Dealing With Disrespect 179

Trying Too Hard 181

Being Her Number One 181

Betatization by 1,000 Concessions 182

Little Indignities 183

The Importance of Remaining Attractive 184

Overlooking Red Flags 189

Remove (Some) Certainty 191

Be a - Playful - "Asshole" 192

Briffault's Law 193

Don't Be a Beta 194

Apologizing 195

Know When She Is "Checking Out" 195

"Why Do You Still Have a Boat?!" 197

Don't Cry (or Even Complain) to Your Woman 198

In Conclusion 199

The Cold, Hard Truth 200

The Three Ity's: Proximity, Familiarity, and Exclusivity 201

Proximity 202

Familiarity 204

Exclusivity 206

In Conclusion 211

The Cold, Hard Truth 212

Hypergamy, a Puzzle With a Thousand Pieces 213

Short-Term vs Long-Term (and the Overlaps) 214

Hypergamy, Mate Choices, and Age 216

Post-Divorce Return to Party Years 218

Hypergamy and "That Time of the Month" 219

Hypergamy and Birth Control 219

Hypergamy and Fame 220

In Conclusion 223

The Cold, Hard Truth 224

How Marriage can be the Sweet Spot for the Average Man 225

Here Are Some of the Top Responses 226

Shared Beliefs 229

Submissive and Traditional Wife 229

Lack of Prior Promiscuity 230

(Dis)Respect 231

Zero Tolerance for Bad Behavior 232

Stays Fit and Feminine 233

Stuck Through Thick and Thin 234

Alternatives to Tying the Knot 234

In Conclusion 236

The Cold, Hard Truth.. 238

PART THREE

Steve's "How To" Guides Preface 242

How to: Leverage Generative AI in Both Life and Business 244

Cut Through the AI Noise... 245

Trust, But Verify 246

Context Is King 247

How to Actually Use AI in Your Daily Life.. 249

GPTs as Permanent Prompts.. 251

Straightforward AI for Your Business 251

Security and Privacy 252

Automate Your Workflow 254

Scripts Over Models for Data Consistency 255

Resource Management (Cost & Scalability) 256

Maintenance and Long-Term Sustainability 256

Version Control (Practical Reality Check) 256

Ethical Considerations 257

Elevate Your Marketing Game 257

Make Smarter Decisions 258

Practical Examples.. 258

Online vs Offline AI Models (the Pros/Cons)...................................... 259

Advanced Use-Cases: The Hybrid Approach 261

Advanced Use-Cases: Fine-Tuning and RAG 261
Lessons From Building My Own AI-Powered CMS 261
The AI Models Starter Kit 262
In Conclusion 263
The Cold, Hard Truth: 264

How To: Document Your Divorce Like a Pro 265

Cautionary Note for All UK-Based Brothers 266
Why Metadata is Your Secret Weapon 268
Scan and Stitch Docs Like a Boss 269
Capturing Emails, Texts, and Audio 269
Leverage Cloud Services for Backup and Sharing 270
The "How to Use.txt" Efficiency Hack 271
Organize With Naming Conventions and Chronology 272
Pick Your Battles: High-Value Proof That Wins the War 273
Leveraging the Power of AI 274
In Conclusion 274
Cautions and Nuances for Documenting Your Divorce 275
The Cold, Hard Truth 276

How to Deal With a High-Conflict Ex-Wife 277

Welcome to AI - The Ultimate BS Handling Tool 279
Fine Tuning Your Responses - The "Yellow Rock" Approach 282
Pick Your Hills to Die On 284
Don't Let AI Become a Crutch 285
AI Doesn't Replace Self-Control 285
Real-Life Prompts You Can Use 285
Quick Reality Check (Legal Disclaimer) 286
What to Expect 287
In Conclusion 287

The Cold, Hard Truth: 288

How To: Navigate Your Life With Nuance **289**

    Eliminating "Black and White" Thinking 290

    Learning to Read the Room 292

    Learning to Sub-Communicate Better 294

    Managing Non-Exclusive Relationships 296

    In Conclusion 301

    The Cold, Hard Truth 302

Acknowledgements **303**

Introduction

Well, here we are, volume 2, and the follow up to my best seller "The Unplugged Alpha."

First of all, I need to thank you for buying the first book, and express gratitude to all of you that left reviews on Amazon letting other men know what value you got from The Unplugged Alpha.

I've read every one of your reviews, and I'm eternally grateful for the overwhelmingly positive feedback that book had on your lives. I've also entertained all constructive feedback, and done my best to incorporate that into this book, to make it as useful as possible.

I love seeing you putting it into practice and living better lives as a result of it. However, a lot has changed since I released the first edition of The Unplugged Alpha in 2020.

I originally started writing it when I was very active in the manosphere years earlier while trying to amplify the voices in that space, but more on that later in the "Manoswamp" chapter.

Today I still love creating content, but I really enjoy speaking to other podcasters, and being interviewed on the topics I cover, regardless of whether we are in agreement or not.

I've also become more selective with who I will work with or amplify; my dad always taught me that if you want to soar like an Eagle, you can't surround yourself with Turkeys so I've walked away from those people.

Since I started uploading to YouTube, and all the various video platforms, I've amassed over 1 billion video views which has secured a strong, and authoritative position on the controversial solutions to problems men and women face in today's modern world. It's an absolute honor to have the attention of so many people, fans or haters alike.

While my message is organically getting out, the forces that try to control the narrative overall are still pushing back harder than ever. It's clear that "they" don't want you to know the truth, and "they" want you plugged into the comforting lies, and unaware of the cold hard truth.

My hope for this book is that it brings a lot more clarity, helps you manage your relationships better over the long-term, shows you different ways to generate more life-changing wealth, and it ties together more of the concepts and ideas I discussed in my first volume while bringing you many new insights that matter.

Personally, I have learned more about life and especially relationships since writing The Unplugged Alpha, than I had known when I wrote the original book.

This volume will take you much deeper down the rabbit hole, and while you may not like everything I have to say, I promise you that if you sit with it, you will find a goldmine of value in every chapter in this book.

The first book was more of a summary of introductory concepts men should unplug on, while this book is more advanced, and talks more about management over the longer term, especially with your relationships with the opposite sex.

As you read this book, you will notice some concepts are repeated throughout the chapters, but tackled from slightly different angles as it applies to each chapter. This is done intentionally.

I believe it's similar to putting a nice car in a setting, and then taking pictures of it from different angles so you can understand its proportions better and how each angle frames it.

As the title of the book "Life on the Top Shelf" suggests, many of the concepts I share with you are there to demonstrate how to beat out your competition, enjoy the most personal freedom, have the best relationships with women all while reducing risks.

The two main keys to enjoying life on The Top Shelf for the unplugged, is to optimize both your attractiveness and your overall value on the sexual marketplace. Much of what I discuss in this book won't work for the plugged-in, or those who are simply unwilling to go do the work to level-up their life enough to enjoy it on the top shelf.

You can read this volume without reading the first book, but I am certain that you will get much more out of this book by starting with the first one.

It has been a labor of love for me and finalizes just about everything I could think of, that I wish I knew as a young man in my twenties. I know you will enjoy this book, so keep printed copies so you can hand it out to friends, family or any man that could use a dose of the cold hard truth about life. As always, if you enjoy this book, be sure to leave a written review on Amazon letting men know what value you derived from it to help spread the word and encourage more brothers to turn their lives around.

Peace,
Richard Cooper

Important Terms and Concepts

The Matrix

The Matrix is the pervasive, often invisible web of societal narratives, institutions, and systems designed to keep men docile, compliant, and disconnected from their true potential. It's the collective lie that prioritizes comfort and conformity over truth and self-actualization.

This includes healthcare systems that profit from treating symptoms rather than promoting genuine fitness, restrictive regulations that stifle entrepreneurial spirit, an education system that churns out obedient workers instead of critical thinkers, and the soul-crushing 9-5 corporate grind that trades time for money while eroding personal freedom.

The Matrix feeds men a steady diet of distractions: mainstream media, consumerism, and false promises of security to keep them plugged into a system that benefits from their submission, not their strength. Unplugging means seeing these structures for what they are and choosing to forge your own path, no matter how uncomfortable the truth.

Oneitis

An unhealthy attachment to one woman where a man desperately pines for her love, attention, and intimacy. The woman in question often couldn't care less about his existence. Men who get "oneitis" often subscribe to the notion of her being his "one true love," only to see her move on to another man. All while he suffers and sulks in misery hoping she will, one day, return.

Spinning Plates

This is a term used to describe simultaneously dating multiple women in a non-monogamous fashion (aka: casual dating). It's a tactic that's often used by men who are disinterested in a conventional monogamous relationship. Or, by someone who knows he is prone to developing "oneitis," or likes vetting women for an LTR/wife by providing contrast - allowing the cream to rise to the top

It's important to note that you never overtly state you are spinning plates. You just do it, and let your actions signal, by the lack of your availability, that you are spinning plates.

Women are, unknowingly by nature, master plate spinners, and often date multiple men at once. Unless, of course, they feel that they've found their best hypergamous option.

Sexual Marketplace Value (or, SMV)

An individual's own value on the sexual marketplace. For example, your physique, style, game, frame, confidence levels, etc. all have a "value" to women. The more you chase excellence, the higher your SMV naturally becomes as you optimize every area of your life.

The Wall

There comes a time in a woman's life when she can no longer really compete on the sexual marketplace with younger, more virile women, and they have therefore "hit the wall" (metaphorically speaking). Women are beauty objects to men and her SMV peak is around 23 years old. After that, she is steadily on the decline.

While you'll never openly hear a woman admitting to the existence of "the wall," if you ever hear 30+ divorced women talk between each other, they'll talk about giving their "best years" and often ask their friends "who wants a 30 year old with two kids in tow?" Like it - or not - they know that their prime asset is on a very steady decline.

Women can accelerate this process of hitting the wall with bad lifestyle habits like smoking, drinking, drugs, or by becoming a single mother. Conversely, a woman can also slightly push back hitting the wall by mastering self-care. Either way, a hot 23 year old will *always* be more attractive to high value men than a relatively hot 43 year old (as the latter now has a lower SMV).

Men also hit the wall, but a man's decline doesn't begin until he's in his mid-late thirties (or much later if he's doing the work to be a top-shelf man). For more, search: "What is (SMV) Sexual Marketplace Value & The Wall" on my YouTube channel.

Soft Next

A "soft next" is where you completely cut contact with a girl for a few days immediately after she displays any really bad behavior (may be longer, depending on how often you see her, or how bad the behavior was). You do not respond to her texts, calls, or attempts to see you. It's essentially short-term ghosting.

The soft next works because it anchors negative consequences/emotions to bad behavior. For women, attention is the coin of the realm, and removing your attention powerfully resets your frame as the dominant frame in the relationship.

However, it's *critical* that, at the end of the soft next, you simply continue the relationship normal and act as if nothing had ever happened. If she took the hint that you're more than prepared to hold your boundaries firm, she'll be more than happy to meet up with you again.

A Shit Test

Also known as a "competency test," women often test men to see if they really are their best option due to their hypergamous nature. It can be in the form of a question, or a behavior that she exhibits to test the frame of the relationship, and she watches closely as to how he responds.

An example of a shit test might be: "Hold my purse for me." But, what she's *really* testing you for, is to see if you are a good little compliant beta male that will do as he's told, and stand there holding her purse like an obedient little puppy.

A simple "No, I don't carry female accessories" with a slight sneer would suffice. Hypergamy means that women will always shit test men (whether that's consciously or subconsciously), but the frequency and severity of the tests will reduce to almost zero when she is fully in your frame.

Hypergamy

Women's primary sexual strategy for millions of years has been to form a sexual relationship with a superior man on the socio-economic scale. It's often said that hypergamy doesn't seek its own level. Rather, hypergamy always seeks better than itself.

This is an evolved survival technique for her and her children to always find the best male she can secure for provisioning and protection. When a woman leaves a man, for another that she deems to be of higher value, it's because of hypergamy (also sometimes referred to as "monkey branching" because they won't let go of their current "branch" (i.e. man) until they have a secure hold on the next "branch"/man).

Many men are furious at women for being hypergamous. However, there's no value in being angry at a woman for wanting the best she believes, rightly or wrongly, that she can get. Understand hypergamy and make it work *for* you. To dive deeper into hypergamy, search for: "what is hypergamy" on my YouTube channel.

Resource Links Compilation

The following QR code/web address will take you to a page with links to all of the studies, recommended books, courses, and videos that I reference throughout this book.

▶ **More Resources found at https://theunpluggedalpha.com/bookresources**

Scan Me →

▶ https://theunpluggedalpha.com/bookresources

Part One

Money, The Modern Woman & Your Place in it All

1

Six Wealth Creation Methods

When it comes to money, the sooner you understand what creates life-changing wealth and implement it into your life, the sooner you will become wealthy. Doing this at 20 is better than doing these things at 50, but there is no better time to start building wealth than today.

However, before I highlight the way most multi-millionaires have created their wealth, I need to spend some time explaining what **not** to do.

There's a lot of garbage peddled online today to young men encouraging them to become entrepreneurs by buying courses, programs, and monthly memberships to something that will teach you to go from "zero to hero" in no time for only $50 per month. Most of these are absolute garbage.

I have seen promises of generating $10k per month within 60 days by getting into programs and courses around affiliate marketing, copywriting, thumbnail designing, video editing, e-commerce, content editing, freelancing etc. all with only a laptop, or cell phone, and from the comfort of a warm beach chair in Thailand.

My inbox is always flooded with emails from young men from around the world, offering to write my emails (aka: copywriting), edit my short form video content (aka: content editing), or perform all kinds of freelancing tasks for me.

Most of these people have almost no personal experience and are just hoping to get rich quick off of me, and others hold out that they're experts in the field of performing these services, when, in actual fact, they have accomplished absolutely nothing of meaning themselves.

With content editing, there is now an oversupply of these contractors in the market (made even worse with the advancement of automated AI tools), which has significantly driven down the cost of many services that I do hire out for. Currently, I can get high-quality shorts edited from my long-form podcast content for less than 25% of what I was paying only 5-years ago.

E-commerce is also saturated (e.g. dropshipping), and unless you are bringing huge innovation to the space, it's a *very* difficult market to compete in. Amazon is virtually a monopoly today and, if you read "The Everything Store" by Brad Stone (which is basically a Jeff Bezos biography), you will understand why.

But you may well make a thousand or two a month, on some obscure product, in a niche that usually performs for a few months, but then fizzles out. Then, on top of that risk, you also have to deal with shipping stock to warehouses (which is a *nightmare* if it has to be shipped between countries/continents), returns, product procurement, lost shipments, damaged products, and the list goes on, and on.

I've had far too many private consultations with aspiring entrepreneurs that are building a business that they hate, that's difficult to manage, and is very annoying to scale efficiently.

These hustles, as they are being sold, are just that - a hustle. You *might* make *some* money, but the truth is, they're hard, annoying, lame, and frustrating businesses to create. I go deeper into entrepreneurship later on in this chapter (and how to actually make it work for you).

But first, let's examine the six main and proven wealth creation methods to make life-changing money, and at the end of each section, I will also explain the cons to choosing that path (because no path is simple and they're all fraught with their own unique challenges).

High Ticket Sales

Sales jobs pay a percentage of the product sold. When I was a teenager, I loved rock and heavy metal music, and I worked in a high-end stereo store selling and installing equipment like amplifiers, speakers, home theaters, etc. I was paid a percentage of the sales I made, and it often amounted to around one hundred dollars a month (if I was lucky), and I sold tens of thousands of dollars a month for them.

If you are going to sell anything, and earn a percentage of the sale, then make sure you sell expensive things like mansions, jets, luxury automobiles, or yachts. The commissions on these high-ticket products can amount to hundreds of thousands of dollars to millions a month.

I personally know a real estate agent that has developed a reputation for only selling luxury estates over $5m and he makes about $3M a year on commissions. It's a *lot* of work, and he is constantly networking looking for sellers and buyers, but he loves what he does, and has built a large supporting team around him.

Cons

The money is good, but the downside to being in this line of work is that you're usually working all the time. Your client will be wealthy, and if he wants to see a house at 8pm on a Friday night, you will need to make it happen. They say "jump", you say "how high." It doesn't matter what your plans are, or if you have a hot date.

You will also need to be VERY good at networking, attending events, gifting clients, befriending them, and asking for referrals to keep a steady flow of customers coming in. People usually don't buy a new house or luxury car every year, so this isn't very likely to create any dependable recurring revenue for you, and you are basically eating what you kill.

People in this profession are the equivalent of hunters, they snipe what they are after, feast on it, and then go back out and do it all over again.

Sowing seeds in increments, and then harvesting regular crops, is one of the reasons why humans switched from nomadic hunter-gatherers into agriculture 10,000+ years ago.

But, if you do it long enough, and build up a solid and dependable team, you'll be able to sell that book of business to a senior member in your team, or to someone else, and one day down the road, you'll be able to draw some passive income off of it.

Licensed Professionals

Acquiring a professional designation in law, accounting, medicine, finance, becoming a pilot, etc. is a longer, and slower road to wealth, but it *is* a path that has created millionaires. The time required in school, then in college with the specialized degree can be *immense*. For example, becoming a doctor (especially where you specialize in one area, such as a brain surgeon) can take anything up to 12-years in total - between medical school classes and gaining experience in different hospitals as a junior doctor. That's a *lot* of time and work.

However, the jobs pay very well. I have a good friend that is a partner in a personal injury law firm, and he makes well over $3M a year. Many licensed professionals can operate in private practices alongside other roles (something many specialist doctors do in the UK for example), and the additional income from the private work often greatly outshines their main income.

Many cultures today strongly encourage these paths for their children because the jobs are secure, are prestigious, and pay very well into six figures. The bragging rights to being a lawyer are real. When women are surveyed on dating applications and are asked what careers are the most attractive, entrepreneurs, doctors, and pilots were near the top, but lawyers (especially a partner in a law firm), were right at the very top. Whether that's the best position to hold is debatable, but - as we all know - women want what they want.

Cons

The downside is you are often overworked and you become a tool of society and the state. Overworked professionals, especially early in the game, are the standard, *not the exception*. Back in my 30s, when I was dating my fiancée - who was a lawyer at the time - it wasn't unusual for my phone to buzz around 11 p.m. on a random Tuesday. I'd be winding down for bed, and there she'd be, calling about her day while scarfing down dinner in 15 minutes flat, all before hunkering down for an all-nighter at the office hammering out some high-stakes agreement for a massive finance corporation.

It's not a question whether being a licensed professional will take a toll on your health - it's just to what degree.

Every licensed professional has a governing body that can limit choices, and state regulators behind governing bodies forcing you to comply with a strict code of conduct that changes over time, and usually not to your favor or to make your job easier. The standards are high, but lately - like most public-facing organizations - they're starting to lean into wokeness and force their licensed pros to jump through hoops in the name of progression.

Also, there were many licensed professionals during the recent COVID scamdemic that were forced to take experimental vaccinations, that later on proved to be neither safe, nor effective - just to keep their careers.

Over the years we've also seen companies and governing bodies slowly begin to compel professionals to use pronouns. It usually starts by a prerequisite of putting them in your email signature, and it eventually leads to more adoption of logic-defying Diversity, Equity, and Inclusivity (DEI) standards. Unfortunately, this insistence on hiring based on DEI quotas (rather than seeing who's actually the most competent at the job in question), ironically often discriminates against the best candidate for the role, so they can offer it to someone who may not even be remotely competent at the job.

This trend may prove to reverse in the future, but it should be something to consider. At the very least, you must understand that you'll be expected to align with their opinions and worldviews - irrespective of what your *true* values and beliefs actually are.

STEM (Science, Technology, Engineering, Math)

Professional degrees in this area are what propel society forward, and advance humanity. Without STEM we wouldn't have rockets, cars, computers, AI, or smartphones. They are noble roles, and they often pay well.

I know several men that work for tech companies that make $800k+/yr. While senior roles compensate well into the millions. Like the other professionals mentioned in this chapter, you will need *years* of schooling, and for many that will come with the burden of a significant amount of student debt.

Cons

On the flip side, the nature of the work – endless hours glued to screens – means a lot of these guys aren't the most masculine out there, or tuned in to what *really* draws women in and keeps them hooked. Truth is, STEM fields often attract a higher percentage of folks on the spectrum, like autism or ADHD, and that can make them prime targets for women looking to manipulate and fleece an easy mark.

STEM roles attract some of the brightest people I know, but for some reason, the *vast* majority of private consults I've had with men on navigating divorce were from STEM roles, and while they are absolute *weapons* in their profession of choice, as well as being good men (all while putting a dent in the universe), they very often struggle with the basics around women.

Also, as stated earlier in the licensed professional section, the organizations that run most of these big tech companies are *considerably* more woke than in any other industry. Take a look at the FAANG group of tech companies (Facebook, Apple, Amazon, Netflix, and Google) and pay close attention to how they are holding themselves out to the public. Many of these companies have been proven to be interfering in elections, and when you look at the campaign donations, the *vast* majority of them seem to donate to the Democrat party and seem to strongly support DEI initiatives and the woke agenda.

Another issue is that they tend to only promote people twice a year (two cycles, via mid-year and end-of-year reviews), and you're promoted into the next pay band which of course has an upper limit. So, it is *incredibly* time consuming to climb and the reward is capped at each level (where you'll find your pay rises slowing down at the upper-end of each band).

Additionally, it's very common to be rejected the first time you go for promotion, so you're operating near the next level for around a year while being paid at the lower rate.

Finally, the real income that puts you above most other jobs *isn't* the base salary, it's in the equity grants (usually spread out over four years with a set amount vesting (i.e. becomes yours) every pay cycle). This can be good because the grant can appreciate by the time it vests, or you can leave for another job if you don't believe the stock will appreciate/stay level. The problem with most seasoned tech companies is that the stock is mature and has already seen tremendous growth, so it's unlikely to have incredible jumps at this stage.

Compare this to a company that can have hyper-growth, like Nvidia, which has recently had *astronomical* gains (in the 10's of thousands of percents over the last few years), so anyone that has yearly share grant in such a company is - more than likely - a multimillionaire.

The big downside however, is that you have less agency and lower ceiling than starting your own business, and - when it comes time for "restructuring" - then the higher cost-areas tend to go first, even more so in 2025, where most of the FAANG companies just made a huge round of redundancies (and this will become far more prominent over time as more and more companies user better, and better AI models for doing work).

Don't get me wrong, they are important, and are often great jobs, but they **do** come with some cons that you need to be conscious of.

C-Suite Jobs (CEO, CTO, COO, etc.)

These jobs are rare, usually very prestigious, and they can pay *exceptionally* well when you land them, but landing one often requires an intersection where luck, opportunity, and preparation all meet together at the same time.

You need to be a master at networking, well spoken, experienced in your realm of specialty and in life, know how to attract/retain top talent, and - most importantly - be a leader that knows how to get the job done (while also being able to get out of the way of good people who are performing critical tasks for you).

I know several C-suite guys out there that run multimillion dollar companies and, while they encompass all of the above, they also tend to be manic/anxiety-riddled, ADD, and sometimes even bipolar.

Cons

It will take a decade or two of commitment to your craft, kissing *plenty* of ass along the way, climbing the corporate ladder, moving to where opportunities lie halfway around the country, and learning how to navigate and add value to the right people at the right time to land one of these roles.

But, if you can stick with it, and find the right company, compensation well into seven, or even eight, figures is not uncommon with larger corporations. However, what *is* uncommon is the number of available roles to fill. **C-suite jobs are few and far between** and thankfully, despite all those DEI initiatives, these roles still only seem to go to the most qualified.

Commanding an Audience

If you can grab and hold the attention of a massive crowd, you're setting yourself up to build serious wealth and influence. Take pro athletes: They're so damn captivating that their fans go all-in, dropping loads of money on overpriced gear, painting their faces in wild colors, shelling out fortunes for tickets and merch, and yeah, even slapping a jersey with another dude's name on their wife's or girlfriend's back.

Actors, musicians, and media influencers pull the same - or bigger - crowds. Dwayne "The Rock" Johnson launches his tequila brand and, thanks to his massive pull, he's moving *millions* of bottles every year. For example, I know someone that paid $7,500 for two Taylor Swift tickets recently in Toronto.

And before you roll your eyes at social media stars, remember this: MrBeast got hit with offers of over $1 billion for his empire - and he straight-up turned them down. Bottom line: If you can master commanding a huge audience, and monetize it smartly, you'll stack wealth like it's nothing.

Cons

It seems apparent that nearly all of the biggest athletes, actors, musicians, and other influencers are controlled by a "handler" of some sort. It's almost like there are strict conditions on what they can and can't say or even do. When Black Lives Matter (BLM) was a strong movement, we saw *far* too many athletes that didn't have a dog in the fight, being forced by their handlers into taking the knee during the national anthem. Only a handful spoke out and they were often dealt with harshly as a result.

Football players (on both sides of the Atlantic) are absolute icons of cardiovascular health, but the rates at which they started dropping dead on the football pitch not long after their mandatory vaccinations after the recent COVID scamdemic, was astounding versus prior years. Even today, if you Google search for the data on this, the entire first page are results Google pushes to the top from MSM or universities claiming this narrative is "misinformation."

However, if you do the same search on a free speech platform for compilation videos of football players collapsing after the COVID-19 vaccine, there's - sadly - plenty to see, and it's very clear that this didn't happen in prior years.

Make no mistake, the vast majority of mainstream influencers that command an audience will be required to comply with their handlers, because if they *don't*, they often find the response to be harsh, and swift.

Look at what happened to Andrew Tate for example, he became a **huge** influence on young men and he had a loud and opposing voice to the mainstream narrative, and he *clearly* didn't respond to any handlers, so they deplatformed him *worldwide* in a very coordinated effort over a 24-hour period in an attempt to steal his voice. When that didn't work, they put him in jail, then under house arrest, had millions of dollars worth of his assets seized, and he was constantly accused in the mainstream media of being a human trafficker, a rapist, and more.

Finally, if you happen to go viral in this space in a very short space of time (which usually means you don't build up a dedicated base of evangelists who genuinely love your message and your personality), then you can - just as quickly - fall out of fashion and be another flash in the pan.

Entrepreneurship

A business is just an organization that solves a valuable problem for another business, or the consumer.

Starting and running your own business is - IMO - probably still one of the most rewarding things you can do today. **When done properly**, it often comes with true wealth, influence, captivation, maneuverability, and more autonomy *than any other option above*. Just look at what Elon Musk has done for himself. Also, because you are the captain of your own ship, there will be no mandate from above telling you to celebrate rainbows, declare your pronouns in your email signature, or even lock down your business and force people to take experimental vaccinations just to keep your job.

You are, if structured correctly (more on that later in this chapter), in charge and captain of your own ship. If you set up your business properly from the beginning and if you can also orchestrate it so that you can maneuver and run the business from any country in the world, (with low or no staff), and you're selling valued information or a digital service (such as Software as a Service, or SaaS), then you can make it Easy, Lucrative, and Fun (which is referred to as an ELF business - one of the best kinds to have). A big shout out to *Joe Polish* for that one.

In the next segment, I'll explain what differentiates a good business from a bad one (so you have an idea of the cons to entrepreneurship, because there are some), but first, I want to explain the perspective that you should **never let school get in the way of your education.**

Going to school and getting an education *aren't the same thing*, you can go to school, and not receive much of a useful education. Conversely, you can skip school, and still receive a valuable education by way of life experience.

However, make no mistake, If you are pursuing a career as a licensed professional, or in STEM, you **will** need that degree.

The point is, you should never let school interrupt your life education. I know *plenty* of people with useless degrees working dead-end jobs, and burdened with loads of student debt, because they did what they were told by family and society, "it's what you do." Likewise, I also know *plenty* of dropouts that never did *anything* with their life either.

It's about holding the man in the mirror to account and doing the work. At the end of the day, if you put your mind to a task, the relentless will find a way to make it happen; the lazy will find an excuse for why it didn't happen.

You can have results, or excuses, but not both.

There was a season of the popular TV show "The Apprentice" where they put university educated men and women up against high school dropouts, and Donald Trump, who was the main character in the show, pointed out that the dropouts often made three times more than the university educated. Food for thought.

The Sad Truth About Most Businesses

Over my lifetime, I've consumed years' worth of podcasts and books on the topic of entrepreneurship and marketing. It's fairly common knowledge that about 50% of new businesses fail after five years, but that's not the statistic that should trouble you; the *real* issue is only about 5% of businesses ever make more than $1 million dollars a year in sales revenue.

What's the point of running your own company if you don't make life changing money?

These businesses missing the $1m/yr threshold are often in pressure washing, driveway sealing, phone flipping, lawn maintenance, dry cleaning, dog walkers, doing handyman work, running a local restaurant, chimney sweepers, running a breakfast diner, etc.

So that means 95% of entrepreneurs have taken on the constant burden of entrepreneurship, essentially to end up just employing themselves, and have a business card that says "CEO" on it. The worst part is these small business entrepreneurs are only paying themselves an average of $68,000 a year.

Sure, you may write off some meals and entertainment, and perhaps a vehicle, but that goes to show you that the vast majority of the sales receipts are going to operational expenses. Factor in the increased risk exposure to lawsuits as an entrepreneur, and the fact that most entrepreneurs in this space are also the cleaning crew, handyman, mover, and IT guy, and you can see it's a relatively unwise and unrewarding way to make money or create freedom.

You'd be better off as an employee with a job that pays $100k, taking your 2 weeks' vacation, statutory holidays, and benefits, without any of the concerns whatsoever of a typical entrepreneur.

The Problem

Most entrepreneurs don't engineer a *good* business, they just create a business.

It's usually one that is annoying, difficult, frustrating, and never has the opportunity to make $1M in sales receipts or more annually because it's built on a terrible foundation.

This $1M/yr mark is extremely important and often overlooked. If you are going to take on the risk of building a business, it's literally the same amount of effort to build a sub $1M/yr business as it is to build one that can scale beyond that.

Beyond that, most business owners either get tired or bored of a business, and they want to exit it at a certain point in time. A driveway sealing business that made $637,462 last year isn't attractive to a prospective buyer, unlike a software business that has 4,428 users paying $97/m which means recurring revenue of $5,154,192 annually.

You are thinking anyway, so why not think bigger?

The biggest mistakes entrepreneurs make are:

1. Not generating recurring revenue,
2. Competing on price,
3. Employing too many people,
4. Being location dependent,
5. Not billing in US dollars,
6. Selling a physical product,
7. Selling a vitamin instead of a painkiller,
8. They still exchange time for money.

Let's take a closer look at each one:

Not Generating Recurring Revenue

At the time of writing this, Netflix has a market cap of $375 billion because it charges so many people a flat monthly fee for its streaming service. You can see how this is scalable, and therefore also attractive to buyers.

When you have a book of recurring business (that is customer's credit cards on file that you bill monthly), you have something of longer-term value. Whether it's a membership, or a subscription, you now have regular income from your customer base.

However, not all businesses that offer subscriptions make money. For example, most gyms charge their members monthly, but barely break even (due to high operational costs). So, you need to do your research. Alex Hormozi made *far* more money selling services and information products to gym owners, than running his own gym. Look him up if you are unfamiliar with his story (his books are great by the way, definitely worth checking them out).

Ideally, you want to apply this model to a business that offers information, software, and sometimes a service, but it's generally a better idea to stay away from physical products, (I'll explain why that is shortly).

Netflix houses data (digital movies) on a server, and then streams that content to multiple customers simultaneously. There are very few moving parts, nothing to return in the mail or get lost (which is how they *used* to operate as a company) - it's just data moving across the internet, and entertaining people monthly, in return for a set monthly subscription fee.

Your typical window cleaning business does not generate recurring revenue. They pay for marketing, booking a customer, and going out to wash their customer's windows once a year, at best. This is not ideal from a recurring revenue perspective.

So, when engineering a business, it's ideal to put time and effort into a business that creates recurring revenue. Potential buyers down the line *love* a business with recurring revenue on the books as it signals steady cashflow. Potential buyers will also pay a higher premium for companies with a proven history of recurring monthly sales receipts.

Competing on Price

Let's get this straight - dropping your prices to compete is a straight-up loser's play, nothing but a desperate race to the bottom. You should *never* build a business designed around undercutting everyone else on cost alone.

Like I mentioned earlier in this chapter, back when I was a teen hustling at that electronics spot called "Stereo Den," the margins were razor-thin - sometimes scraping by on just $15-20 bucks from a $1,000 sale. Brutal doesn't even cover it. Customers would stroll in, zero-in on what they wanted, jot down the model number, haggle for a deal, get our quote, then bolt out the door. Five minutes later, they'd be pulling the same stunt at the next shop down the road.

Somebody eventually closed the sale, sure, but nobody was stacking real cash.

Do not compete on price!

Focus on creating your edge elsewhere - things like superior value, rock-solid warranties, and top-tier customer service. These are the *real* hooks that pull in customers who actually give a damn, way more than pinching pennies ever will. There's a killer book on this called *"Creating Competitive Advantage: Give Customers a Reason to Choose You Over Your Competitors"* by *Jaynie L. Smith* - every entrepreneur worth his salt should dig into it.

On top of that, customers have this built-in habit of convincing themselves that pricier options are just better quality - call it post-purchase rationalization. And if your product or service *truly* outshines the competition? Charging more actually highlights that superiority. When the reviews and feedback back you up, word spreads, and more folks line up to see what the hype's about.

Employing Too Many People

Employees have become increasingly expensive, ineffective, burdensome, disloyal, unappreciative, and inefficient. If you start a business, it's IDEAL to build one *that needs as few employees as possible*.

Paul Jarvis wrote a great book titled: *"Company of One: Why Staying Small Is the Next Big Thing for Business."* I **strongly** recommend reading it and considering whether or not you really need employees, and if you can replace them with automation (such as AI), contractors, or just not performing the task at all.

When you limit your payroll, you limit many of the cons associated with hiring employees. Theft, HR conflicts, office romances, feelings, sick days, poachers stealing your staff, re-training, wrongful dismissal lawsuits, employee error, employee incompetence, employee espionage, etc. The list of potential problems that you can avoid go on, and on.

I've hired and fired *hundreds* of people, and I've also offered some of the best compensation packages and retention plans in my industry, and I've also implemented a world-class culture that received industry awards. And, I can tell you from extensive personal experience, that I definitely prefer to run my business today as a company of one.

We live in a digital world where most tasks can either be automated (especially with the rise of AI), outsourced (Fiverr or Upwork for example), or just simply engineered out of the business model, and it's possible to create a business without having many, if any, payroll obligations.

Being Location Dependent

The vast majority of businesses are dependent on the location in which they operate. The problem with that though, is that you cannot maneuver out of a hostile business environment when it comes your way.

It's not a question of "if," it's more of a "when." Restaurants, gyms, dry cleaners, day care, auto mechanics, and every brick-and-mortar store rely solely on their location for their business.

With the advent of the internet, mobile devices and the global marketplace, you can now start a business that can be run from *anywhere* in the world.

For example, when the recent COVID scamdemic hit Canada, within 12-months of lockdown, all of my friends with a location independent business took their business and moved out of Canada to a less restrictive business environment. They all ended up enjoying *far* more personal freedom again and, in many cases, *much* lower taxes.

A region may look appealing today, and for years to come, but nothing is permanent, and having the ability to quickly and easily pack up your laptop and belongings and then run your business from anywhere else there is power and an internet connection is a *very* powerful position to be in. Legislative changes, political, tax, the next "scamdemic," and environmental changes that swing outside of your favor, are all reasonable reasons to pack up your bags and go to where you, your business, and customers will be treated better.

But, you'll never have the option to maneuver if you create a business that anchors you down to a specific location.

Not Billing in US Dollars

Today the US dollar is currently strong, and it's widely regarded as a reserve currency (although, that may change in the future). When I set up my content creation business, I made the decision to invoice only in USD, and it proved to be a wise choice, even though I live in Canada.

It's a more stable way to do business, bank, collect revenue, and pay service providers.

Canada has a population of just over 40M, the United States has 335M. So I knew that the US was going to be my target market. If you live outside of America, but half (or more) of your customers are Americans, invoice them in USD.

Finally, if you're based outside of the US (but receive any funds in USD), then it may be worth looking at either opening up an international business account that you can make USD deposits/withdrawals from directly, or find an account with near-perfect exchange rates into your national currency. This minimizes your risk to any sharp fluctuations in exchange rates.

Selling a Physical Product

Of all the headaches I see entrepreneurs take on, this is the one I get the most arguments on. It's usually some version of "well Jeff Bezos made billions moving physical products."

Yes, he did. But again, if you read *"The everything store: Jeff Bezos and the age of Amazon"* by *Brad Stone*, you will quickly realize the sheer volume of issues he faced, how unprofitable it was for **years**, and how today you will struggle *immensely* to compete against a behemoth like that with the massive infrastructure they have now built out.

That's not to say people don't make money selling a physical product, Bezos proved it's possible, it's just harder. We all need cars, electronics, clothes, food, supplements, etc. *Someone* has to sell this stuff, I'm just saying let someone else deal with the headaches.

When you sell a physical product, you must source it, warehouse it, display it for sale, ship it, accept returns, deal with lost items, broken items, warranty issues, defective products, and many more potential headaches.

For example, Netflix no longer deals with any of this, they swapped from physical to digital delivery many years ago - and look at where they are now. That switch alone makes setting up, running, and scaling the business much easier.

As another example, Shopify (a software as a service provider), has a market cap of $201 Billion, and while Amazon is worth well over a Trillion dollars, Shopify operates in a similar space. They handle everything except the physical product, which is genius, and that allows for far greater profit margins.

Now, profit margins may not mean a lot when we're talking about *billions* of dollars, but as a start-up generating less than a million a year, you ideally want to bootstrap (which means to keep your costs really low), to be able to generate strong profits off the bat.

Vitamins vs Painkillers

Humans, by a wide margin, are motivated to take action more when they are dealing with pain. It's always harder to sell a vitamin that offers health benefits, than it is to sell a painkiller like Advil.

It's the carrot v the stick argument.

When possible, sell a painkiller. Pharma companies are *notorious* for targeting this market, and they make HUGE amounts of money off of dealing with people's pain points.

They have the capabilities to sell prevention, but - crucially - they also aren't generally in the business of curing diseases - they are, in fact, in the business of managing diseases over the long-term. A cure would eliminate much of their subscription revenue. And that would be bad for their business.

They can clone sheep, but nobody is in the business of cloning your hair follicles to cure baldness. Instead, hair transplants (but more importantly monthly products like pills, lotions, potions, dyes, and powders) are sold more often due to their higher profitably instead.

Also, with rampant obesity (especially in Western societies), there is plenty of room for drugs which need to be taken monthly to deal with diabetes (i.e. a monthly subscription is required to pay for them), along with cardiovascular issues, cholesterol, etc.

Likewise, divorce and personal injury lawyers are some of the most profitable niches in law because they solve pain - and that translates into hefty fees.

The problem with painkiller businesses is that your company will likely be viewed as nefarious, or evil. Consider that the next time your car breaks down and three tow truck drivers show up to save you. They don't have the best reputation for a reason, but people will *always* be motivated to open their wallets when it comes to solving their own painful problems.

Exchanging Time for Money

Most entrepreneurs making under $1M in annual sales receipts fall into the category of exchanging a block of time, for a specified amount of money. Unless you are a lawyer running your own firm invoicing $1,000/hr or more an hour with a stacked calendar, you aren't ever going to easily crack $1M in annual sales.

Painters, window cleaners, dog walkers, lawn maintenance, electricians, plumbers, car detailers, nail salons, personal trainers, etc. are *all* exchanging a set price for some of their time.

To break out of the 95% that never really create wealth or personal freedom, you will need to engineer a business that makes you money while you sleep, eat, and are in the shower.

To use myself as an example, when I am asleep, someone somewhere in the world is watching a video (earning me some ad revenue), buying one of my books, or is joining one of my memberships, looking to learn more in a concerted effort to level-up their life.

Amazingly, we live in a permissionless economy today. You don't need a publisher to write a book anymore (but you will need an audience to sell it), and you certainly don't need a TV or radio station to broadcast your message. There are *plenty* of opportunities right in front of your face that will allow you to engineer a great business for very little cost.

Business Idea Generation

Now that you know what *not* to do and you will hopefully have begun to define your non-negotiables. You can now get clear on what elements need to exist in a business. For me, it needs to be a service, or even better, an information product that generates recurring revenue, is location independent, and needs minimal or no employees.

The next thing to consider is that a good business needs a healthy balance of:

1. Strong income,
2. Doing something you are good (ideally, world class) at,
3. Doing something that you *truly* enjoy.

Otherwise, you may create something you hate, and if you don't like what you are doing, your chance of failure will be much higher.

Use a note taking app on your mobile phone, and as you go about your day, make notes of business ideas you can cook up. The more the better, don't worry about if they are good or not, you can figure that out later.

Inventing a niche can be very powerful. Being first in a niche is a *very* good place to be.

I didn't see anyone making YouTube videos in their car while driving in 2014 when I started my channel, so I created that niche, now it seems like I've created a small trend, and many others have followed suit.

The point I am making here is that, in the absence of clarity, do *something*. More specifically, do something aligned with what it is you are trying to accomplish in your life

Have you ever seen one of those robotic vacuums that bounce into walls and pivot in another direction, until they hit something and repeat the process over again? In the absence of clarity, be like a robotic vacuum - keep pivoting in another direction until you find something that works.

I spent eight years in collection agencies learning the ins-and-outs of the business. It was in the last few years in the business that I made copious notes on paper during my lunch hour after reading the business section in the local newspaper, trying to cook up business ideas.

It wasn't until I got a package, went home, and had a massive "AH-HA!" moment that I thought to myself "I could settle people's debt, and charge a fee on what I save them." It was a true frying pan to the forehead moment and it was obvious that it should be my next move. Remember, every "overnight success" you see out there, more-likely-than-not, took *years* to realize. All you get to see are the end results of all the years of hard work that you *didn't* get to see.

Problem Solving

On a final note, I am leaving this until the end of this chapter because, in my opinion, it's the most important skill a man must develop. You need to be a great problem solver for all these methods above, but it's *especially* true for entrepreneurship. Your entire life as an entrepreneur is going to be solving problems that come your way in a business.

Marketing, operations, human resource management, logistics, legal issues, tax issues, planning, company culture, etc. I can't stress enough the importance of being able to work through obstacles that get in the way of you, and your company's goals. Sometimes, you will go around, under, or even over obstacles. Other times, the obstacle itself will become the solution. A great resource that defines the essence of problem-solving and critical-thinking is a book titled: "*The Obstacle is the Way*" by *Ryan Holiday*.

It's important to note that problem solving is like a muscle, it needs constant use to strengthen. Otherwise, it will waste away and become useless. Speaking of which, if you are a parent reading this, and you have children that you want to be successful (and why wouldn't you?), put real problems in front of them, and ask them to work through them in front of you.

In life and business, I encourage you to get good at R&D, and that doesn't stand for "Research and Development," it stands for "Rip-off and Duplicate." Most solutions to the problems you are experiencing have already been solved - you just need to look around, find them, and then look for ways of solving them more efficiently or find ways to add additional value that you can charge for.

Using a prior example, during my time in my debt relief business, I remember this annoying lawyer that had a nasty habit of writing disparaging content critical of anyone in the debt relief business, and he had optimized it to rank well on search engines to drive traffic away from your business to his. He eventually wrote a piece that was brought to my attention that required me to have a serious talk with my board of advisors.

He'd crossed the line big time - suing him back to the Stone Age was a solid option, and that was our initial plan. But, rather than spending tens of thousands of dollars to teach him a lesson, instead we decided that, since he likes writing so much and running his mouth, why not hire him to write articles on the industry that were critical of those that actually deserved it. In the end, this approach cost us just a tiny fraction of what a lawsuit would have been, we also created a conflict of interest to protect our position, and we used him to improve our business and make it more antifragile.

Finally, a note for parents, and soon-to-be parents. *Nothing* infuriates me more than parents putting their kids in front of a screen, consuming mindless garbage, because they don't want to engage with their children. Take your kids away from screens and teach them life. For example, if you are swapping your summer tires for a winter set, and your child is old enough (five or more), show them how it's done, how to jack up a car, why bolts are tightened with a torque wrench, and in a star pattern.

One of the best tools you can use to teach kids problem solving, and to exercise your own problem-solving muscle, is to play chess with them. My dad did this with me for years in my youth; I also joined a chess club after school and played with other kids. I got good at the game, and it played a role in developing the problem solving muscle I use today. If your kids are too young to play a complex game like chess, start them with something simpler like Connect 4.

Your problem solving skills need developing as soon as possible. So, get good at solving problems (as early as possible), and then share your new-found skills with your children and encourage them to use their new skills to add value to their lives, and to the lives of others.

Box, What Box?

As I mentioned earlier on in this chapter, many entrepreneurs either have Attention Deficit Disorder (known as ADD) or ADD-like traits. While this often means that they **really** struggle to remain focused on tasks that they don't enjoy (i.e. the task isn't generating any dopamine for them), they rarely ever struggle to come up with very creative solutions to problems. This line of thinking is often referred to as "thinking outside the box." It's a very helpful skill to harness.

Likewise, those further along on the spectrum have a tendency to *not even see the box.* This doesn't just lead to them finding very creative solutions to problems - these are often the people who uncover genuinely innovative answers, diving deep into uncharted territories.

While exploring the coping methods required for dealing with ADD, Autism, or the like is far outside the scope of this book, in the context of becoming an entrepreneur, it's imperative that you at least keep the following two points in mind as much as possible:

1. **Hire people to do the tasks you absolutely deplore:** For example, if accounting isn't your bag, find an accountant that can help you significantly simply ways of keeping your bookkeeping in order and then pay them to do their job well. Find ways to off-load (or automate) the tasks you don't excel at to others, so you can remain hyper-focused on the tasks that you **do** excel at.
2. **Develop an ELF business:** Earlier in this chapter I discussed what an ELF business is. It's one that you find *Easy*, one that is *Lucrative* financially, and - importantly for those of you on the spectrum - one that is ***Fun***. If your business bores the life out of you, then you'll struggle to stay on track and remain focused when your business needs you most. If you can find problems **that you really enjoy solving**, then - assuming it's a problem that can be easily scaled, and can hopefully offer recurring payments - you're more likely to turn your traits into a super-power that can turbo-charge your growth and success in business.

Invest in Yourself

One of the greatest investments you can **ever** make is the investment into your own skills and experience. Those skills (if used often and are kept up-to-date) will - literally - last you a lifetime and their benefits compound greatly over time. And, unlike with money, it's one asset that can't ever be taken away from you. It's why many super successful people can rebound back to their prior positions of wealth. The retained skills, experience, resilience to challenges, and their rock-solid network of reliable friends will get them back to where they were *far* quicker than those just starting out.

Luckily for you, it's **never** been easier than it is now when it comes to learning new knowledge and up-skilling. The advent of the internet has seen to that.

It's also been said that finding a mentor is one of the true shortcuts in life. Their *decades* of personal experience can be passed down to you *in a fraction of the time*. And, as someone who's had mentors in the past, I can attest to just how much valuable time a great mentor can save you.

However, many people have shared their decades of personal experience online for you to learn from. This very book is a perfect example of that. I've condensed **many, many** years of life lessons into one easy-to-learn package. There's also countless YouTube videos and tutorials on any number of subjects, just waiting for you to learn from. There's no excuses, go do the work.

You Can't Save Your Way to Wealth

Finally, while many people focus on paying religiously into their tax-free retirement investment account every month, it's critically important to know that you **can't** just save your way to true life-changing wealth. Sure, you may be able to stash away a few hundred thousand into that retirement account (assuming the government hasn't changed any of the rules on when/how you can access your money when you retire), but that won't create *true* wealth.

Likewise, it takes just as much time and energy finding better ways of making money as it does finding ways to save money, think: cutting out coupons, scouring online feverishly for the best deals, grabbing your groceries from different shops (just to save a few bucks), etc.

It's a *much* better return on your time to invest it in looking for ways to make money, rather than save it. That doesn't mean be reckless with your money, but it *does* mean that focusing your energy in the right ways allows you to continue enjoying a higher quality of life, rather than trying to find ways to "just get by" and sustain a much-lower quality of life.

In Conclusion

You can become quite wealthy by taking on any of these wealth creation methods, but entrepreneurship is by *far* my favorite. It offers the most freedom, flexibility, maneuverability, speed, and - most importantly - income potential. There isn't anyone on the list of the world's richest men that got there as a real estate agent selling mansions, from STEM, or as a licensed professional; almost everyone on these lists did it through entrepreneurship, owning real estate that appreciates in value (or they can rent out en-masse for recurring income), or via an inheritance.

The Cold, Hard Truth

Never forget:

- **Become a key problem solver:** People experience problems every day. Look for ways on how to solve them more effectively than others have, and see how quickly your solution can be scaled.
- **Get what you need and move on**: There's useful info out there, but most of it is noise. Take what helps, ignore the garbage, and don't let it drag you down.
- **Stop chasing pointless drama**: Gossip, controversy, and online fights don't make you money or improve your life. Focus on things that actually move you forward.
- **Be skeptical of so-called "experts"**: If someone isn't living the life you want, why would you take advice from them? Most are just selling a dream they haven't lived.
- **People selling shortcuts are selling lies**: Get-rich-quick schemes, crypto scams, and "secrets" behind a paywall are usually just traps. If it sounds too easy, it's more-than-likely a scam.
- **Fix yourself first**: Envy, resentment, and complaining won't get you anywhere. Build your own skills, money, and mindset instead of worrying about others.
- **Guard your reputation**: Who you associate with matters. Stay away from toxic people and places that drag you down. Surround yourself with those who push you to do better.
- **Focus on what really counts**: Don't waste time on meaningless numbers or shallow validation. Put your energy into building something real - your health, wealth, and future.
- **Stop trading time for money:** Doing so **severely** dampens your ability to build generational wealth for you and your loved ones. We're now in the digital era, where anyone with a laptop, internet access, and enough savvy can solve problems for people on the other side of the world, allowing them to constantly earn money *in their sleep.*

2

The Four Quadrants

In my first book "The Unplugged Alpha," I put together a loose guide on what I learned during my unplugging process. In this book, beginning with this chapter, I'm going to take you even further down the rabbit hole and I'll be even more specific on assessing where you stand, how to become that top-shelf Unplugged Alpha, and live a fully optimized life.

A distinct pattern has emerged with the men I've worked with over the years, and it's become obvious they all fall into one of four - very distinct - quadrants. In this chapter, I'll discuss the four quadrants, so I strongly recommend that you look at this chapter as an opportunity for both an honest self-assessment and to understand where you currently are - and what you need to change to get to where you want to be.

It's been said that, in order to first start dealing with a problem, you first need to identify the root of the problem. It's why the first step for an alcoholic to resolve their issues is to admit they are an alcoholic.

Every man starts his journey living in one of these four quadrants, often completely oblivious to how he got his belief system, how he's currently navigating his way through life, and how other people see him.

The *vast* majority of men live in the bottom half of the chart; plugged in to comforting lies, sleepwalking through life. While the remainder live in the top half of the chart; they're unplugged living in the cold, hard uncomfortable truth, but as a consequence of that, they can see the world for what it truly is (and they accept it's not how they "feel" it should be).

Here's a quick overview of how those quadrants look:

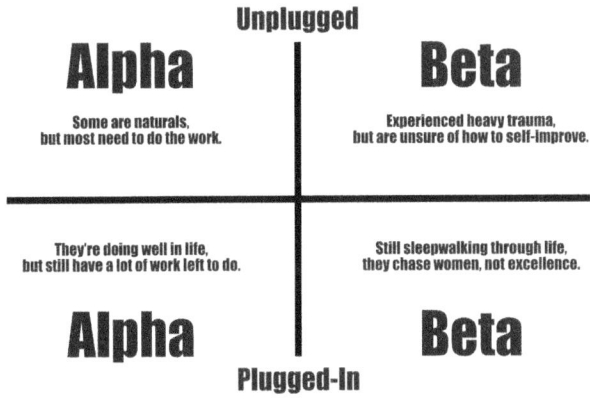

The four quadrants.

To dive deeper into the four quadrants (as well as find links to every study and book recommendation I make in this book), be sure to check out my comprehensive resource PDF, which is available from my website:

▶ Scan the QR code for Book Resources

▶ http://theunpluggedalpha.com/bookresources

Let's examine each quadrant, starting with the "Plugged-In Beta" and move up from there.

The Plugged-In Beta (70% of Men)

The following characteristics are strongly associated with the Plugged-In Beta male, they:

- Willingly bend the knee to others, think: women, government, and other societal narratives,
- Are far more interested in chasing women, not excellence - which is what *actually* attracts women to men,
- Are seen as unattractive to the majority of women, often being labeled as "creeps" in the process,
- Are the "nice guys" and tell others to "just be themselves,"
- They listen to, and blindly accept women's words at face value, and ignore her actions,
- Will try to negotiate desire with women, think: "Choreplay," and they do *everything* women dislike in men, such as being: submissive (rather than assertive), overly agreeable, without a backbone, devoid of personal standards, etc.,
- Are insignificant, invisible to most women, and - where possible - are avoided by Unplugged Alphas,
- Are usually physically out of shape, and are generally unhealthy,

- Are fragile across all domains in life and, as they're not natural problem solvers, they're prone to experiencing difficulties when chaos enters their lives,
- Will invite problematic, low-desire women with red flags into their life because they value waving their "Captain-Save-a-Hoe" flag over peace and passion,
- They frequently complicate their life, and then justify why they do it afterwards,
- Believe everything the Mainstream Media (i.e. the MSM) narrative is,
- Vote for big government, and look for their control over their life,
- Do what women tell them to do, and are generally people pleasers by nature,
- Can, sometimes, also be influential aka: "useful idiots" that can be used by the Matrix to control the current narrative.

Western society is doing its best to manufacture Plugged-In Beta males, with culture, religion, Hollywood, government, education, television, marketing teams, and medicine leading the charge. I don't think this is accidental; it's clearly well-orchestrated, and is working *very* effectively. The vast majority of men today are, in fact, Plugged-In Beta males.

It keeps men agreeable, soft, without purpose, and happy enough to comply with everything they are *told* (by everyone else) to do.

Given that this is about 80% of men, then it's fair to say that we all know someone in this category. You might even be thinking to yourself, "yeah, that's me."

Plugged-In Betas were made most obvious during the recent COVID scamdemic. There were the men that were fully aware but were forced under duress to take jabs to keep their jobs, and then there were the "others." They went with every narrative they were sold. Hook, line, and sinker. Wearing masks everywhere, social distancing, and standing on those little dots like sheep.

They also, often angrily, ostracized their own family and close friends when it came to holidays, and gatherings; boldly regurgitating media lies, and telling their siblings or parents that they weren't welcome in their house because of their vaccination status.

When it was time to take their 3rd shot, they proudly lined up, and then didn't hesitate to boast on social media about how well they were conforming to the comforting lies, and they mocked anyone that didn't form up on their social-warrior pedestal. They didn't ask **any** questions, they just simply complied.

The Plugged-In Alpha (15% of Men)

The following characteristics are often associated with the Plugged-In Alpha, these men are generally more naturally attractive to women, but they:

- Struggle to retain them for any length of time,
- Will regurgitate soundbites like "happy wife, happy life" or, "let me check with the boss,"
- Will negotiate desire with women, and perform "choreplay" in exchange for intimacy,
- Still openly support big government control and interference in their life,
- Are still fragile (across most domains) and they're still susceptible to chaos disturbing their life,
- Are at least getting *some* of what they want out of life, but they're still *blissfully* ignorant of how the world *truly* works.

These men are rare, often natural Alphas, but they're still subscribed to the plugged-in mindset. So, they are often men that women usually find physically very attractive and who other men look up to, but they're ultimately still plugged-in and are a tool of "The Matrix."

However, the biggest difference between the Plugged-In Beta and the Plugged-In Alpha, is that they are ***more physically attractive to women***, and have also achieved more success in life in general, but they're still the type to "go along, to get along."

Just like the Plugged-In Beta males, they often still subscribe to comforting lies, and do all the things they are told to do, but they are higher in status than the Plugged-In Betas because more women are naturally drawn to them.

Using the scamdemic to illustrate this further, the Plugged-In Alpha was the guy calling into my podcasts, and emailing me with something along the lines of, "I'm a successful blah blah blah, but my employer is going to terminate me if I don't take this vaccine, what do I do? I have a wife, a mortgage, and kids."

The Unplugged Beta (10% of Men)

The following characteristics are often associated with the Unplugged Beta, they:

- Are often brought to the point of "Unplugging" through a traumatic experience (e.g. Divorce),
- Remain mad at the world once they begin to see how it *truly* works, where they struggle to understand and accept such facts,
- In turn, either become Men who Go Their Own Way (MGTOW), or they remain *extremely* jaded,
- Don't like how much work they need to do to level-up their life and instead, they prefer to remain the victim in the chaos they created for themselves,
- Like being the "smartest man in the room," but they won't take the uncomfortable step of looking for the rooms where they are no longer the smartest there,
- Love to complicate their lives and then gaslight themselves into justifying "why" afterwards,
- Are unable to make solid friendships as their plugged-in friends won't share their views, and unplugged alpha men won't stand for them not doing the work needed.

This category is where things start to get interesting; you start to see a small fire burning, there's *almost* a glimmer in his eye because he has begun to move away from the comforting lies. The largest migration to this category is from Plugged-In Beta males (with a much smaller percentage coming from the Plugged-In Alpha category). Those Plugged-In Alphas beat themselves up hard to end up in the category, and they often found that women and success came to them reasonably consistently, but they never really understood *why* women were confusing, difficult, and fleeting in nature.

Once they see the world's raw truths, anger takes hold; they're raging at the system, struggling to digest facts that don't fit their old narrative. This either pushes them to check out as MGTOWs, or leaves them jaded, stewing in bitterness with no exit plan.

They constantly dodge the hard work needed to level-up (focusing on more comfortable hobbies), clinging to the victim role instead of owning their path, and they puff up as the "smartest man in the room" without the guts to step into tougher arenas where they'd get humbled in a heartbeat.

These men thrive on over-complicating their lives, then twist their own minds to justify the chaos, while their social game crumbles; Plugged-In friends ditch their new views, and Unplugged men won't waste time on their half-assed effort.

However, Unplugging isn't optional and it's just the first damn step to forging a stronger, more successful you. Those cozy delusions? Torch them. Remember: facts don't give a damn about *anyone's* feelings, so quit whining and start building.

Take it from the men in my community who've clawed their way out; real change hits when you stop making excuses and start putting in the work. No shortcuts - doing the work to improve your health, personal freedom, create wealth, and form strong networks takes effort and consistency.

The Unplugged Alpha (Top 5% of Men)

The following characteristics are often associated with the Unplugged Alpha, they:

- Have truly come to terms with how the world *actually* works and they make it their goal to learn how to navigate life accordingly,
- Chase excellence and not women.
- Live their life on their own terms and focus on making their own mental point of origin the one that they invite others to join them in,
- They take great care of their body, their health (nutrition, at a micro and macro level), they dress well, and naturally signal high status,
- Look for problems to solve, find scalable ways to make money from it and understand the importance of building a solid network of like-minded men,
- Understand the importance of being "antifragile" in life and take steps to remain outcome independent,
- Don't want to be the smartest person in the room, so they constantly look to surround themselves with people much smarter than them in key areas,
- Only allow women into their life if they *genuinely* compliment them and offer them consistent value. They'll also quickly get rid of any women who try to invite drama into their lives (see the "Hire Slow, Fire Fast" chapter from my first book).

The best way I can explain this category is if I take you on my personal journey. If I am being perfectly honest, I've lived in **all four** of these categories. I definitely started out as a Plugged-In Beta (until I hit adulthood), I then went on to become a Plugged-In Alpha in my 20's, to becoming an Unplugged Beta (during my divorce), to ultimately becoming the Unplugged Alpha that I'm known as today.

Antifragility

A key component of the Unplugged Alpha is becoming as **antifragile** as possible. *Nassim Nicholas Taleb* wrote a book called *Antifragile – Things That Gain from Disorder*. The subtitle says it all, and every Unplugged Alpha I know lives this way.

To clarify: fragile people collapse when chaos hits their world. Disorder breaks them, and many never recover. The antifragile are the opposite - they **gain** from chaos and disorder.

Here's a real example. Years ago, a washed-up former lawyer from the collections industry tried hijacking search traffic from my debt business (and others). He wrote slanderous blogs designed to trick consumers into using his services.

My board and I looked at options. We could have sued him into the stone age for slander. But that would've been costly, dragged on for months, and even if we won, the guy was broke. No collectable damages, no payoff. Just wasted time and money.

Instead, we flipped the script. We saw his unstable mental state, his desperation for money, and his love of writing blogs. So we hired him. For a fraction of the cost of a lawsuit, he started writing content for *us* - factual comparisons of debt relief solutions that we signed-off on before publishing.

We turned a potential enemy into a cheap advocate. We also created a conflict of interest - once he worked for us, he couldn't legally spread lies about us anymore.

Most people would've struggled in that chaos, but it didn't weaken us, it only made us stronger and more resilient. By being antifragile, we gained from it.

Plugged-In Beta (Years 0-18)

As a kid, I dealt with a stutter, and third-degree burns across my upper body (that I received in a horrible accident as a toddler), and buck-teeth challenges that left me far from comfortable in my own skin. Looking back, I was the definition of a Plugged-In Beta. I was low on confidence, feeling utterly insignificant, and basically invisible to women.

For the most part, I kept to myself, avoiding the spotlight. Skateboarding was my outlet as a boy, but if there was one thing that started pulling me out of that shell in my teens, it was diving into heavy metal music and hitting the gym. I'd lose myself in live concerts, blast powerful tracks non-stop, and grind through heavy weight sessions on the regular; it lit a fire that began my unplugging process.

The heavy metal song lyrics were all about bucking the trends and being a rebel. I remember the lyrics from a band called Suicidal Tendencies, from a song called "You can't bring me down." They hit hard:

> ...*Can you say, "Feel like shit"?* Yeah, maybe sometimes I do feel like shit, I ain't happy 'bout it, but I'd rather feel like shit than be full of shit, And if I offended you, oh, I'm sorry, but maybe you need to be offended, But here's my apology, and one more thing, Fuck you!
>
> — Suicidal Tendencies

Plugged-In Alpha (Years 19-37)

By the time I hit 19 I had found my stride, and a way to remedy those things that I thought had held me back. I rode motorcycles, went to the gym six days a week, and I got jacked. I'd stay out to 3am with friends on sports bikes and we'd do unspeakable things on the roads with our bikes. I lost my virginity at 19 to my first girlfriend, and shortly after had a fantastic, and very enthusiastic threesome with her and her best friend - at this phase of my life, women came easily to me.

By the time I was 20 I stood 6'3", weighed 198lbs with under 10% body fat, and I was absolutely *ripped*. I remember another girlfriend at 24 that would get visibly upset when her friends fawned, and called me the "Calvin Klein underwear model." At the time, I never really understood her jealousy and anxiety. However, *now* I do.

As a boy, I was afraid to take my shirt off at the beach because of my scars. However, in my twenties, I actively sought out the sun, and I proudly displayed what I was building with my work in the gym. I realized that chicks actually liked my scars, and that these scars were just proof that I was stronger than what tried to kill me. A **real** shift in how I saw myself started to take place.

I also attended a college business course for a few years, which I subsequently quit when my dad invited me to join him on a sales road trip to the US to sell fans, circuit boards, and switches in a new company he had founded. His business ultimately failed, but I learned more in that one week traveling with him on business calls than I ever did sitting in a classroom for **years**.

From that point on, I started to consume the biographies and books of every successful man I thought I should learn from: Richard Branson, Donald Trump, Brian Tracy, Og Mandino, Stephen Covey, and so on. During this time, I rapidly climbed the corporate ladder in the collection agencies I worked at, and learned how creditors really operate, what their motives *really* were, how a business makes money, and how people are successfully managed in those large corporations.

I also indulged in women. Attracting women really wasn't a problem either at this point (one of the aspects of being a Plugged-In Alpha), but managing them over time proved to be the biggest issue. Nothing I learned from family, sitcoms, Disney, religion, or school ever seemed to work. So, during these years that I dated, I went to bars, clubs, and had a few long-term relationships.

Then at 30, a few weeks after I bought my first home (with a big mortgage), I received a severance package for not fitting into the corporate structure, went home, sat around, and I finally realized that I needed to start my own business if I was *ever* going to make life-changing money. So, I did just that, and I founded TotalDebtFreedom.ca which ultimately became Canada's most successful award-winning debt negotiation company. I was recognized three times by *Profit* magazine as one of Canada's fastest-growing companies, and I was also nominated by Ernst & Young for Entrepreneur of the Year.

Later that year I met a lawyer on a dating app that worked at a big law firm, who became my wife and the mother of my daughter. We built a *spectacular* custom home, and I did everything that I was told to do my entire life but, again, *nothing* I did seemed to work in my benefit long-term. I stopped putting myself first, gained weight, lost muscle, wasn't able (or equipped) to lead my relationship, and a few years after my daughter was born, it became clear that our relationship had run its course, so it became time to untie the knot. Look, I'm definitely not proud of those years, but I will absolutely own them.

As it is with most men, it was going through the divorce grinder that started the unplugging process, when I saw how women, lawyers, and family law treats men with disdain and subjected them to grossly unfair court orders when it came to matrimonial assets and access to their own children.

The Unplugged Beta Years 38-42

Those unplugging years hit me **hard** - painful as hell and full of lessons I didn't ask for. By that point, I was a shadow of my former self, drifting without direction, and straight-up embodying beta male energy. Divorce almost wrecked my resolve, my business faced nonstop hostile attacks, and to make it worse, I pulled the ultimate beta move by getting involved with a single mom who turned around and betrayed me.

What really opened my eyes during the divorce was just how vicious family law can be toward fathers - it straight-up despises us. On top of that, I was battling new business regulations packed with bullshit lies and manipulative crap, all pushed by competitors and creditors hell-bent on killing my industry. The lobbying group I dumped over $50k into nailed it when they said the proposed bill should've been titled "The Protect Creditors' Profits at All Costs Bill."

We lost that fight in the end, and it damn near wiped out the entire sector, but we scraped a win by hustling hard, benefiting from the chaos and pivoting fast. My brother successfully runs the business I built to this day, and I stick around as an advisor.

Looking back, that chaos was exactly the kick in the ass I needed to step into this upgraded version of myself. For most guys, it's some brutal trauma or total upheaval that forces us to unplug - divorce, getting cheated on, a pandemic, or the massive lies society and mainstream media shove down our throats. It's that unstoppable force that flips your world upside down and makes you rethink everything.

In those red-pill years, I dove deep: reading every evo-psych study and book I could get my hands on, watching countless videos, and soaking up podcasts that broke down women's nature. I absorbed takes from every dating guru out there, pored over thousands of pages of divorce case law, and jumped into events and masterminds to surround myself with top-tier entrepreneurs.

It was a considerable amount of time and effort, but:

I needed to rewire my brain to see things as they are, not how I hoped they would be.

I started creating content on YouTube in 2014, and those who were around back then saw me shift my type of content, and I started working through many of these newer ideas from late 2015 onwards.

The Unplugged Alpha (Year 43 Onwards)

This is the quadrant and age where I've seized the most personal freedom, forged ironclad friendships, built world-class networks, racked up life's best experiences with women, sculpted a peak physique for a seasoned man, fortified my mental game, and stacked the most cash. No excuses here, just visible results from owning my path.

I also came to learn the value of participating in combat sports during these years, and during the scamdemic, I found a dojo that was willing to ignore those lies, and help me put a 4-year focus on boxing. I had my first three, two-minute round fight at 49-years-old. I won.

I'm pretty hard on myself. So, if I am being honest, I'm still not maxed out in every area; for instance, my sleep isn't as great as I'd like it, I should be a little bit leaner, and I *really* should stop being afraid of eye surgery and get my eyesight permanently fixed so I can eliminate (or at least minimize) my reliance on glasses to (not only look more attractive) but also enjoy the more adventurous activities that life has to offer.

Sometimes I slip up in business, in life, and with women (I'm only human after all). But even when I do, I am *far* less prone to allowing this chaos to ruin my life (compared to how I failed to handle it properly in the past).

Most importantly, I'm now antifragile, so for any problems or chaos that enters my life, I'm *more* than equipped to deal with it, I also have a strong network that I can lean on if needed, and, at the end of the day, that chaos actually ends up *benefiting* my life, and it ultimately makes me **better**.

Look, it's **our** responsibility as men (and ours alone), to make something out of ourselves, and solve our problems. When you *truly* understand and accept that nobody cares, or is coming to save you, you can surrender fully to that truth, begin to take ownership, and actually **do the work that needs to be done** (because **no-one** is going to do it for you).

In Conclusion

I've just mapped out the battlefield for you; four quadrants that define where men stand, from the sleepwalking masses in the Plugged-In haze, to the elite few owning their reality as Unplugged Alphas.

If you're honest with yourself, you've pin-pointed your spot on this grid and, if you're not and Unplugged Alpha yet, then it's time to face the uncomfortable truth: staying stuck is a choice, *and it's a loser's one*. My own journey through these stages proves that it's possible to claw your way up. Divorce, betrayals, and chaos didn't break me; they forged me stronger, made me antifragile, and kept me laser-focused on chasing excellence.

But talk is cheap; this isn't about feelings or fairy tales - it's about grinding through the discomfort, torching delusions, and building the life you demand. Assess hard, act harder, and join the ranks of men in my community who've turned potential into power. No one's coming to save you - so unplug, begin to level-up, and start dominating your life.

The Cold, Hard Truth

Never forget:

- **The four quadrants:** There are four quadrants that men can, often unknowingly, find themselves going through. Assess your current situation, see which quadrant you're currently in and, if you're not an Unplugged Alpha, make a note of what needs improving.
- **The most likely beginning:** Most men begin as Plugged-In Betas due to growing up in single-mother households, or homes with weak fathers, and it sadly often takes some *severe* blunt-force trauma to force that man to take a long, hard look at themselves in the mirror.
- **"Red pill rage":** Unfortunately, most men who begin to "swallow the Red Pill" can't ever digest it fully. They - metaphorically - spit it back up because the exposure to the uncomfortable truths scares them too much to do the work. Do NOT be one of those guys.
- **You CAN level-up your life:** If you're not getting the results you want out of life, and if you're willing to look hard at yourself in the mirror (without an ego), and are willing to do the work, then it truly is possible to live the kind of life you only dreamed about.

3

Acceptance and Understanding

By: Steve From Accounting

I learned what I found to be the most significant and hard-hitting lesson through my less-than-amicable divorce: nothing lasts forever - not my marriage, not the way things were with my kids, **nothing**. And you know what? That's honestly OK. For years, I was always angry; "red-pill rage" had me by the throat; I was blaming her, the world, and - most of all - myself for believing society's BS and lies.

But then I realized something: getting mad at life for changing, for not being what I was told it was going to be, is like getting mad at the sun for being hot or the sea for being wet. It's a losing battle.

The sun's going to shine whether you want it to or not, so you can either look outside, bitch and moan that it's "too hot out there" and stay inside, or you can put on some shades, maybe a fitted tee, apply some sunblock, and step outside with a quiet smile. Relationships? They all shift, they fade over time, and they all end.

Every last one of them ends in either death, or a break up. **Without exception.**

When you're able to ***truly*** take a step back and fully accept that cold, hard truth - and then learn to navigate it properly - you'll find a kind of inner peace that makes life *so* much better. Once I fully internalized that my relationship with my kids will also end one day in death (which, I won't lie, fucking sucked to think about), I was able to reflect on why my marriage failed. I could *genuinely* understand why my ex-wife made the choices she did. It doesn't mean I forgive her for making them (far from it), but I at least *understand* her thought process now.

Learn to Let Go

I've seen too many guys unplug - take that metaphorical red pill - only to watch them get permanently stuck in the anger phase. They see the hard truths, and it hits them hard. I get it - it hit me hard too. I spent *way* too long thinking, "I should've stayed for my kids," or "my kids should still need me like they used to." But reality doesn't care about what you think *should* happen, and - as Rich has constantly said over the years - "facts don't give a fuck about your feelings." Staying angry at the facts is like beating your head against a wall; it doesn't change a thing, it just hurts *you* more.

Here's a way to start moving past it: the next time you feel that anger bubbling up, take a deep breath, physically take a step back, and think to yourself, "This feeling won't last,". It sounds simple, but do that every time it hits, and it'll soon become second nature. What changes everything is **accepting what's real and finding a way to make it work *for* you** - flipping the script so you're not stuck in that rage state forever.

Stop Being a Hypocrite

Here's an irony I've noticed: when you're stuck in the "anger phase," you end up letting your emotions dictate your choices. That's something we often call women out for - making choices based on how they feel in the moment, "I feel like" instead of "I think that." But when you're wallowing in your anger, letting it control your mind, you're doing the ***exact same thing***. You'll *never* make good choices if you're constantly letting your emotions run the show. Don't criticize women for making emotional choices if that's what you're doing too. Knock that bullshit on the head **right now**.

Here's how to catch yourself: the next time you're about to make a choice out of anger - say, sending a heated text to someone - pause and ask yourself, "What would sending this message actually achieve?" If sending it achieves nothing (other than it making you - very temporarily - feel better), then *immediately* walk away until you're clear-headed. That simple step can save you a lot of regret. I've learned to do that with my ex-wife, and I'll teach you how to do that yourself near the end of this chapter.

My Approach: Letting Go With Grace

I've also found it's *so* much better for my mental and emotional state - not to mention minimizing any drama coming back on me - to look back on a relationship that's ended and appreciate it for the good times we had, then look for lessons learned, and finally for places where I can do better in the future. No one's perfect - I'm definitely *fucking miles* away from it still - but that just means there are countless opportunities for personal growth and for letting people go in a way that doesn't make me look like a dick.

For example, when women told me they didn't want to date me anymore, especially over text, I'd simply reply: "I understand. All the best." Nothing more. No begging, no questions, no anger - just an acknowledgment. Here's the crazy part: the number of women who tried to come back later after a response like that was *way* higher than when I reacted with any kind of negative emotion. It worked for me, showing me the power of letting go with some form of grace (whilst also significantly reducing the odds of her trying to come back at me in the future and try and fuck me over out of spite).

But let's be clear here - this approach is very much situational. If she went full-on psycho on you and did something **truly** unforgivable, like hurting someone you love, or trying to get you put in jail, then you *certainly* don't owe her any kindness. In those cases, letting her go might mean cutting her off completely, no words needed. If wishing her well doesn't seem right to you, that's fine - sometimes indifference is the best move to make. The key though, is to let them go without letting the situation drag you down with it.

Where Anger Catches Hold of You

I've seen a few places where anger *really* grabs hold of guys after they unplug, and I've felt them myself. First, there's hypergamy - women are wanting to "trade up," always looking for the "better deal." *Countless* men have slaved away like horses for the benefit of their wife and kids - only for her to tell them that she "loves him, but isn't in love with him" anymore, before jumping ship to another man who she "feels" will offer her an easier life (which is rarely ever the case, he just makes her feel excited again).

It stings, and the anger comes fast: "Why can't she just love me for me?!" The truth is, women have been hard-wired through evolution to chase the best option they can get. It's biology, not a personal attack. Will **all** women "trade up"?

No. But all women **definitely** have the propensity for doing it if they don't see you as their best option and they feel like they can do better. Granted, some will jump sooner than others, but *very few* will stick it out with someone who isn't actively working on getting (and then keeping) their shit together.

Then there's betrayal - she cheated, lied, or just straight-up disappeared. Rich has coached **loads** of guys who have found their girlfriend in bed with someone else - it's a tale as old as time. The anger is real: "I deserved better than this." Maybe you did, but you didn't get it. People let you down - her, him, sometimes even the people you trust most. Loyalty isn't guaranteed in life. Or maybe you ignored the 21 Red Flags from Rich's first book. In which case, that's squarely on you.

Another big one is the loss of control - you can't stop life from changing, no matter how hard you try. For example, my daughter used to come to me for *everything* - now she's 13 (going on 16), calling me "old," no longer coming to me for hugs, or even actively smiling in group photos. Instead, she's growing up, searching for her own independence, wanting to see her friends more than me, chasing her own path.

I won't lie, it *really* fucking hurt - especially as I can see my ex-wife's negative influence creeping out in her more and more as the days go by - and I found myself becoming selfish, wanting to spend as much time with her as I could when she was with me. But, I'm not in control of how she grows. Control over anything but yourself is an illusion, and father time marches on regardless. So it's my job to be there for her and ensure I continue to lead by example and provide any guidance (and boundaries/discipline) where needed.

Flipping the Script

The way out of all these common traps is the same: let go, focus on what you can control, and navigate life with competence (which breeds natural confidence). Life's a storm - don't curse the rain, grab an umbrella and keep walking. Hypergamy stings? Use it as fuel - get to the gym, build your career, sharpen your skills, and become the winner women are hard-wired to chase. Then watch as she inevitably checks in to see how you're doing, only to see that you're smashing life, and leaving the door open for someone better who *truly* wants to be with you.

Betrayal cuts deep? Let her go to "discover herself," reflect on where you can do better next time, and walk away knowing you dodged a bigger mess - now stronger for it. Loss of control weighing on you? Focus on your own growth and your own mental and emotional frame.

My daughter pulling away? I've come to realize she has enough comfort in my love for her that I'll always be there for her (while I'm alive); that's my win, *not* my loss. I'm finding ways for her to hang out with her friends, even on "my" time, because I know she'll come back when she needs advice, and I'll be ready to give it. If *you* can learn to let go of what you can't control, then you'll also find the strength needed to keep moving forward.

The Shift

After my divorce, I was a wreck. I thought my ex owed me a lifetime, that my kids would always be little, needing me to fix everything. I was wrong. She moved on, they're growing up, and I spent too long feeling angry about it - angry at her, at life, at myself. Then I stopped fighting. I looked at what happened, not to blame, but merely to understand.

She wasn't the blood-sucking enemy, and I sure as fuck wasn't perfect. We drifted, we messed up, and it ended. I thought about the good stuff - my kids, the laughs we had, the wild times - and I saw my own misguided mistakes: I checked out too often, didn't work out, had zero frame, and I didn't lead anywhere near as well as I could have. That was it. No fairy tale to cling to, no grudge to carry. Just the unvarnished reality.

Here's the thing: **nothing lasts** - not your relationships, your friendships, not even the way your dog looks at you. Things inevitably fall apart; that's just how life works. Getting angry won't hold it together, but accepting it will. And I'm not talking about giving up - I'm talking about seeing things for what they *are* and finding a way to work **with** them. You're not chasing women or some perfect life; you're chasing your own excellence. When someone comes along for the ride, enjoy it for what it is, knowing it's not forever. That's not a loss - *it's a mindset that sets you free*.

The Payoff: Inner Peace and Magnetism

Here's the real value in all this: when you stop fighting reality, you find a kind of inner peace that changes **everything.** I used to be bitter - every day felt heavy, like I was carrying a grudge against the world. But once I accepted that my marriage ended, that my kids' lives would evolve, that life doesn't owe me *anything,* the weight suddenly lifted. I started enjoying my days again - **really** enjoying them. A sunny afternoon wasn't a reminder of what I'd lost; it was a chance to feel alive, to smile, to be present. That bitterness was gone, and in its place came a lightness I hadn't felt in *years.*

That peace makes you a better man to be around. People can really feel it - your friends, your kids, the women you meet. You're no longer the angry guy who drags everyone down with his complaints; you're the guy who's calm, grounded, and genuinely positive.

After I let go of my anger, I noticed how people gravitated to me more - my energy shifted, and it drew others in, especially women who could feel that I wasn't rattled by life's storms anymore. Acceptance doesn't just make *your* life better - it makes you better for *everyone* in it.

Ways to Break Free

Here are some ways to check where you're currently at mentally and ways to move forward:

- **Own your part first:** Think about your last breakup - what's one thing you did wrong? For me, I realized I stopped leading in my marriage - I got far too comfortable. Write your failing(s) down. It'll sting, but it's also the honesty you need to be better.
- **Catch yourself dwelling:** If you're stuck replaying "she did me wrong," ask yourself: "What's this fixing?" If the answer's "nothing," let it go.
- **Feel it, then move on:** Give yourself five minutes to feel the anger - like, *really* feel it. Then, when the timer's up, walk away. You're done.
- **Find one thing she didn't ruin:** What's one good thing she left behind? I looked at my ex and saw she gave me my kids - and I love them more than life itself. If you can't name one positive thing, you're still stuck. Work on that.

- **The opposite of love *isn't* hate:** Can you think of her - or hear stories about her - and remain indifferent about her? If you can, you're on the right track.
- **Flip the script:** Next time life throws you a curveball, accept the challenge and deal with it head-on. If a storm hits (which it inevitably will), assess the situation, make a plan to deal with it, and then execute it - you're untouchable and unflappable. *That's* the shift.

Why it Matters

That shift doesn't just give you peace - it makes life better in every way. I used to wake up heavy, carrying my anger around with me everywhere like an invisible bag of heavy rocks. Now, I wake up light, ready to take on the day, smiling at the good stuff, being grateful for where I am now (compared to where I was a few years ago), and I manage my fucks carefully by shrugging at the stuff I can't control.

That *true* inner peace makes you someone people *want* to be around - your kids, your friends, and the women in your life. If someone asks me the timeless "How's things?" question I usually reply "Amazing thanks, and you?" I can see the surprise in their faces as it's not the kind of answer people usually give these days to such small talk.

Hold Yourself Accountable

Today, taking action and holding yourself accountable to your peers is *invaluable* in finding your own way to letting the BS go and unlocking your own inner peace. Being a part of a dedicated community (or brotherhood) of guys that share their "Flipping the script" wins, lifting each other up (and, respectfully, calling each other out on their BS), will give **you** the accountability needed to stay on course.

I'm grateful for the ability to do just that as a part of Rich's community, and when someone there with infinitely more experience in an area than me talks, I'm happy to shut the fuck up and listen to what they have to say and apply that advice to my own life.

And, if I drop the ball somewhere and I fuck up (which happens on occasion), I know the guys there will 100% call me out on it, and I appreciate their honesty and candor. Forcing me to step up more and be better.

Ultimately, anger's an emotion that shouldn't last forever. It's certainly real, and it's an expected part of the process when you unplug. But, it's **not** where you want to stay. If you stay there for too long, you'll end up a bitter shell, *not* the man you're meant to be. Letting go of the bullshit gets you out of that hole - whether it's a relationship, a betrayal, or something you can't control.

Don't mourn what's gone, enjoy what was, and then look forward to what's next.

In Conclusion

I don't resent my ex or the fact that she's gone - she gave me two incredible kids, memories that'll last a lifetime, and some hard-hitting (and much needed) life lessons that I'll carry with me forever. I no longer resent my daughter for pulling away - she's building her own life, and I'm proud of that. She'll call when she needs me, and I'll be there, steady as ever.

I've thanked my ex-wife (in my head) for what we had, learned where I went *massively* wrong, and I've now moved forward with all of that behind me. You too can do the same - I promise. Navigate life - whatever it throws at you - and you'll find it's not just about surviving. It's about *thriving,* with a **true** inner peace that makes every day better than the last.

The Cold, Hard Truth

Never forget:

- **Nothing lasts forever:** Relationships, kids' bonds - *everything* changes and *everything* ends. Accept it and then work with it.
- **Anger's a phase, *not* a permanent destination:** Use it to wake up, then learn to regulate your own emotions so that you too can let it go.
- **Flip the script:** Learn to take life's curveballs, analyze them thoroughly (from different perspectives), then flip it around to use the circumstances to your advantage.
- **You messed up too:** Learn to hold yourself accountable for where you are and start owning your shit; learn from your mistakes, and then **do the work** to get better.
- **Peace is power:** Accept the truth for what it **IS** (and not what you want it to be), and learn to adapt quickly so that *everyone* in your inner circle (and beyond) will feel it and benefit from your progress.

4

The Manoswamp

When I would frequent Las Vegas in my early 30s for weekends out with friends, it became a place you were as happy to arrive on a Friday night, as you were to leave Sunday evening. The manosphere is a lot like Las Vegas: it's a crazy place that you are usually happy to discover, but once you see it for what it *truly* is, you are also happy to leave it behind.

If you search up "manosphere definition" you get:

*"The **manosphere** is a collection of websites, blogs, YouTube channels and online forums promoting (to varying degrees) masculinity, dating advice, misogyny, and strong opposition to feminism. Communities within the manosphere include men's rights activists, incels (i.e. "involuntary celibates"), Men Going Their Own Way (or, MGTOW), pick-up artists (or, PUA), and fathers' rights groups."*

Both men's rights activists and fathers' rights groups are actually trying to do good work by highlighting blatant injustices, but they're also proving to be ineffective, mostly because nobody cares when men complain and point to said injustices because we live in a matriarchy, and as I discussed in my first book, a "female first primary social order."

Meanwhile, incels (and "Black Pillers") struggle to overcome their limiting beliefs and, according to some evo psych researchers, seem to prefer wanting others to acknowledge their struggles, and express sympathy (i.e. Victimhood). But they rarely do the work needed to level-up and become genuinely more attractive and valuable across every area of life (to therefore get the genuine, burning desire and intimacy from women they crave). For more actionable info on how they could be leveling-up in life, see the "Seven Spokes of a High-Value Man" chapter in my first book, The Unplugged Alpha: 2nd Edition, for more).

Likewise in my last book, I covered MGTOWs in its own chapter, and pick-up artists have a collection of some useful information (when you spend the time to sift through it), but they focus too much of their lives on harassing women on the street (aggressive "cold approaches"), with regurgitated (often cringe-worthy) pick-up lines, and - if we're being honest - any truly unplugged man would never want to have them over to dinner with your family and kids.

The manosphere, according to the Wiki page, has also been associated and blamed for online harassment, and has been implicated in radicalizing men into misogynist beliefs and the glorification of violence against women. Some media sources have associated manosphere-based radicalization with mass-shootings motivated by misogyny.

I don't think the blame and association is *entirely* fair, because there is at least some decent information out there to suggest otherwise. However, as the old saying goes: "where there's smoke, there's fire."

To say the manosphere has a bad PR issue, is an understatement. There's a reason why I've nicknamed it "the manoswamp." I'm grateful for what I have learned, but I'm also glad I left.

Mind you, I didn't go looking for the manosphere, it found me in late 2016 when I was already making content on my YouTube channel on topics around dating and masculinity. It was then that I was invited to speak at a manosphere convention in 2017, which I accepted, and spent the next four years there interacting with, endorsing, and helping many of its creators get exposure.

At that time, I'd already crushed it by running Canada's largest credit card debt-relief company for 12 years. We were pulling in over a quarter-million in monthly sales.

My "Entrepreneurs in Cars" YouTube channel? It had a bigger audience than most of the manoswamp *combined*. Back then, those guys were mostly still just cranking out blogs on Reddit or Twitter and they mostly hid behind aliases, pen names, or fake profiles. No faces shown, no real names dropped. It was all explained to me that "doxxing" (revealing their real names, address, etc.) was a serious issue for these men.

You'll come to learn the reason for that last one later in this chapter.

The Obsession With all the Different Colored Pills

One thing you'll notice quickly in the manoswamp is the obsession with "pills." Red pill, black pill, white pill, blue pill, purple pill - you name it, someone's carved out a niche around it. Each color supposedly represents a worldview, a brand of "truth," or a solution to male struggles. In practice, it's just marketing. It's jargon designed to sell you on a tribe, keep you consuming content, and - more often than not - they want lock you into someone else's defeatist frame.

The red pill was useful when it first broke through mainstream denial about female nature. But somewhere along the line, it stopped being a tool and turned into a badge. For some men it became less about self-improvement, and more about parroting bullshit. Instead of unplugging fully, they get trapped into their own echo-chamber and get stuck in the "rage phase" for *far* too long.

The black pill is even worse. It pushes a doomsday mentality: e.g. "you lost the genetic lottery, so give up." It feeds on hopelessness and an unrelenting narrative of being a victim with no room to improve or grow - which is the exact *opposite* of what men need. Spend too long in those circles and you'll see nothing but bitterness, nihilism, and confirmation bias dressed up as "reality." It's quicksand for men who could've climbed out if they just lifted heavy weights consistently, fixed their money issues, or learned some social skills.

White pill and purple pill camps try to soften the edges, rebranding the conversation as optimism or compromise. Again, it's mostly wordplay. They package up what's already obvious - work hard, stay positive, adapt - and slap a color on it like it's a revelation. It's not. It's recycling basic truths to keep the brand fresh.

Here's the reality: obsessing over pill colors is mental masturbation. It distracts men from the only thing that matters - the results of doing the hard work. The man grinding in silence, building his body, his bank account, and his frame, doesn't care what "pill" he's on. He cares about whether his life is moving forward.

So, when you hear someone trying to drag you into the pill wars, stop and ask: does this serve me, or just feed someone else's ideology? The real unplugging isn't picking a pill - it's rejecting the need for one at all.

If it's not Drama, it's "Red Meat"

I've been a member of several entrepreneurs' organizations in the past, and have many great friends I remain in contact with to this day. But, the manoswamp *really is* something else; when I picked up and left, I cut almost all contact with everyone in the manoswamp (bar a handful of exceptions).

Bickering, infighting, strawmanning, ad hominem attacks, doxxing, and underhanded childish behavior is - sadly - commonplace. People will befriend you, only to betray you just as quickly. It's a disloyal place filled with arrogance, lies, and - frankly - a lot of stupidity.

Creators often use their platforms to manufacture drama between other creators and, as a consequence of that, a good portion of their audience will mobilize and viciously attack opposing creators and, in some cases, harasses their family members over things as simple as a disagreement, or even a popularity contest for what can only be described as "clout chasing."

Quite frankly, the behavior I witnessed was *embarrassing*.

Why I Played in the Sandbox in the First Place

When I first got involved in the manosphere (long before the issues became obvious), I saw an opportunity to collaborate with creators, help amplify their message, and improve the lives of men still plugged-in to the comforting lies that were negatively affecting their life.

There were three events that from 2011 to 2015 had a compound effect in my own unplugging from the matrix. I went through the Western divorce grinder, chaired a lobbying effort with politicians on legislation (and saw what the government was *truly* about), then had a toxic three year relationship with a single mother after my divorce.

After experiencing my own unplugging from society's comforting lies, I saw too many men getting destroyed by family law, being kept away from their kids, being taken advantage of emotionally in relationships, routinely being taken advantage of financially, and ultimately getting betrayed by women and a system they were told they should just trust.

I've had tens of thousands of men contact me and let me know that my videos, and book, had literally saved their life from toxic relationships, money issues, and even suicide.

When men contemplate suicide, you know things are very bad in their life. Women often "attempt" suicide, but these attempts rarely succeed, and what - more often than not - appears to merely be a bid for attention on their problems. Men on the other hand, are *far* more serious and, as a result, are far more "successful" at ending their lives early than women.

Never EVER contemplate a permanent solution to a temporary problem in your life.

If you are ever feeling down and can't see a light at the end of the tunnel, and are **seriously** contemplating suicide, stop, take a **deep** breath, and invest in seeking guidance from a brotherhood of like-minded men (such as those in my communities), or from a pro-masculine professional. You'll soon see that, not only are your problems **not** unique (which is good news as it means they're solvable), but also, such a group of good like-minded men often come together to pull each other through their darkest hours, while also holding each other accountable for turning their lives around.

Hang in there. There's almost always a solution to a problem (even if it isn't easy to see at first). Ultimately, as harsh as it sounds, you must **ALWAYS** get your life in order first and **NEVER** play the victim card.

As I've said before to too many men in my private consultations: "I can guarantee you that there's another man somewhere out there who would swap your place with theirs *in a heartbeat*.

Look, men have constantly been lied to about what women *actually* respond to (versus what they *say* they want), and also lied to about what a good, healthy relationship looks like. As discussed in my first book, unplugging men is difficult work when almost everything they were doing, and ego invested in, was detrimental to their own success and happiness.

I had a new purpose, and was excited to roll up my sleeves, get to work, and get what looked like an underground goldmine of resources and information, to the masses of men that needed it.

I already had a platform with my YouTube channel, with around 30 million views, when I decided to get involved.

I'm generally a giving guy when it comes to anything I am passionate about, and I was more than happy to introduce my audience to tools, authors, and other small creators by mentioning them, and bringing them on my shows.

I even considered changing my YouTube channel name to align with this purpose, and I'm glad I didn't, because what happened over the next four years was both an accomplishment, and a disaster.

I just wanted to get to men, and get them the clarity that I found so useful in my own life.

Why These Underground Groups Stay Underground

The manoswamp remains fringe, and underground, because it cannot organize, agree, and collaborate in a productive manner. It's like a full bus, with every passenger trying to be the driver, and fighting constantly over every little, insignificant detail.

A good portion of the manoswamp doesn't even offer solutions. It just talks about the problem, which is a good way to recruit persuadable men, and then creates more angry, bitter men that form nihilistic and deeply unhealthy views of both women and intersexual relationships. For more on that, see my chapter on MGTOWs, in my last book.

While they focused on descriptions, I only wanted to focus on prescriptions and solutions.

However, red meat sells, and it sells well. If you are a manoswamp creator, the easiest way to get views (and therefore ad revenue) is to manufacture drama on topics, as well as between similar content creators, i.e. "Red Meat."

It's also a simple formula to copy; point at a popular name, craft a clickbait thumbnail, talk about why they are wrong, dig up some dirt on them and, if you can't, just lie, create some dirt, and BOOM!, just like that, you get views.

Look… if you're a liar and a fraud, you *will* be factually exposed at some point. But it's the lack of solutions, or prescriptions that are provided (which is often blanketed in endless hours of "gobbledygook") and constant drama-led "clout chasing" that I take issue with. Character assassination livestreams that run for 4-8 hours were commonplace, and it's just exhausting trying to pick out the useful information during the endless blah, blah, blah.

Driving views via drama-led "clout chasing" is *very* common. It usually appears as trying to alter your optics, by character assassinating another person (usually someone with a higher social status and platform ranking than their own).

By way of watching their actions discussed in this chapter, it appears that few people in the manoswamp are creators, with the primary intention of genuinely helping men get better results out of life. It's all about riding the coattails of others, lying, cheating, and building up your own name or brand while disparaging others to make money, and gain an audience.

It turned out, the *only* thing I had in common with these manoswamp creators, was the fact that we all experienced dramatic trauma in our life with women at some point, and we all went looking for answers.

There was also one key thing that I DIDN'T have in common with almost all other creators. I was already accomplished, before I started creating content. I wasn't aware of any accomplished men in real life creating content. My professional success, money, health, and influence was sorted, but it was just my mindset around women and managing those relationships that wasn't.

Within the manoswamp, I saw guys running from the law with *extensive* criminal records, others were disowned by their family, straight up broke, previously bankrupt or still in loads of debt, were physically unhealthy, had homes foreclosed on them, were failures in their original career choices, and more.

It would appear that, instead of focusing on genuinely trying to help men sort themselves out so they can truly live a better, more fulfilling life, a lot of these creators are in the manoswamp for the wrong reasons (usually for popularity, and to make money).

Think about it, when you are broke, insignificant, and start to realize these things are one of the biggest attraction cues to solving your woman problems, you will do almost *anything* to solve that.

Look, I don't think there is anything wrong with getting paid for the value you create in life. I've always maintained that nobody should deliver genuine value for free, but with video creation, all you need is an internet connection, a mic, and you too can be an expert by saying clever-sounding things, or by parroting and reacting to the latest soundbites. You don't even need to show your face, or use your real name.

Until such creators can learn to collaborate effectively, stop the drama and victim-blaming, and own who they *really* are, then the manoswamp will stay underground and significantly fewer men will get the support they really need to help them turn their lives around.

Sirens (Women) of the Manoswamp

It's no secret women will invade male spaces, and the manoswamp is no exception.

Normally it's not a big deal when some girls want to play video games with the boys for attention, but men already have difficulty with understanding both attraction and female nature fall for what can only be defined as a "thirst trap." A thirst trap is a woman seeking the attention of men by using her beauty, with no real exchange in value to the men.

These sirens are good at regurgitating content men have thought through, organized and collected, but it's now delivered on camera with their hair and makeup done, and their low-cut tops and breasts presented front and center.

Female solipsism doesn't allow them to fully comprehend what men struggle with. Again, by way of watching their actions (especially if you read any of their social media posts, or just dig a little deeper online), these women are mostly there for the validation, attention, and the money.

As I've pointed out many, many times in the past: women don't *really* care about men's struggles, they simply hang out at the finish line and pick the winner.

I've also noticed that it's mostly women approaching, or just past, the prime of their sexual market value that enter the manoswamp, and they're using these confused and thirsty men for attention, validation, and a source of revenue. The old British saying of: "Mutton dressed as lamb" springs firmly to mind when it comes to these women.

If any of them got married, I guarantee that it would be to a man who they view as superior to them (i.e. hypergamy) and if the knot were to untie, like most divorces, she would likely initiate it, and use her enhanced understandings of the power of family law to firmly gain control their kids, and enrich her purse in the process.

Seriously, there are **no red pilled female unicorns out there**, but men *constantly* fall for this bullshit fantasy, and a lot of men of the manoswamp are now also openly supporting this, because female beauty gets views and views = ad revenue.

These men in turn actually believe there are genuinely pro-male "red pilled" women out there and they essentially simp for them in their comment section. Below is just one example of what you'll read.

"What an amazing woman, you define the word sweetheart like no other, eyes are confident and full of life, her voice is angelic, kind hearted to name a few. That happiness and Heath may follow you everywhere you go. Thank you sweet girl, I hope one day to find a woman like you."

— Typical Simp

It's beyond clear that these sirens don't *ever* want to be friends with, have any sort of relationship with, or ever fuck any of these men who watch them; they just want the validation, views, and their money. It's just OnlyFans for the red pill.

Look, the bottom line is this: A man looking to catch fish *doesn't ask a fish how to catch fish*, he asks a seasoned fisherman instead.

Truthfully, women can't understand the plight of men today, and because of women's solipsistic nature, neither do they really care. Women only want men that "just get it" when it comes to forming any kind of relationship with them.

In the past, I saw many male manoswamp creators share this opinion above, and were vehemently opposed to collaborating with women in a men's spaces. Today however, these same manoswamp creators now actively put these sirens on their channels, some of which are *clearly* batshit crazy, all in the name of getting views from thirsty men, and making money off them.

Look, some of these women do try to see things from a man's angle. But - let's be honest - unless you've got a penis with high testosterone pumping through your veins, and you've lived through the crap men deal with from bitter, angry women firsthand? You'll never *truly* get the struggles today's guys face. And that means you can't drop accurate advice from real experience on what women *actually respond to*.

We know this because women don't even know what they want. How many women do you know that have said they just want a really kind and stable Mr. "Nice Guy" but go off and fuck "Mr. Exciting" instead?

For me, it's really simple. If these women *really* cared about men's struggle, then they would openly recognize that the men that came before them who attempted to fix these unjust laws were publicly mocked, and not taken seriously by our female first primary social order. If they *truly* cared, they'd willingly organize themselves, get thousands together, and start protesting on Capitol Hill about changing the hostile laws that ruin men with the abuse of false DV or #metoo charges and unjust family laws. But, they don't (and they likely never will). They just want your attention and your money.

Sadly, very few see the reality of it, but for the most part, it's a grift.

The Manoswamp's Obsession With Notch Counts

In my experience, there's two types of men you cannot trust:

1. The guy that obsesses over his notch count and is getting laid all the time, and
2. The guy that can't get laid at all.

Both types of men will always throw you under the bus when it's convenient for him to scratch his itch.

As far as I'm concerned, it's an unhealthy obsession.

I've never kept track of my "notch count." I lost my virginity at 19, only a few weeks before my 20th birthday, and proceeded to count my notches on my hands, but after I ran out of fingers to count on, I abandoned any notion it mattered.

To me, it was like the first time I rode a motorcycle, it's thrilling and an accomplishment at first, but after you ride a few bikes, it just feels normal.

Why it matters so much today to grown men in the manoswamp, some well past 40 years of age, counting numbers into the thousands, is beyond me and only seems unique to these obsessed men. I've never seen an obsession like this anywhere else before. There's *far* more important things in life to work hard on - gunning for a super-high notch count *isn't* one of them.

Should I count the number of times I've had a bowel movement, or how many times I exhaled in a day? Even as a young man, I found the notion of tracking such a metric simply absurd.

It became clear to me I was in the wrong room when I was on a panel of six and the host asked us all what our notch count was, and everyone but me could provide an exact number, and the others had an odd look of confusion on their face when I said I legitimately didn't know or care.

I'll say this again: if you are the smartest guy in the room, *you are in the wrong room*. They say "birds of a feather, flock together" well it was then that I realized that I was not with my flock. I concerned myself more with leveling up every area of my life, instead of seeing how many notches I could etch into my bedpost.

Posers

When I used to ride sport bikes in my 20s with friends, we rode hardcore and really enjoyed racking up the miles. I talked fondly about motorcycles in my first book, and why a man should own one at least once in their life.

Bike tires are rounded, to allow grip, as you lean the bike over around bends. The faster you went, the more lean angle you needed and subsequently, the outer tire would wear closer to the edge, the harder you rode. We'd frequent a café only bikers would go to, and when other new riders would ask to join us for a ride, we'd always inspect their front tire to see how hard they rode before we would take them with us. This was how we fact checked them. We didn't want any posers holding us up, or getting hurt trying to keep up with us.

Looking the part on the surface, but ultimately lacking the skills, is the very definition of a poser.

Posers (or liars) exist everywhere - there are no checks and balances, you will never see them in a business organization with entrepreneurs, because the market exposes all posers quickly.

I've learned the following holds true: women lie to protect their value; men lie to amplify their value.

It's why women use older photographs, cropping techniques and filters on dating apps to lie about their age, their facial beauty, and their actual weight. Whereas men will round up their height, and lie about how successful they are.

In the manoswamp however, posers are *everywhere*, and they aren't as easy to spot as looking at the front tire of a motorcycle. The dichotomy of posing is interesting to me.

Guys brag to amplify their value but exist in the shadows, shilling lies - and there are *plenty* of shadows to hide in.

By the way, these are the same guys that have been exposed for:

- Claiming that their dating systems allow them to only date "gorgeous women," but are revealed to be in a relationship with "average at best" looking women, many of them older than them, and some are even living with single mothers.
- Having a criminal record and, in some cases, have been forced to move from their home country, and are still running from the law.
- Claiming to be a multimillionaire, with several successful businesses, only to be shown to be living at home with family, completely broke.
- Getting socially awkward men incarcerated for following their dating systems & techniques.
- Saying they are a "world class" Pick-Up Artist (PUA) that can teach you to seduce, and sleep with beautiful women, and is then exposed for hiring prostitutes to be paid actors in "boot camps" to seduce, and sleep with paying "students." In many cases, these disgusting PUAs will even sleep with the prostitutes prior to placing them for students to scratch their itch first.
- Telling you to "do the work" and lift weights, eat well, and get restful sleep, yet he stays up all hours of the night, and gets liposuction to remove belly fat because they are too lazy to actually "do the work" themselves.
- Saying he has an amazing bi-sexual girlfriend, that is compliant, loving, and brings other women into the bedroom for threesomes, yet has been exposed in a recording to have an abusive girlfriend that physically assaults and batters him.
- Telling men they are "legends" for bedding 1,000+ beautiful women, then admitting that some of the "women" they had sex with were transsexuals that were biologically born as men.

- Calling men that send money to "OnlyFans" women "simps," yet is found out by the manager of an OnlyFans agency, to be sending money to his OnlyFans girls.

These bullet points above are all factual events I came across while in the manoswamp over the four years, and I could go on, but I will save you from any further disgusting examples.

Ultimately, I've always asked myself one simple question when it comes to taking advice from others. "Would I trade places with this person dispensing this advice?" This is the gold standard only unplugged men use, when evaluating a source of information and advice.

Once I saw these discrepancies pile up over time, it changed how I looked at those creators moving forwards, and it really forced me to rethink what I was doing in that space.

Advice is a Form of Nostalgia

Baz Luhrmann wrote a popular song when I was a younger man, called "*Everyone's free to wear sunscreen*", I suggest you pay close attention to the lyrics; this particular verse stood out:

> *"Be careful whose advice you buy, but be patient with those who supply it. Advice is a form of nostalgia. Dispensing it is a way of fishing the past from the disposal, wiping it off, painting over the ugly parts and recycling it for more than it's worth."*
>
> — Baz Luhrmann

This brings me to my next point about how manoswamp creators today lay claim to ideas and concepts that they purport to have invented, and also own the rights to certain language and phrases used.

I've gone deep into the rabbit hole, and many of the creators today are doing exactly what Baz describes above. I've come across material from *Chateau Heartiste*, *Pook*, *Alan Roger Currie*, and even *Ross Jeffries* from the 80s that is all used today, and claimed as a brand new concept by the modern manoswamp creator.

Now, there's nothing wrong with reminding men of what works, but don't claim it to be your own original body of work, when it - clearly - isn't.

I'm pretty sure men several thousands of years ago, after a hunt and sitting around a fire, likely had a conversation about how women didn't care about their struggles as men if they failed in a hunt, and how they preferred the winners who were bringing home the spoils.

No Honor Among Thieves

I've recommended *Jack Donovan's* books to my audience for some time. *"The Way of Men"* was a great introduction into masculinity, and the tribal nature of men throughout history.

Jack says that the way of men is the way of the gang. Men have always formed tribes, and from those strong brotherly bonds, come the gang. When the gang is formed, and tested, there is a distinction between "us," and "them." Men will draw a perimeter around "us" and define who is "them." This cohesion is what creates brotherhoods.

Men of honor will protect their tribe, men of honor also have no patience for weak members of the tribe, or men that disparage their tribe.

It's been said that the mark of a true friend is that he will insult you to your face, and defend you behind your back. Those that you can't trust will never insult you face to face, but always disparage you behind your back.

Remember, gossiping is a feminine trait, and he who gossips to you, will gossip about you.

<u>Never</u> trust a man that gossips.

With the manoswamp, which is primarily either obsessed with who's getting laid, or who isn't getting laid, it has no real cohesion and, as mentioned earlier in this chapter, will openly disparage, or throw anyone under the bus for clout or views.

At some point, when the underhanded behavior is discovered, they start playing the victim in the chaos they created, and the creator uses their YouTube platform to manufacture drama, and then they character assassinate that man, and others around him.

Maybe I'm just used to always having solid men who have my back - or hell, maybe I'm a bit too trusting - but you must figure out when you go all-in to help other dudes, build a real tribe, boost their businesses and clout, that they'd return the favor. Unfortunately, not in the manoswamp.

The notion of a brotherhood and honor is absent in the manoswamp. There is no honor among thieves. It's never about who is real to your face, it's only about who is real behind your back.

Pen Names

From the start, I've used my real name. I stand behind it, what I say, and I'm proud to carry my family name.

Much of the manoswamp uses pen names, or an alias. Some on YouTube don't even show their face, and will just use AI voice-overs and generic stock images to narrate their videos.

Sure, there are spots where an alias - that fake name swapped in for your real one - might make sense. Like dropping a hot-take opinion that could get you canned from your day job. But let's face facts: Historically, it's mostly criminals who've pulled that to shield their identity, dodging the fallout when they get exposed.

So that raises the question. What are they hiding?

From what we've learned thus far, quite a lot. For a short time, I thought when I was calling many of these manoswamp creators by their name, I was using their birth name, but it turns out that I wasn't. Most of the creators and authors in this space use an alias, or pen name and although there are some exceptions, it's mainly for the reasons mentioned above.

I want to look into the eyes of a fellow man, know his family name, and see his soul. If you haven't got the decency to be honest about who you are, then in my opinion, you have no business holding out to the public that you have solutions to men's struggles in life.

> ***Editor's Note:*** *From my personal perspective, I've chosen to use the alias of Steve From Accounting (instead of my real name) as the family court system in the UK are still often very biased towards the mum, and if my ex-wife caught wind of my work in this space (who's still very bitter about losing out heavily in our divorce), then I've **zero** doubts she'd weaponize this against me in a legal-setting, potentially removing my (near daily) access to my kids. It's extremely frustrating having to use an alias (as I stand by Rich's viewpoints and use them to live my best life to-date and I'm extremely proud of the work I've done to help shape the (audio)books, but I also know that learning how to navigate - potentially very nasty - rigid frameworks in a prudent and pragmatic way is super important to ensure that I don't shoot myself in the foot with regards to my kids.*

My Golden Rule

I've been part of many organizations, and groups over the years. Some of them exposed me to some elite performers, and the common denominator was all of those that excelled in life, understood one thing: If you lay with dogs, you'll get fleas.

As a result, and as insurance against complicating my life unnecessarily, I created my own golden rule: ***Don't work with losers or people that work with losers.***

To more clearly define that, I stay away from people that are obviously frauds, liars, posers, incompetent, and - worst of all - dangerous.

Additionally, beyond that, I won't collaborate or work with anyone that works with such types of people.

Although some manoswamp creators have useful content, and fair observations, it's quite difficult to assess who is the real deal, what is made up for drama (aka: red meat), or just straight up clickbait.

That disqualified a large part of the manoswamp, which is absolutely okay and it's why I choose to distance myself from the manoswamp at the end of 2021.

In Conclusion

Sometimes in life, we need to prune, to grow. I still talk about things that matter to men, I just won't collaborate with, or amplify, other men that I wouldn't invite over to my home for a family dinner.

Too many men today wonder why their life is a circus, but fail to see that they've gone and surrounded themselves with clowns.

I've been away from the manoswamp for some time now. Again, my advice is to cautiously pay the manoswamp a visit, get what genuine value you need from it, but leave again quickly if you value your name and reputation. You will find *far* more applicable information to women, attraction, relationships, being a good man, *and being good at being a man*, by reading evolutionary psychology books, my books, and watching my catalogue of free videos on YouTube.

In closing, a good friend from my community summed up the manoswamp like this:

"The biggest problem with this space is that so many guys out there, their income is tied to their following... so they have to sell hopium/coaching to keep their lights on. That's what I always respected about you Rich, is that you made your money first, so you can speak/coach from a place of "I don't need your money" so you can give actual, helpful direction without compromise"

The Cold, Hard Truth

Never forget:

- **Take what's useful and leave**: The manosphere can offer valuable lessons, but it's filled with bullshit. Visit cautiously, extract insights, and leave before it drags you down.
- **Stop chasing drama**: Avoid creators who thrive on conflict, gossip, and "red meat" content. Instead, focus on those offering proven solutions and actionable advice.
- **Don't idolize frauds**: Vet anyone offering advice. If they're not living a life you'd trade yours for, then they're not worth following. Fake success stories are all around; stay skeptical.
- **Women don't "fix" the manosphere**: Female creators catering to male audiences are usually playing for attention, not offering real solutions. Don't fall for it.
- **Control your envy**: Hating others won't solve your problems. Work on improving your fitness, finances, and mindset instead of wasting energy on resentment..
- **Be real and demand authenticity**: Avoid advice from those hiding behind fake names or personas. True leaders stand by their words and live by example.
- **Protect your reputation**: Don't associate with toxic individuals or environments. Surround yourself with people who lift you up, not drag you down.

5

Finding Your Tribe

Once men have unplugged from society's comforting lies and begin updating their beliefs, they begin to level-up in life after taking ownership for themselves. While doing the work, they will stop, look around, and soon realize that they are now the smartest guy in the room and that they're surrounded by Plugged-In Betas.

To put it bluntly, they no longer fit in.

As I've always said: "If you find you are the smartest guy in the room, you're in the wrong room."

I view people that come into my life a lot like how I view sailing. People around you will often behave like either anchors, or sails. One holds you back, the other fills with wind, and takes you on a passage to your next port of call. The magic is in identifying who is who, and then cutting those anchors loose. For more advice on ways on how to do this effectively, see the chapter in my first book: "Hire Slow, but Fire Fast."

As a result, one of the most popular questions men ask me is: "How do I find like minded men to hang out with and network with?"

In this chapter, I want to deal with the question of brotherhood.

Jack Donovan, author of the highly recommended "The Way of Men," writes on topics of masculinity, and one of the conclusions he's drawn is: "The way of men, is the way of the gang", meaning men are tribal in nature, and they need to form a strong brotherhood in order to strengthen and grow.

How I Found My Tribe

As an entrepreneur for many years, I've been a member of several organizations. Most of the successful entrepreneurs in the organizations I was a member of were Plugged-In Beta males, or women that you could classify as successful entrepreneurs, or "boss girls."

They were all plugged-in to comforting lies, and they all served a "female first primary social order," as I described in my first book.

In 2014, I vividly remember sitting in a private meeting of nine peers in an entrepreneurs forum. I consider them all great people and, as far as I was concerned, they were friends (although some of them may not feel the same way about me today, because of the conversations I openly have online).

They were all high-net-worth individuals, running businesses doing high seven or low eight figures in sales receipts annually, and they're really good people. But, I had a genuine feeling of unease when I heard my friend complaining about his sexless marriage, then closing with the - now infamous - "happy wife happy life" soundbite. At that point, I just *knew* something was off, and that I was now sitting in the wrong room.

I couldn't put my finger on it at the time, but here I was, looking at an absolute weapon in his own business, but who was a total Plugged-In Beta in his private life. He could solve problems and make life-changing money, but he was in a marriage where he was run by his wife and he openly admitted that he wasn't having sex.

A race horse should **never** *be giving pony rides.*

Then, a few years later (when I was well on my way through the unplugging process and had joined another "men's group for entrepreneurs,") one of the members in the chat group, who was quite successful in his business, announced that he was getting married. While everyone was smothering him with approval and asking for an invitation to the wedding, I waited to see if anyone was going to chime in and ask him the obvious question about doing some prudent financial planning and structure a prenup to minimize risk of the hostile divorce courts getting involved in his life.

Everyone piled on me like a bunch of fat kids attacking cake, accusing me of everything under the sun with the standard soundbites like: "Who hurt you?!" and "That's just setting the marriage up for failure," etc.

I thought these people were my tribe, having shared multiple retreats together, broken bread together, but the mere mention of a prenup turned them all against me.

That was the straw that broke the camel's back for me. I swore from that point on that I wouldn't get involved with *any* community of men that aren't unplugged. Being around successful entrepreneurs didn't matter to me anymore, if they were plugged into society's comforting lies.

Cautionary Note

There's so many men's groups out there that hold themselves out to be about masculinity and brotherhood, that are really just filled with complete posers. As I've seen with my own eyes, if someone raises a problem around their cold wife and sexless marriage, the "plugged-in men" in these groups start offering ideas around "learning her love language" or, "doing more chores around the house" (aka: "Choreplay"). None of which have *ever* led to making a woman feel true, genuine attraction.

Ultimately, the people I was going to surround myself with going forward needed to be of a higher caliber and of sound mind. I only want to spend my valuable time around good men, who are also good at ***being men***.

Let's take a look at some of the best places I've found some of these men.

Fight Gyms

I discussed the imperative need for men to learn the art of how to fight and being lethal in my first book. One of the additional benefits of joining a martial arts dojo, and learning how to fight well, is the caliber of people that such sports often attracts.

No clearer example can be shown than watching a few podcast interviews of Dana White - who is the CEO of UFC. I have also met several professional MMA fighters over the years that are clearly unplugged, and who also share very similar opinions and beliefs to me.

Not all men that fight are unplugged, but *far* more than you'd expect are, and I think that's a great group of men to spend time around and socialize with. I don't think that it's the fighting discipline which you choose to learn that matters, it's the notion of combat training in general that I've noticed brings out stronger men of character who enjoy seeking out challenges and are comfortable being uncomfortable.

Motorsports

Being an avid petrolhead myself, I've talked to a lot of men over the years that own motorcycles, and fast cars. Again, not all of them are unplugged, but there is a disproportionate amount of men that participate in motorsports, whether professionally or casually, that seem to subscribe to the unplugged mindset I talk about; and at the very least, people that love fast vehicles are always fun to do social events with.

Diving into the engineering of a car or motorcycle has a pull. That drive to test its limits - or find where they end - fires up curiosity across the board in life.

Libertarians

On the "Left versus Right" political spectrum, most of the guys are plugged in to lies (although I find the more conservative leaning people to align more with my content). I still hear people like Dr. Jordan Peterson telling men to "man up," "stop being babies," and to get married without offering any of these men any prudent guidance on how to vet the woman, or on how to structure a prenup to protect their wealth in case they were to untie the knot.

Libertarians on the other hand seem to "get it," and when I was asked to speak at a recent Rebel Capitalist event I was a little hesitant at first, as I wasn't sure if my message would be appreciated by the audience, but - to my surprise - it was. On top of that, some speakers there seemed to know me and my content, while expressing some curiosity about it. Some of these men even had an appreciation for my work and how I was trying to help men.

I think my content, and the notion of unplugging aligns well with libertarians and their beliefs around questioning the narrative, more personal freedom, less taxation, and less government involvement in our daily lives.

Other Groups

I've also met some unplugged guys in gun clubs, cigar lounges, a few crypto communities, ranchers, tradesmen, private gentlemen's clubs (*not* strip clubs), whiskey lounges, and powerlifting gyms. I've also heard from friends that the mining community is very unplugged, but you're hardly going to move to the middle of nowhere to hang out with miners.

However, the problem with most of those environments, is that if your goal is to be part of a community and join a tribe of like-minded unplugged men, then you're still going to run into a lot of Plugged-In Beta males that *will* cause problems for you (**especially** if they disagree with your unplugged opinions).

I've learned that people don't really want to debate, or hear your opinions; what people *really* want is to hear their opinions coming out of your mouth.

I ran into the same problems that most guys do when looking for a community of like-minded men, there were still quite a lot of rotten plugged-in apples.

I've caught other dudes I'd call red-pilled building communities and slinging memberships. But too often, their "leaders" end up in deep shit - hot water with the law, or worse. Definitely not the kind of guys I'd link up with.

What Makes a Man Unplugged?

Look, with social media blasting radical BS at warp speed since 2010, it's no wonder everything feels like a battlefield – politics, culture, even health choices turning folks into enemies overnight. Both sides wield it to divide, pushing in-groups that serve agendas over truth, leaving average guys scrambling to adapt or getting radicalized into echo chambers. But unplugging isn't about picking a side in that noise; it's about owning your integrity, uplifting yourself, family, and tribe through hard questions and real work - not blindly enforcing (or caving to) shaming tactics from feeds or "experts."

So, if you're wondering "Does believing X/Y/Z make me unplugged?" - then no, it's more nuanced than that. Instead, ask yourself: *"Am I deciding based on facts that serve my mission, or am I reacting to just fear or hype?"*

Being unplugged isn't about slogans. It's about personal freedom, less blind obedience, and more strategic curiosity. If a man's uplifting his circle without drama or lies, he's tribe material. Vet by results: does he push you forward like a sail, or drag you back like an anchor? That clarity keeps your path clean.

How I Solved My Own Problem

I remember looking at the booking stats one day where my YouTube viewers could book me for one-on-one coaching and I noticed that only 1% of the people that landed on my page actually booked a call.

While it was such a small number, it was also a very significant one, because it represented the men that wanted a meaningful connection, and to genuinely change their lives.

While reflecting on this 1%, I also realized how much I enjoyed the conversations I had with these men I'd been coaching from around the world, and I noted how often they asked for a tribe. So, I decided to offer my own community to my viewing public and I called it the 1%.

Since 2017 we have grown to a global community of like-minded men, and throughout the different membership tiers, we currently have over 1,000 members - and rising.

Membership starts from as low as $50 per-month for well curated classroom lessons helping you unplug, and with those members in the higher tiers we have done the following as a group (with more planned events and meetups for 2025 and 2026 in the pipeline already):

- Ski trips,
- Supercar rallies,
- Hiking excursions,
- Navy Seal firearm training,
- Fishing and hunting trips,
- Yachting trips,
- Back-country canoe trips,
- Stayed in beach houses in Panama,
- Big city, formal dinner events,
- And more.

Brothers, Breaking Bread, and Building Bonds

The following photos capture just some of the highlights of brothers from my community traveling the world to meet, connect, and do cool shit together:

1% and TUB members, Europe meet-up (2025). Faces blurred for privacy.

Sharpening my gun skills at the range.

Brothers at the end of our inaugural Algonquin trip.

"Buds Experience" at our annual Full Spectrum Warrior training. Blood, sweat, guns, and bonds.

Every year now we have a three-day annual forum event open to all community members with a line-up of incredible speakers who want to share their expertise with others, and help them find ways to make their own dent in the universe.

We have everything from unplugging students looking to level-up, to world-class entrepreneurs, to professional athletes in our community.

Life-long friendships have been forged at these events and many professional connections have been sparked, which has led to a wealth of business deals being made.

You can find the link to my community at the end of this chapter.

In Conclusion

All healthy men who've unplugged will seek a tribe of some sort. Call it a gang, a brotherhood, or a community. That drive to join something bigger than yourself - and surround yourself with like-minded grinders - it's always there.

As an aside, the "Sigma" idea often stands out. It's that "lone wolf" type who skips validation and group ties. These guys get painted as introspective, strategic, and detached from the pack. They prioritize personal freedom over fitting in. Think how we romanticize 'em through characters like John Wick.

The truth of the matter is, wolves - like men - are pack animals, and men always have, and always will, form hierarchical gangs (even unplugged men inevitably into a hierarchy). That's just the way it is.

It's often been said that a Sigma is just an Alpha without friends and there will always be introverts, but men can accomplish *so* much more when we work collectively and lift each other up.

So, get out there, chase masculine pursuits, and try to engage in social activities with these like-minded men. By all means, look for ways to form your own tribe where you live, but always know that my community can always use a few more good men and is always open to men who're looking to level-up their lives.

The Cold, Hard Truth

Never forget:

- **Frequently assess your surroundings:** If you're now the "smartest guy in the room," then you're no longer in the right room. It's time to move on and find a group of like-minded men where you can not only learn new skills and perspectives from, but also share your expertise with.
- **"Anchors" versus "sails":** If you find you've got people in your life that are being anchors and are holding you back, then either find a way to remove them from your life or, at the very least, hold them at arm's length. Spend more of your valuable time on forging relationships where you both put wind into each other's sails and push each other forwards.
- **Not your monkey, not your circus:** Keep in mind that if you're doing business with men who are absolute machines at business, but are Plugged-In Beta's in private life, do so with extreme caution. Keep those relationships firmly business-only. There's nothing to be gained from trying to "red pill" them in their relationships.
- **Find *your* tribe:** Irrespective of whether or not that's within one of my communities or not. Men are tribal in nature - they always have been. The right tribe will not only lift you up and want you to succeed, but they'll also - firmly but fairly - call you out on your own BS and hold your feet to the fire. And they'll be open to you doing the same to them. Join a dojo, a gun club, or another club where men of character and integrity reside.

- **Bonds are forged in adversity:** For those of you who are more introverted, then the thing to keep in mind is that the strongest bonds are *always* forged in the flames of adversity, overcoming challenges together, and in embracing being uncomfortable. So, be prepared to challenge yourself and look for groups where you can listen, learn, and share your expertise.

6

Becky, Today's Modern Woman

The term "modern woman" has been thrown around a lot now that women are getting degrees, are working in higher paying professions, buying their own homes, paying more in taxes, and are "strong and independent" (more on that later in this chapter). Let's call this avatar "Becky," and *every* guy will meet women like Becky at some point in his life.

The Rise of "Becky"

Becky is usually older than 27, has a degree, and is a working professional.

At no time in history have so many women ever parroted the phrases "I don't need no man" or, "a woman needs a man, like a fish needs a bicycle." But today, it's become common for women to remind other women that they too are "strong and independent."

Women are earning more degrees than ever before. In both colleges and universities across the US today, women outnumber men by a large margin. *Source: QR Code and Link at end of chapter*

Women are also more financially independent today than in any other time in history. In large urban cities especially, Becky is *everywhere*.

Becky, is far more common than the more traditional woman that wants to be protected, and provided for as a mother and wife by a strong, virtuous man. Becky is the type of woman that uses hashtag soundbites like "#boss-girl," "#baddie," or "#bossbabe" in her social media posts.

Becky gets up in the morning, usually as her "fur babies" jump on her bed as the alarm goes off looking to be fed, and taken for a walk. She makes her bed, aligns 17 decorated pillows in just the right fashion, then stops for a brief moment to admire the bed.

She then has her coffee, usually posts a picture on social media of it, the sunrise, or one of her pets, scrolls through her screen looking to see who's liked her posts, catches up on her horoscope, her favorite group chats with her family, friends, and then comments on how much she loves them, her nieces, nephews and godchildren.

Praise by everyone in the group chat is dispensed on cute pictures of little children the group chat doing something simple (like wiping their own ass).

She then goes on to read messages from several men (that she chose not to reply to), all of them telling her just how "pretty" she is, calling her a "queen", only to reply with something like: "Oops! Sorry I didn't reply, I fell asleep early!" even though she was out last night on a date with another man. She then messages the men that have ghosted her with a "good morning handsome" message, desperately hoping one of them will reach out for another date after they hooked up together and then went silent on her immediately afterwards.

Becky then takes a shower, puts on her power suit (with padded shoulders no-less), then admires her degree with little letters after her name (framed in beautiful mahogany) for a fleeting moment, reminding her that she is important; sometimes Becky wishes she was made out of mahogany.

She then scans around her home, and admires her décor selections and recites her affirmations reminding herself that she is "strong and independent," and "what a total boss babe she is," and "how lucky any of the guys she is chasing would be to be with her."

She then says good-bye to her fur babies in her best baby voice, and commutes to work to "smash the patriarchy," often - ironically - by willingly serving a male-owned "patriarchal" corporation. Becky doesn't see this obvious irony of not prioritizing family in her 20s and wanting to serve a husband and family at home, but she's perfectly okay with serving a man at work, working longer hours, and paying taxes to the state for the imaginary prestige she carries in her mind.

After a long day smashing the patriarchy, Becky now finds time to fill one of her rotating weekly hobbies. Drinking with her other "strong and independent" girlfriends, or maybe having a workout class, or returning some décor she brought home that didn't fit her style, or spending more time working to climb that corporate ladder slaving away at the machine, just to pay even more in taxes, and maybe get a possible promotion next year, and be an even bigger "#bossbabe."

By the time Becky gets home, she often finds that the loves of her life, the fur babies, have either vomited, defecated in her home somewhere, or chewed a hole in her mattress.

After cleaning up the mess, she takes the fur babies for a walk. All while yapping loudly on her phone in public (while on speakerphone) - venting to her mom, sister, or BFF about her big day "smashing the patriarchy." And don't forget she's trashing that "lazy bitch" part-timer on her team who clocks fewer hours now that she's a "mom."

She then returns home, fixes a salad, microwaves some chicken from the freezer, and sits on her couch swiping on dating apps for her "equal" (only to be disgusted by her options), and sits wondering "where all the good men have gone?," and talking to several men totally out of her league hoping that one will be her knight in shining armor, and eventually be her soulmate and make her a mother.

Time Waits for No One

What Becky fails to understand is that she is no prize, she is past her prime, has spent her early 20s partying, drinking, smoking, and doing too many drugs. She's slept with so many men, she has forgotten most of them, and when one of her girlfriends asks what her notch count is, she only remembers the men she was in longer-term relationships with (but has, conveniently, forgotten the names of most of the men she had one-night stands with, was in a "friends with benefits" arrangement with, had threesomes with, gave blowjobs to, or women with which she had blackout drunk lesbian encounters).

Becky knows that she is incredibly interested in a man's future ability to provide for her burning desire for a family, but she's unfortunately unable to see that the men who she wants, don't want her. Instead, these top-shelf men are *very* concerned about her past, and the baggage she - clearly - doesn't see, but nevertheless, likes to bring to the table.

You see, one of Becky's biggest conundrums, is she was sold the feminist lie, of the "strong independent woman" but she also painfully feels the ticking of her biological clock, and is counting every egg that isn't being fertilized monthly, all while watching through teary-eyes at her friends and family of hers getting married and having babies.

Becky Is Delusional

Becky's expectations are so incredibly high, only a handful of men could meet her requirements, yet every "Becky" has nearly the same expectation and when men ask her what she brings to the table, she tells them that she is smart, funny, educated, has style, has her own place, is a responsible pet mom, has a car, and a career. Or, even worse, that she IS the table!

What Becky doesn't understand is that she's basically describing a successful man, and what makes him attractive to her.

Setting aside her confusion around what she - incorrectly - thinks men want, she has a lot of the red flags I mentioned in my first book like: debt, a large notch count, is disagreeable and bossy, a feminist, not fit, obsessed with décor and returning things, is very masculine, has tasteless tattoos everywhere, is sometimes a single mother, and - in some cases - comes with multiple children from multiple different fathers.

Becky certainly knows what she "wants," but she doesn't understand that the men she wants don't want her or why ("Where's all the good men gone?!"). She's trying to attract bees with vinegar, but doesn't understand that they want pure, sweet, 100% natural honey.

The Painful Truth

I always get flack when I correct women, and explain that men don't want boss girls, or that beautiful women aren't the prize, it's the high-value men who are putting a dent in the universe who are. Beautiful women are reasonably common, but the top-shelf men they all want (and are chasing on dating apps), certainly aren't.

Top-shelf men have their own struggles; truly feminine, beautiful, and agreeable women are rare - even scarcer than before in today's world.

However, it's Becky's disconnect from the reality of what men want, and her impossibly-high standards for a man, that keeps her single, lonely, and perpetually angry. Her own solipsism prevents her from seeing the flaws in her thinking. Inner reflection isn't a skill that's in her wheelhouse.

When Becky Settles

At some point, Becky eventually does settle, and she makes concessions when she realizes she can't have it all. This is when things can go very badly for the plugged-in men she hooks her wagon to.

You see, Becky hits a phase in her life, usually in her 30s where she can no longer ignore her biological imperative shouting at her about having kids.

Becky desperately wants to have kids, but she doesn't really want to be a hands-on mother. She just wants to pop them out, take a few weeks off on maternity leave, drop them off at daycare, and keep climbing the corporate ladder. Sometimes, Becky cooks up crazy ideas like not even carrying her own children (using a surrogate instead), or insisting that she skip natural childbirth completely and use a c-section, because she's "too posh to push."

She wants to be a bride with all the wedding-day glitz and glam, (she just doesn't want to be a loving and caring wife, or even a mother). She wants all rewards and social praise for all of this, but without any of the accountability that comes with it.

When Becky finds her "equal partner" he often isn't her first, second, or even her third choice, he is merely just "good enough." He is usually a beta chump, plugged into society's comforting lies, who'll unwittingly go through the very slow and soul-sucking process of "betatization through a thousand concessions" during the time he spends with Becky, the boss girl who "has it all."

She complains to friends around her that he's: not quite tall enough, not quite handsome enough, not quite rich enough, not quite competent enough, not quite good enough in bed; but she has run out of time (and therefore out of options). After all, every guy she had pined for (and even pursued diligently in the past), didn't want to commit to her; so settling is what she often now has to do.

After the months leading up to the big fancy wedding, the brutal dieting to get into decent shape she got in for her engagement and wedding photographs, a honeymoon for two weeks in an exotic destination (just so she can get all the pictures she needs for social media clout), and an extravagant home purchase (with a large mortgage they can barely afford), Becky might eventually get pregnant (assuming her husband's testosterone levels haven't tanked over the proceeding years of nagging).

Fast forward a few years. Becky has her kids out of the way now. She's put on more weight and become all about the kids - even when it's not about the kids. She henpecks her husband into a complete "happy wife, happy life" beta male. She stops being sexually intimate with him on a regular basis - sometimes only using it as a weapon to get what she wants. He starts googling: "How do I get my wife to fuck me?"

Becky lacks any self-awareness. She often blames hormones or her "baby weight." Or she claims he "doesn't do enough chores around the house" to make her want sex - so three times a year or so ends up being the frequency if he's "lucky" enough. Becky closes her eyes and assumes the starfish position. Very reluctantly she grants her husband sexual access. Yet, she used to enthusiastically give that access to her "first true love" Chad - no less than three times in one night - after the foam cannon party in Cancun when she was 22.

It's usually at this point that she watches a film like "Eat Pray Love." She has a conversation with her girlfriends and does what many Beckys do when they've gotten together with other divorced friends. She files for divorce by announcing something that sounds like: "I love you but I'm just not in love with you. I want a divorce." She thinks she'll find a much better man. A high-value man that will want her very average looks and now worn out body. And who will want to take on the burden of raising another man's children as if they were his own.

Don't ever be that man. For more on why smart men don't marry, read my first book.

I am, of course, being facetious with this description of Becky. Or… am I?

The Six Sixes

I was talking to a friend's wife once, and she was very interested in introducing me to one of her friends, she said: "Rich, you look like you have the six sixes" I must introduce you to my girlfriend.

When I asked for clarity, it was revealed that these sixes are:

1. Six ft tall,
2. Six inches in the pants,
3. Have six pack abs,

4. Drive a 600hp car,
5. Be six months out of a relationship,
6. And, most importantly for some, have a six-figure income.

So "this" is what women want I thought?

But the truth of the matter is that a woman's laundry list for what she expects in a man is often much much longer than six items.

She also wants him to be: funny, kind, loving, strong, smart, resourceful, competent, humble, alpha, sweet, thoughtful, romantic, a good father, love her family and friends, a poet, handy, be stylish, have great hair, smell great, and the list goes on and on to another hundred points.

Women's expectations of men are now often so high, less than 1% of the male population can meet their requirements. Sadly, all these women are also under the delusional impression there are plenty of these types of men out there, they just need to wait for them to come along.

With the vast majority of women competing for the top 1% of men, it's no wonder the biggest complaint these women have is that these very in-demand men aren't sexually loyal to them.

It's almost like these men at the top have options, wow, who knew?

Let's just take a look at one of the sixes, height. Only 14.5% of men in North America are over six foot tall. But women's expectations of how tall they want their man to be are often much higher. When men read the bios of many women's dating apps, they discover the expectation seems to be 6'2" and only 3.9% of the North American population is that height or higher.

Have you begun unplugging from the Matrix yet and seeing how disconnected modern women are from reality?

Top-Shelf Men

I'm going to be generous here, but I'd estimate only 5% of men fall in the category of being a "top-shelf man." But this is what most women (especially the Becky's) are pining for, more-so when they hit their late 20s to early 30s and they suddenly realize their beauty is on the decline, and they need to lock down a man (i.e. the "Epiphany Phase").

The sad reality is, in order to avoid the Becky avatar I just described, the best position you can be in is to do the work and be a top-shelf man. As I've stated many, *many* times before (and as I'll continue to reiterate):

"Men are success objects to women, and women are beauty objects to men."

If you want a feminine beauty who's going to willingly be in your frame, have true Genuine Burning Desire (GBD) for you, and compliment your life, then your ideal position is to be on the top-shelf. Or, to be more specific, be at the finish line as a winner because, as I've also stated many times prior:

"Women don't care about a man's struggle, they wait at the finish line and pick the winners."

Are Women Really "Strong and Independent?"

Let's define strong first: Strong is about having power or resilience - physical, mental, or emotional. Physically, it means you can lift heavy stuff, fight off an attacker, or endure tough conditions - like a soldier. Mentally or emotionally, it's about holding it together under pressure - think someone who doesn't crack during chaos, or keeps pushing through grief. It's not about being invincible; it's more like you've got a solid core that doesn't snap easily.

Let's take a look at independent: Independent means you can stand on your own. You don't need someone else to prop you up - financially, emotionally, or otherwise. It's not about isolation; it's about self-reliance. You pay your own way, and don't cling to others for validation.

Let's be honest, if the Beckys of the world were as "strong and independent," as they always claim to be, they'd fight in wars, refuse alimony and child support beyond the child's needs, pay for their own dinners on a date, and not vote for big government, huge tax rates, and free social programs.

Raising a Daughter to Avoid the Becky Trap

If you're a father of a daughter that's unplugging, then the real win is steering your daughter clear of that mess in the first place. Raise her to respect her father (that's from her seeing you leading by example) and men in general - not as superiors, but as complements in a balanced life.

Remember, it's about modeling respect through actions, not lectures, so she internalizes it as natural. Done right, she'll chase excellence her way - feminine, accountable, and hypergamy-smart without the delusion. Finally, make sure that she has a better relationship with you as her father, than with her screens, her friends, the mainstream Media, etc.

Start Early With Your Own Frame

Be the rock she looks up to. Set boundaries calmly - "No means no, kiddo" - and follow through. When she pushes, hold firm without anger; it teaches her men aren't pushovers but fair leaders.

For example, if she throws a tantrum over screen time, don't cave or yell - explain once, enforce, then redirect to something fun. She learns respect flows from strength, not weakness. This builds her trust in masculine guidance, prepping her for healthy dynamics with men later.

Encourage Femininity (Without Forcing It)

Praise her when she shows nurturing traits, whether that's cooking a family meal or helping her siblings. Positive reinforcement builds identity far better than lectures. At the same time, don't ignore the cultural noise. Call out the media BS together. Watch a "strong independent woman" flick, then challenge its message with something like: "It's a cool-sounding story, but *real* power is balancing smarts with heart."

Guide her gently to value her sexuality without cheapening it. A subtle reminder works best: "Your body's a gift; share it wisely with a top-shelf man who earns it." The point isn't to scare her, but to frame her choices as valuable.

When the teenage drama hits - those crushes, gossip, and the boy trouble - give her a simple filter. Advise: "Look at him the way I look at deals: does he bring value, or does he bring drama?" That simple frame lets her see herself as the prize, confident in her worth. Over time, it helps her attract winners without hiding behind the boss-babe armor.

Teach Accountability and Self-Reflection

Never allow a victim mindset to take root. The rule is simple: own your choices, and fix what you can. If she blames others for a bad grade, don't let it slide; nudge her with a question like, "What could you do differently next time?" This shifts her focus from excuses to solutions.

Model the behavior yourself. Admit your own slip-ups openly and show how you course-correct. Growth isn't about pretending to be perfect; it's about demonstrating how responsibility builds resilience.

When it comes to how she views men, highlight the positives. Point out examples she can respect: "Your uncle's hustle built that business from the ground up." If she disrespects a male relative's opinion, intervene with something like, "Hear him out; strong people listen before they fire back."

Over time, these moments shape her into someone who values accountability over entitlement. That mindset makes her a partner men will crave, not compete with. Just remember: keeping a woman accountable is one of the hardest things you'll ever do. Do your best, reinforce the lessons, but don't expect miracles.

For Divorced Dads

Lead by example in your time together - show strong, kind masculinity she won't get elsewhere. If mom's filling her head with "don't need no man," don't bash - redirect: "Everyone needs good people; find ones who lift you." Use time alone for real talks and if alienation creeps (mom badmouthing you), stay steady - "Actions over words, kid; you see how I show up."

Document bullshit calmly for the courts if it's needed, but focus more on bonding: Do joint activities that build trust, like teaching her how to cook a few solid meals. Be sure to keep planting seeds that mom's narrative can't uproot, keeping her unplugged despite the split-home tug-of-war that's going on in her mind.

Finally, if your daughter is already into her mid-teens/early-adulthood years and she's showing signs of turning into a Becky, then you need to find that balance of being there for her (which may just mean listening to her), and giving her guidance should she start asking you for it. As long as you haven't been shutting her out of your life, then they often do come back to their dads in the later years. Which may mean you are playing the *very* long game while you wait. Time together is key, your kids watch your choices more than listening to the words you speak. Actions *always* speak louder than words and your kids are *always* watching your actions - so lead by example **at all times**.

In Conclusion

Becky is a very common avatar today. But make no mistake, there still are some conventionally feminine women with very low notch counts. And they aren't covered in hideous tattoos. They want to complement a strong virtuous man's life. She wants nothing more than to be a wife and a loving present mother of his children.

But as the old saying goes "you need to dig through a lot of dirt to find gold." So don't expect her to come to you. Especially if you haven't done the work on yourself and maxed out your own SMV.

You'll need to vet all women against the 21 Red Flags listed from my first book, then let time, and sunlight, sanitize any deceptions and lies to see if they really do have the true virtues of a loving mother, and a submissive and faithful wife.

Once again, women don't care about a man's struggles, they are naturally hypergamous (it's a feature, not a bug), so they'll naturally hang out at the finish line and pick the winners. If you've done the hard work to become such a high-value man, then take confidence in knowing that there are fewer of you at the finish line than there are beautiful women waiting there, so YOU will be the one that's spoiled for choice, not them - IF (and only if) you do the work.

I'm not describing Becky to discourage you from dealing with women, Becky is a tale of many women combined and of my own experiences personally, through the thousands of men I've coached, and the tens of thousands of call ins I've taken on my podcasts.

In today's world, she IS the "modern woman" and is - unfortunately - very common.

However, it's my view that "Beckys" should be avoided, especially if you are a top-shelf man, and you want and value a peaceful, fun, and prosperous life. Becky won't add any value, she's delusional, bossy, struggles with pair bonding, and - because most of you will never meet her delusional high expectations - you will never be her first choice. She has a high probability of divorce raping a man (most likely an unassuming Plugged-In Beta chump), all while taking his kids and a large chunk of his net worth when she gets bored of him.

The Cold, Hard Truth

Never forget:

- **Becky's trapped in a lie:** They're now all being sold "strong, independent" as a prize. Today's Becky's are being molded by (social) media, algorithms, and economic pressure, and they're blind to how their bossgirl vibe repels true high-value men.
- **Social media amplifies her delusion:** Dating apps and social media inflates her ego (making her more picky), while simps offer her money and validation with nothing of comparable value in return.

- **Sky-High standards and heavy baggage:** Chases the top 1% of men while ignoring her own red flags that high-value men see clearly (keeping them strictly in the "fun zone"). Cue the age-old "Where have all the good men [I'm Attracted to] gone?" soundbite.
- **Settling spells doom:** Becky molds her "good enough" man into a beta, loses interest, often divorcing him, chasing a fantasy that doesn't exist.
- **Dodge and thrive:** Vet Becky's social media feeds, goals, and actions. Become a high-value man, seek rare feminine women, and sidestep her chaos for a better, and more peaceful life.

Part Two

Retaining & Enjoying The Company of Women

7

Green Flags

In my last book, I outlined my top "21 Red Flags" to look for and avoid in women if you want a peaceful and fun experience as a man with women. Here are my favorite green flags I look for in a woman when I'm vetting for a Long-Term Relationship (or, LTR).

Some of the most obvious green flags to look out for in women come from the field of clinical psychology, and are considered *especially* important for an LTR, they are known as the **"bright triad traits."**

More specifically, the traits that make up the bright triad are: **clarity, emotional maturity**, and **stability** (also known as high agreeableness, high conscientiousness, and low in neuroticism).

Clarity

Clarity means that she won't waste time quarreling or fighting about who is right, but you talk like adults and go to the source of the issue. She can express herself constructively, avoiding tantrums, hissy fits, aggression, and passive aggressiveness. She is also inquisitive, and has the curiosity and drive to understand what is going on, sets aside the need to be right, and focuses on solutions rather than blame. She must also be able to assert her desires, openly without manipulation, gaslighting, or the use of underhanded tactics and without being bossy and overly assertive.

Emotional Maturity

Emotional maturity means she accepts personal responsibility, copes with challenges well, and positively. An emotionally mature woman can calm herself when she is angry or sad, and doesn't blame you for her emotional states. She also accepts that life can be unfair, and doesn't go through destructive patterns of idealization and vilification.

She is resilient. She understands herself, and works on her own limitations. She keeps her commitments. She doesn't base important decisions on her impulses or feelings, but on her values instead. She understands and enjoys taking care of herself physically, and she has an emotional and positive mental regime that allows her to see the cup as half-full, rather than half-empty. She also functions well with co-workers, family, and friends.

Stability

Stability is probably the most important of the three. Men should look for stable women and avoid those who have mental health problems as the odds of divorce go up *exponentially*. Avoid common mental disorders like: depression/anxiety, substance abuse, unresolved emotional injuries, personality disorders (psychopathy, sociopathy, BPD, drama queens, and OCD). Unstable women all have intense and inflexible experiences and are ineffective, and are often poor at human relationships (especially intimate ones).

Neuroticism

Neuroticism is characterized by emotional instability, anxiety, moodiness, worry, envy, and frustration. Individuals who are highly neurotic are more likely to experience negative emotions like fear, sadness, embarrassment, anger, guilt, and disgust. If you are going to invite a woman into your life, you want her *really* low on neuroticism.

Conscientiousness

Conscientiousness refers to the tendency for individuals to exhibit self-discipline, act responsibly, and pursue goals with determination, often aligning their actions with external standards or internal values. It involves traits like organization, dependability, diligence, and the ability to plan and follow through on commitments. You want a woman high on consciousness.

Agreeableness

Agreeableness reflects individual differences in concern for social harmony. People scoring high in agreeableness are typically compassionate, cooperative, empathetic, and considerate, while those low in agreeableness might be more competitive, critical, and less concerned with others' feelings. You definitely want a woman that's high on agreeableness.

Moving away from psychology, there are a number of other green flags that have become increasingly obvious to me, and are present in better women, which are important for men who are looking for an LTR.

The Other Green Flags

She Adopts Your Interests & Views

When a woman is in love with a man and sees him as her best option, she will adopt his mannerisms, hobbies, musical tastes, political opinions, and interests (this often occurs at a subconscious level and usually happens over time). If she doesn't adopt them, she at a bare minimum respects them, and the time he spends enjoying them. His mission and purpose will become her interest. He won't be dragged to pointless events and have his schedule filled with an agenda of conflict, she will look for ways to adapt to his calendar and schedule.

It's preferable that she agrees with your political opinions, and world views or, at the very least, respects yours. Adopting them is obviously ideal, but not always possible. So, look for a woman that, at the very least, genuinely respects your political positions and values. Women find it very difficult to respect a man she disagrees with politically.

She Takes Care of You When You Are Sick

A real test of a woman's love, loyalty, and sincerity is how she responds to you getting ill. Does she become distant and cold, or does she embrace her feminine imperative to care for a man that matters to her? In my life, I have seen women that truly loved me bend over backwards to take care of me, and nurse me back to health. Even when there was nothing she could do, she found a way to put a smile on my face.

I recall lying in the hospital with appendicitis - with excruciating pain ripping through me - one summer in my twenties. My girlfriend at the time left work early to be with me, dressed in a nice skirt. After checking in on me, and doting over me in my weakened condition, she excused herself to the bathroom, slipped off her panties, came back to my bedside, handed them to me, and whispered a reminder of what awaited when I got better.

When a woman *truly* loves a man, and sees him as her hypergamous best option, she *will* go out of her way to care for him even if it's just to put a smile on his face. The real test is if something devastating or serious happens to your health. Many women will abandon a man and quickly move on. But, if she sticks around and is there for you, *that* is a **big** green flag.

She's a Complement to Your Life

I've often said that a woman should be a complement to a man's life, not the focus. When in the dating phase, you should ask yourself, does she compliment your life? If you are on a purpose, and grinding, but lack culinary skills, or time to prepare healthy meals, does she step in and feed you well, and prepare your meals for the week, or lunches before you go to work completely unprompted, with a smile on her face? If she sees laundry piling up, and you're super busy with projects, does she take care of it, again, unprompted, all with a smile on her face?

A woman that loves you will not only crave your attention, but she'll also be calibrated enough to give you space when your schedule is busy. She will likely ask you what she can do to be helpful in your life. Another often overlooked, but important complement to a man's life, is how does she make you look in front of your peers, family, and friends? Women are usually *much* higher on agreeableness, tending to side with the opinion of the masses and trends, so a bright green flag is when a woman is willing to fully support, and stand by you, no matter how unpopular your opinion (or other people's opinion about you) is.

Watch How She Reacts to Not Getting Her Own Way

I've often said that you can *really* see what someone is truly about when you tell them "no." If she throws a tantrum, becomes abusive, passive aggressive, or calls your names, then you are far better off avoiding her over the long-term. You want a woman that is calm, inquisitive, and curious that wants to figure out why you said "no" and not someone that throws emotional hissy fits, and that creates drama in your life. Women who are inquisitive are also often self-reflective in nature, which is a strong sign of possessing a growth mindset - another green flag.

She's Agreeable to You

Women are - by a wide margin - more agreeable than men. But today's women (via the toxic feminist narrative) have been encouraged to act more like men, they're told to: chase excellence, get degrees, climb the corporate ladder, delay motherhood, and be "strong and independent." A woman that is disagreeable, or one that tries to compete with you, will make your life very difficult. It's a green flag when a woman understands that she must make his life easy, and his dick hard. **Not** the other way around.

She Seeks Connection With Your Family and Friends

This is a test of her character, but when the opportunity presents itself, does she actively seek a connection with your family members or friends (and maintain it) or, does she try to push you apart and cause havoc in your family and social networks? For an LTR, you definitely want a woman that integrates effortlessly into your life, and you see her family and friends the same way. It's a bigger green flag if her family and friends also see your value, and do everything to support your purpose, and your boundaries.

She Subscribes to the Idea of Blue Jobs & Pink Jobs

When it comes to forming a family unit, you want a woman that subscribes to what each gender is good at, naturally gravitates to and generally seeks that from the other. Signing up for a woman that insists on cutting the lawn, shoveling the snow in the winter, and having you cook and clean inside isn't a good idea. You *will* grow to resent each other, and she should understand that men and women *aren't* the same, but that they really can be a great complement to each other.

It's critical though that you, as the leader, step-up and handle the gender roles that you're good at (i.e. the blue jobs) and that she sees the value in your ability to be a competent masculine leader. If she sees that you've got a solid handle on your tasks, then she'll be naturally more inclined to become a warm, feminine complement to your life when it comes to handling the pink jobs. The last thing you want after a long day of chasing excellence, making money, and putting a dent in the universe, is an argument over whose turn it is to cook dinner because she did it last night.

She Doesn't Put the Relationship in Jeopardy.

A woman that has asked you for your commitment, should have no time in her schedule to do things that would expose your relationship to unnecessary risk, like taking a girls party weekend to Las Vegas, attending bachelorette parties with a bunch of single and/or divorced friends, or even having lunch with an ex-boyfriend (or any man she was intimate in the past with for that matter).

I often get a **lot** of push back from my female guests on my Ladies Night podcast when it comes to this boundary, with rampant accusations of being "insecure", or "unfair." As I often remind them, it's important to take a look at what they're proposing to do. An example I often use is that going away with her closest girls to a spa for a weekend to chill out, relax, and finger paint or just gossip, isn't anywhere *near* as concerning as her wanting to go away to a bachelorette party in Ibiza for a week with a bunch of drunken single friends.

Ultimately, a woman that does any of these things shouldn't be considered for an LTR, and if she asks for your commitment, it's at that point you tell her that you can't take her seriously, or love her the way you'd like to if she likes to behave like she is single while in a relationship with you. A woman that *truly* loves you, **will** respect your boundaries (even if she doesn't like it), she'll defer to your judgment and follow your lead, and she'll *never* intentionally put herself in a position where she puts either herself (especially when around drunken, horny men), or the relationship at risk. In fact, the idea of scheduling these types of trips away from you shouldn't even cross her mind.

Finally, always keep in mind that you (and you alone) get to define what you find acceptable and what boundaries apply in your life. No-one gets to make that decision but you. Always calmly (but firmly) give her the choice to either respect the relationship that you're building together (and therefore stay home if the planned trip violates your clearly stated boundary), or make it crystal clear that - should she choose the trip over your relationship - there won't be a relationship to come back to. You want to be with a woman who values you, your time and your relationship more than such trips away that expose your relationship to risk.

She's Younger Than You

This may not seem so obvious if you are both 35, but if you take care of yourself, by the time you are 50, she won't look nearly as good as you. Women lose collagen, and skin elasticity faster than men, gravity affects her body more than yours. Childbirth can do a number on older women, and menopause can also take quite a toll on women if she isn't managing the aging process with a hormone clinic.

Fertility, which is a woman's primary benefit to men, declines dramatically after the age of 30, whereas a man can remain fertile well into the autumn years of his life. It's why some of the best LTRs are with women younger than you, especially when you are over 35. Younger women naturally look up to, and defer to, a seasoned man, *especially* if he has his life squared away.

For a man over 45, a good 7-15 years younger can be ideal, as you get older, the age gap can increase as long as you have similar energy levels, and can still perform in the bedroom.

She Takes *Some* Accountability

Taking full ownership for all of her results in her life, is something that you're unlikely to find in any woman. But, expect a better woman to take *some* accountability for her results and choices in life. If she takes at least half the ownership you take, you are doing okay. Remember, men and women are very different in this regard, so don't expect to hold her to as high a standard when it comes to accountability. A woman that can apologize, and say "You are 100% right, I fucked up, I am sorry" is a smart woman.

She Takes Care of Her Appearance & Health

Aside from the obvious optics of attraction and sex appeal, you don't want to be in a committed relationship with a woman that doesn't make self-care a priority. Diabetes, cardiovascular disease, obesity, anorexia, etc will all become burdensome on you, your time, and your finances. She will also be more unable to bear your children (if that's important to you), or be useful in your life if she isn't looking after her health. So, seek women that prioritize a healthy lifestyle over indulgences in vices like overeating, smoking, drugs, and alcohol.

She Makes Plans Into the Future With You

If a woman is blocking off dates several months, or even years, into the future for a vacation, or some other special event, it's a green flag because she is telling you - in no uncertain terms - that she is *fully* committed to you over the long-term. The deeper into the future the plans are, the greener the flag is.

She Wants You to Drive

It's a big green flag when a woman comes to my house, parks behind my car, and when we are going out, she hands me her keys and says "you drive" completely unprompted. It shows you that she values you as a man, your skills behind the wheel, and that she feels safe in the passenger seat of her own car. Take a look around when you are driving and you will notice a lot of men sitting in the passenger seat of the family car, while their wife drives and they look absolutely foolish doing so. There is only one driver's seat in cars and, unless you are unable to drive temporarily for whatever reason, you should *always* lead and sit behind the wheel.

Genuinely Happy, Positive, and Doesn't Play the Victim

You want a woman that is *genuinely* an upbeat, happy, and positive person. If you are traveling to the Caribbean and the luggage gets lost, does she throw a hissy fit, yell at the airline staff, and have a complete meltdown? Or, does she just turn to you, smile and say "let's go grab some bathing suits, it's all we need for the week anyways." Seek women that look at the cup as half full, have a positive mindset, and "can-do" approach to life.

She Genuinely *Craves* Sexual Intimacy With You

Too many men get into relationships with women that don't have a true, genuine burning desire for them, and the men just become a tool in her toolbox, or an accessory to her life like a handbag. I covered the importance of GBD in my first book, but its importance truly cannot be understated enough.

 Choose women who choose you!

Sex is the glue holding relationships together. If she isn't craving you - your body, your touch, that raw intimacy - if you are a healthy male that craves sex, there's *zero* point in a long-term setup with her.

Way too often low-value betas pull in women who've partied hard with one too many guys in their 20s. She settles for him as a "better long-term" option - that's reliable, steady, and committed - after chasing sexy alphas who pumped her full of enthusiastic, filthy fun but wouldn't commit.

Nobody likes to overpay for something handed out free and easy to others. And like I've hammered on podcasts before - never be her second choice. Ever.

If you don't want to be used for your resources, only invite a woman into your life if she has genuine burning desire for you. She should *want* to enthusiastically have mind-bending sex with you, and frequently (although, it's critical that you actually spend time learning how to blow her mind in the bedroom. It's a competency skill that will pay unparalleled dividends if you're willing to level up your bedroom game, so be sure to check out Stirling Cooper's YouTube channel for some solid mind-blowing tips).

Every man's ego enjoys getting a text that says "be naked when I get there" but you'll have achieved God mode if you hear the soundbite "you're the best I ever had!", or "OMG! I've never cum so hard before! How'd you do that!?" Do the work to become that guy.

> *Editor's note:* I truly can't stress enough how essential it is to choose a woman for whom you naturally "tick off all of her boxes." The more boxes you tick off, the higher her GBD will be for you, and the easier everything becomes. Having a woman who - more often than not - turns up for you in surprise lingerie is the flip-side of being with someone who looks for excuses not to have sex with you. I can tell you from personal experience that such a woman will do pretty much anything for/with you - and she'll do so with a massive smile on her face.

She Keeps Her Social Media Private

If a woman wants to claim you, she must have a private (or even better, no) social media account. She cannot use social media to post provocative posts designed to attract men, and get validation from strangers. It's rare today to find a woman that doesn't have an interest in social media, but if you do find one, it is also a big green flag.

We know that attention (of men specifically) is a valuable currency to a woman, and such women inherently know their true value is in their beauty. So, if she's actively posting on social media to get attention from men (by blatantly leading with her beauty or sexuality), then she is *actively marketing herself* and she's clearly indicating her availability - even if she has asked for your commitment.

Always watch what women do, and listen to less of what they say.

A woman who **truly** sees you as her best option doesn't market herself to others - or even bother keeping options open. Attention-seeking stops cold in a committed relationship. Some women get hooked on the free hits of validation from social media, so you might need to step up as a strong man and set firm boundaries. Tell her straight: you don't date or take seriously a woman who's provocative online.

Modern women today might protest, and call it controlling or jealousy (I get that all the time on my Ladies Night podcast). However, it's not. Like with setting your boundary regarding salacious trips away, it's about protecting a woman that you love, and that you are going to invest your time, love, effort, and resources into. Only a fool would invite a woman into his life that is actively marketing herself to other men on social media, and acting as if she is still available.

Social media use is fine, as long as it's private, and not used to post scantily clad photos on the internet.

Some women *do* need to use social media to promote their business online, so if you get involved with a woman that runs a bikini business, don't be surprised if she models them on her Instagram publicly. But, for most women, it should be private and respectful of your relationship.

In Conclusion

I spent a considerable amount of time on the red flag chapter in my prior book, and I still believe it is easier to use red flags as a sorting tool to eliminate women that would be a bad long-term choice, but it **is** important to look for the good in women - it's up to you to look for these flags too, know what you will - and won't - tolerate in your life, and then communicate that in a very clear and calm manner.

In this chapter, I outlined what therapists, and psychologists put emphasis on, and then offered you some other green flags to look out for based on my own personal experience, and that of the thousands of men that I have worked with and coached.

Be sure to use the red flags from my first book to repel misery, and then use the green flags to invite effortless peace into your life.

The Cold, Hard Truth

Never forget:

- **Vet positives as hard as negatives:** Red flags tell you who to avoid, but green flags tell you who's worth keeping. Most men only screen for trouble; smart men screen for both.
- **Consistency matters more than intensity:** Anyone can fake good behavior for a month. The women who are worth your time show it over the long haul, with steady, predictable actions - not bursts of charm followed by chaos.
- **Stability is non-negotiable:** If she's unstable, anxious, or thrives on drama, your life will be one long firefight. Love doesn't fix instability; it just chains you to it.
- **Respect is binary:** Either she respects your time, your mission, and your values - or she doesn't. There's no middle ground here. A woman who won't follow your lead **will** eventually resent you, and then she'll resist you.
- **Choose women who choose you:** GBD isn't something you can bargain for. If she doesn't crave you (your touch, your presence, your leadership), she's with you out of convenience, not conviction.
- **Boundaries aren't negotiations:** If she thinks partying with single girlfriends, posting thirst-traps, or grabbing lunch with exes is "no big deal," then she's not serious about protecting the relationship. A woman who values you won't put your bond at risk, period.
- **The right woman complements your life:** She plugs into your mission, makes the ride smoother, and adds value. The wrong woman drags you into her orbit and drains you dry.
- **Health is wealth:** Looks fade for everyone, but a woman who values her health keeps her vitality and attractiveness far longer. If she doesn't, her decline becomes your burden to carry.

- **Accountability separates women from girls:** A keeper can say, "I messed up, I'm sorry." A pretender with a victim-mentality will *always* point the finger at someone else.
- **And finally, reward the keepers:** High-value women are rare, and even they need to feel seen. A simple thank-you, a deep kiss, or a word of recognition every once in a while is all it takes to reinforce the frame. She leans in more when she knows she's genuinely appreciated. It's always feelings over facts when it comes to women. Learn to work with it.

8

His Game, Her Game

A grave mistake men and women make when it comes to the game of dating and heterosexual relationships is blurring the lines when it comes to what's best for each gender, and it's very much my opinion that these vanilla approaches to dating and Long-Term Relationships (or, LTRs) aren't serving *anyone*.

In this chapter, I'll dive deeper down the rabbit hole of what I have learned by reading many evolutionary psychology books, published studies, and through the careful observation of human behavior from personally speaking to thousands of men and women through my private and podcast consults.

The grim reality of "the game" is that **men and women are not the same**, and what's good for the Goose isn't necessarily good for the Gander.

Our sexual strategies clash by design - competitive to the core. Sadly, men get conditioned to "do what's right" while women hear "do what's right for you, girl." That leaves guys stuck with raw deals that rarely pay off. As you'll soon learn in this chapter, if she wants to optimize her hypergamy, she - more often than not - doesn't prefer a man yielding entirely to her sexual strategy.

So, in this chapter we'll examine these differences, and I'll offer some actionable advice on how to navigate these waters.

An Epiphany Moment

Like you, I think I spent the majority of my life plugged-in to the lie that men and women are pretty much the same and that, aside from the obvious physical differences that separate men from women, we also think the same, approach relationships and life (in all its forms), the same way.

Nothing could be further from the truth.

Honestly, it's probably taken me over 20,000 hours of consuming books, studies, and content to show me that **women inherently primarily view men as success objects**, and *men primarily view women as beauty, and sex objects*.

When it comes to prioritization for long-term mate selection specifically, women put a **strong** emphasis on getting the best they can (i.e. hypergamy) and men mainly just prioritize her availability to him, when in fact, *they should be prioritizing her enthusiasm for him (i.e. Genuine Burning Desire, or GBD)*.

When it comes to the notion of "availability," you can see this unfold in real-time in those social experiments where they send a reasonably attractive woman to a college campus walking around with a hidden camera and concealed microphone asking random men if they want to have sex with her.

Most of the men will oblige. However, when you reverse the experiment and send a reasonably attractive man to ask the same question, zero women respond positively.

Most men will have sex with most women; whereas most women will *not* have sex with most men.

Pre-Selection

There exists a *strong* conflict between women's stated preferences in men and relationships, and what they actually respond positively to, which are their *true* preferences or revealed preferences.

We know through study after study (and by watching female behavior) that women have a very strong preference for men that other women also want, and who are also the types of men that other men want to be.

It's why women will routinely pursue a successful, fit, competent - *married* - man over a fat, broke, loser who's still living in his mom's basement.

Pre-selection is a *very* reliable, and efficient way for women to evaluate men that are unknown to her quickly.

More specifically, pre-selection by *attractive* women is what women use to really evaluate men.

When a woman sees a man that other attractive women have selected, it's a strong indicator that he has been pre-assessed, and has already been determined to be a man of value. In a woman's eyes, if an attractive woman has picked him, then he **must** be worth having - as she could have had "her pick of men."

Believe it or not, this even applies to her own group of close female friends. They're usually quite happy if their friends also find him very attractive (in a "look but can't touch" kind of way). It not only confirms that they can "pick a good one," but if the man is clearly of high enough value, then it boosts their ego in front of her friends.

It's often been said that, behind every successful man, is a woman. But, the tragic comedy behind that statement is that women, *far* more often than not, don't stand behind unsuccessful men (this also includes previously successful men who then lost their wealth through any number of circumstances).

To put it bluntly: ***Women want what other women want***

First and foremost, the quickest and surest way for a woman to judge a man's worth, is by looking at the woman - or women - already in the company of that man. The more attractive, and abundant the women surrounding him are, then it's far more likely that other attractive women are also going to want to be with that man.

Some women will say that they are put off by the idea (a stated preference) that she would ever share a man. But, in the sexual marketplace, women's revealed/true preferences (i.e. her choices) reveal that she routinely does share her man, and her actions should *always* be trusted over her stated preferences.

Women have led men to believe that because a man has a wife, or a girlfriend, that he is "off limits," or that they would never interfere with that.

That simply isn't true.

The fact of the matter is that being in a relationship with an attractive woman isn't repulsive, or even a turn off to other women. Another woman has already pre-selected him, so it actually makes him more attractive to most other women. This is why a lot of women actually like hitting on married men - irrespective of what his wife is like, or how much his wife actually fancies him anymore.

It's a Feature, Not a Bug

Pre-selection has been hardwired into women's DNA because it makes identifying a good man very quick and easy. One of the surest ways to have access to attractive women, is to be pre-selected by *other* attractive women.

Men don't even necessarily need to be selected by a beautiful woman for the notion of pre-selection to be activated in women. Although, while it's not *quite* as effective, being openly admired, or praised by other high-value men, will make you more attractive to women, especially if those men are the strong, and masculine men that women would typically choose.

She begins to ask herself: "If these attractive men are admiring, or praising this one man, they *must* know something I don't."

You don't even need to be a handsome man to be pre-selected. Pete Davidson, Jay Z, Lyle Lovett, Marc Anthony, and Serge Gainsbourg have *all* pulled genuinely beautiful women, time and time again, because of pre-selection, status, fame, and visible competence in their given realm of expertise.

A man's looks are certainly a big factor, but it's far from the *only* factor.

This may be frustrating for some to accept, but until women choose single, broke, fat, losers over already pre-selected, taken, successful, and handsome men, we must accept this grim reality of female nature (see the chapter on *Acceptance and Understanding* if you're struggling to come to terms with life's bitter truths).

It appears to be an evolutionary survival mechanism hard-wired into women to compete for a top-shelf man with other women, because men exchange resources for sexual opportunities, while women exchange sexual opportunities for resources.

Being "Nice" to Women (and Expecting the Same in Return)

At some point, most plugged-in men will find themselves being too "nice" to a woman, and then find themselves getting punished for it.

We've always been told to be nicer to our sisters, our mothers, and to the women that we are attracted to. I'm not exactly sure where this notion of being a "nice guy" to women we're attracted to started, but it *clearly* wasn't coming from the men who had an abundance of beautiful women that were enthusiastic to be with him.

When I lived in England in my early 20s, I remember hearing the phrase "Treat her mean; keep her keen" and asking myself: "Who cooked up this nonsense?" After marinating on this phrase today, I can tell you it's accurate. Being a bit of a "meanie" (also known as a "cocky asshole") does solicit a far more positive response from women you want to be intimate with than just being a nice guy. Note that, tempering the asshole part with confident humor is the preferred blend, but even being a straight-up asshole usually yields *far* better results than being the classical "nice guy."

Gentlemen, you should aim to be a ***kind*** man, but not a nice guy. The latter will never, EVER be chosen by attractive women for the kind of relationship men desire from them. "Nice Guys" don't have a backbone and will flip their stance on a topic just to appease a woman that they want to sleep with. It's disingenuous and women can smell that BS from a mile away. At least an asshole will stick up for his opinions and won't care if a woman challenges him on it. And women will respect men who hold firm on their views - they actually feel **safer** with a man who can stand his ground.

Nice guys are also the type of guys that get absolutely **destroyed** in family court, have their wealth stripped clean from them, and are then alienated from their kids - because he wouldn't stick up for himself.

These are the same men that think divorce is a time to be chivalrous, because that's how "nice guys" think.

For most men out there, they need to lean into their inner asshole, be slightly more disagreeable, and learn to say "no" far more often than saying yes.

To use a somewhat more extreme example, Gary (a good friend of mine), wouldn't walk around overtly calling himself a stud, yet he somehow has plenty of options with attractive women.

Gary isn't someone who I'd call a "nice guy," but he's a kind man that looks out for those around him and he's successful in life because he has learned to only do the things that he wants to do when it comes to dating women. If she wants a stronger commitment, to do something different, or go to an event that Gary isn't interested in, he politely declines, and - if needed - he replaces her if she throws a massive hissy fit, or if she tries to shame, insult, or guilt him into doing it.

His openly nonchalant attitude towards women (and what they want from him), and towards his relationships is very clear. He puts himself first, is 100% unapologetic about it, and women *still* pursue him.

Ultimately, whether you like it or not, if you want to be treated well by women, you're going to need to be willing to put *yourself* first, and stop being such a people pleaser.

People Pleasers: The Kings of the "Covert Contract"

Being kind isn't the same as being a "nice guy." Nice guys play the "sneaky fucker" game: they do "nice" things expecting a payout - sex, loyalty, love - without ever saying it out loud. *That's* a covert contract, and women can smell the desperation from a mile away. They'll dodge it, or exploit it, leaving you pissed off when your unspoken deal falls apart. You've set yourself up to fail.

Unlike Gary. Gary's generous, looks out for his crew, and gives without strings attached - but he's no pushover. He tells women upfront: "This is how I roll, take it or leave it." Women will step up or they'll leave. Believe it or not, women trust and respect Gary a whole lot more for being like that. Meanwhile, I've seen "nice" guys crash and burn chasing a woman's approval, getting butt-hurt when she doesn't reciprocate his feelings.

Ditch the covert deals. State your terms like a man and let her prove she's worth your time and commitment.

The bottom line is that giving women what they want too often, rarely gets you what you want, or the kind loving, and sweet behavior that you expect from women.

Like you I wish being a "nice guy" and chanting that infamous "happy wife happy life" mantra - buying her flowers and chocolates - would land us a woman who *truly* adores, respects, and craves us. But sadly, it doesn't. Until it does, we've got to unplug from those lies and adapt to what *actually* works - not chase blindly after what we think should.

The truth of the matter is, and I really can't stress this enough, **being as attractive as possible, while being valuable to both women *and* society**, is what keeps women around, enthusiastically. Then, how we manage the frame of that relationship over the longer-term is what keeps women treating us well.

The Importance of Building Value

Since we know that women want what other women want, and since we also know that women behave much better when they **know** that you're attractive enough to replace her (i.e. "Dread"), I would argue that it makes sense to build your value, become more attractive, and foster such optionality.

Attraction is the *key* in both appealing to women and in retaining them for the long-term.

In my first book, in the revised second edition, I talked about how doing the work on yourself and developing the seven spokes of a high value man, especially by improving your looks, money, status, frame, game, captivation, and unplugging will **naturally** make you more attractive to far more women - purely as a side-effect of you doing the work.

This is what women value and respond positively to and, despite what you have been told about "just being yourself" which usually means, "you are fine as you are" (which is a load of BS), there is **no** woman that wakes up in the morning obsessed with a man, that is "just being himself."

I've *always* made it clear that you do these things for yourself, so that *you* can improve your own options (in every area of life), subsequently giving you a better experience in life, and with women. It's about increasing your value, and becoming the best version of yourself.

A man - without any sort of value - is useless to not only himself, but also to those around him, and to the women who he wants that all-important GBD from.

Level up visibly: sculpt that V-shaped body, fitted clothes to showcase it, sharpen competence across fields, stack financial resources, own a rock-solid masculine frame, and build influence in life and business. These spokes sync up in synergy to explode your options.

This was covered in great detail in my first book, so make sure you read it, really take it to heart, and do the work to make it *your* reality.

As men, we *all* start out as a nobody. When I was 19, I was a lanky, skinny, poor, awkward, and insignificant young man with average looks. All I had to show for myself was a great head of hair, and a $5,000 motorcycle I couldn't even afford to insure.

Developing a strong masculine frame, becoming a multi-millionaire, building a network, learning how to fight, and socially calibrating myself, **SIGNIFICANTLY** improved my standing in the pecking order among my competition.

Never underestimate the importance of doing the work, and in creating a strong reputation for yourself.

Notice I said a "strong" reputation, not a "positive" reputation. The man with a strong reputation is respected by default, but not all men with a *positive* reputation are respected in the same way.

Men are born with nothing, but are more valued when they consistently do the work over a long period of time; women are born with their value upfront and are more valued when they preserve their beauty and purity over a long period of time. More on that later.

Men: The Gatekeepers of Commitment

When you speak to enough men about their relationship issues, you soon realize how quickly a man will commit to a woman is alarmingly fast. For the men that aren't as familiar with my work, it's not uncommon for most men to ask for her commitment within a couple of weeks to a month of dating.

Most men today are *so* starved for female attention and intimacy, that when a woman positively responds to his text messages in a timely fashion and then offers him sexual access to her - often less-than average - body, and finally expresses some faint interest in his personal life, then these men's scarcity mindset will kick into overdrive and they'll often pounce *far* too quickly on this and then ask her for her commitment before she "changes her mind."

Again, to put it bluntly, even a leathery stale hunk of beef jerky looks like prime Wagyu from a three-star Michelin spot to a starving man with zero other options.

Many of men's problems in relationships can be reduced ***dramatically*** if they focused more on being *far* more diligent when it comes to gatekeeping who they allow into their life, which begins by them improving the initial selection and screening process (see my *21 Red Flags* chapter in my first book for more detail on how to do this).

This takes time to refine and master, and by giving yourself a few years to evaluate what a potential woman is made of, you'll see if she's up to scratch - but *only* if you are willing to slow things down.

Editor's Note: *Men, vet your partners like the Special Air Service (or, SAS) picks its elite. The 22 SAS regiment's selection is a brutal gauntlet - it's only open twice a year; hundreds try, but most can't handle it. The Directing Staff (or, DS) don't care who makes it; they want proof of unbreakable drive and commitment. Candidates get crushed mentally and physically, pushed past their current limits in the initial Aptitude Phase. A few survive to face the jungle (the second phase), vetted for their grit, smarts, and heart. Even after all that, passing the third (and the toughest) phase isn't always enough - some men still get rejected for not being a good fit. Those who do earn the sandy beret prove they belong and can be trusted by their squad to risk it all. That's your standard for commitment. Choose women who show up, prove their worth and their commitment, and have earned your trust. Half-measures simply don't cut it, so guard your life and time like the SAS guards its infamous winged-dagger badge.*

Again, I can't stress enough how important this extended vetting period is, because women can be like actors. They don't show you their *real* self until at least a year (or sometimes more) into dating. My recommendation for men, especially for those looking to have children, is to watch her *very* carefully for 1-2 years and see what she's *really* made of when challenges inevitably arise during the relationship.

How does she respond when you tell her "no?" Does she have a massive and public meltdown when you travel if the luggage gets lost? Or, does she calmly shrug it off and suggest buying a few simple items while the airline figures it out, focusing instead on enjoying her time by your side?

A man must be *very* careful with who they offer their commitment to.

I've noticed that men only give away their commitment quickly when they have low value and a very toxic scarcity mindset; whereas a man that is a top-shelf Unplugged Alpha, understands that his marketplace value is high, and is therefore both *very* selective and super slow to give his valuable commitment away to a woman, if he even gives it away at all.

So, it's critical to remember the following:

Men are the gatekeepers to commitment, and women are the gatekeepers to sex.

Therefore, if women decide when sex happens, and men are the ones looking for sex, *then it's men who decide if a relationship should happen, and it's down to women to ask him for his commitment.*

This is **extremely** important, and it establishes several things unplugged men want in an LTR specifically - and most importantly - that he has to be her **first choice**.

If women are hypergamous, and they naturally want the best they can get, then if you are dating a woman that you like, *she* must ask *you* for your commitment, *not* the other way around, because this functionally ensures that you'll also get her best in return.

I have often referred to this stage in the dating phase as "the talk." It usually sounds something like: "Where is this going," "What are we?", "I love you and don't want to share you," etc.

It's some version of her asking you: "where do we stand?"

This is good, because a woman that sees a man as her hypergamous best option, *will* want to know how he views her, and ask him for his commitment (before another woman comes along and "snaps him up").

Once you reach the top shelf, don't listen to anyone telling you that you must always ask her for her commitment for an LTR before she does. These men do that because their scarcity mindset is at play and they also inherently know that their value is lower; therefore, their commitment doesn't have much value. High-value men know that their time and commitment is extremely valuable, which is why they guard them *very* carefully.

One of the common complaints you hear from women (about men), is that she dated a man for far too long that wouldn't either move the relationship along, commit to her, or marry her. Here's the thing: he probably *wasn't* some "narcissistic asshole" as she likely implied to everyone who'd listen.

It's more likely that:

1. She was chasing a man out of her league that understood his value (hypergamy) or,

2. He saw too many red flags to take her seriously or,
3. Family law was too hostile towards men where they lived, and he set a firm boundary to keep the relationship where it was.

Believe it or not, you really *can* love a woman and not marry her (especially if the laws are too hostile towards men and fathers where you live). In extreme cases, I've seen many men have children with multiple women, and not live with them, while they all know about each other. This caliber of men are *so* rare, women know this instinctively and they will literally accept any boundary he sets, and do anything for him. There are two videos that go out on my email list with private interviews with *Casey Jones*, and *Tristan Tate* talking about this in detail, opt into the list at found at the end of this chapter and they will be sent to you.

When Women "Settle"

So what often ends up happening is that these women are functionally forced to settle for a man that isn't her first choice, because the high-value men that she **really** wants won't ever give her what she wants in the way she wants it (i.e. his exclusive commitment).

I catch a *lot* of heat from women when I say this to them, but the truth of the matter is, top-shelf men don't often pass on great women that are agreeable, pleasant, useful, respectful, beautiful, offers him novel and enthusiastic sex, and didn't have a promiscuous past.

These women are very rare today. If you are a woman, and men are routinely refusing to offer you their commitment, you need to take a look at the common denominator in all of these relationships - which is **you**.

Women settling for men that weren't their first choice is functionally how most men end up in horrible, sexless marriages that either stay miserable, or end in a bitter divorce where the father is milked for what he is worth through family court, all while she uses that money and sole custody time to poison the well and alienate him from his own children.

These women will then take that newfound freedom, and hit the road running, with the primary custody of his kids, his financial support, and then hope they can move on to a higher value man. But I'll cover that more a little later in the chapter.

I *really* can't stress this enough: a man that has genuinely done the work to be clearly attractive, and has created true value, shouldn't be asking a woman to become exclusive with him. *She* should be the one asking him, and he should get to decide (only after thoroughly evaluating her over a long period of time and also after studying the laws that govern relationships where he lives), if he sees her worthy of committing to her, or where the laws are reasonable enough to take on the risk of inviting the state into your home.

Most Women Would Rather Be the King's Mistress, Than the Peasants Wife

Most women demand sexual exclusivity from the men they want, but I don't believe it's a good idea to give this away too soon, or even with 100% surety to women when they *do* ask for it.

This is a grave mistake for most men because they often blend commitment with sexual exclusivity. These things can be navigated independently, but it's usually only the attractive men with real value on the top-shelf (that most women are chasing) who fully understand the significance of this fact.

A high-value man can pour his strength into leading his family - providing, protecting, and staying loyal in his commitment - but women shouldn't expect him to be 100% sexually exclusive.

Plugged-in men and women often balk at the idea that men can separate commitment from sexual exclusivity but - morality aside, attractive, powerful, or high-value men can, and have done so for thousands of years.

Throughout history, men like King Solomon, Genghis Khan, Suleiman the Magnificent, and Louis XIV built empires while openly balancing committed relationships with sexual connections to multiple women. In modern times, figures like Hugh Hefner, Warren Beatty, Mick Jagger, and Jack

Nicholson followed suit, maintaining primary partnerships - sometimes even marriages - while navigating less exclusive, physical relationships on their own terms.

I'm often challenged, usually by women, suggesting that women throughout history have enjoyed the same optionality, so why shouldn't they today?

But when I dug in with the latest AI models, only a handful of names popped up: Cleopatra, Catherine the Great, Marie Antoinette, Clara Bow, and Elizabeth Taylor. And those surfaced mostly in the context of extramarital affairs - no real love or commitment to their husbands.

Morality judgments aside, men with multiple women are often more respected, but women with multiple men are usually condemned. That's just the way it is.

Few women ever like the idea, but sometimes the very things women don't like are actually very good for her, the relationship, and their genuine burning desire for you because - once again - women want *what other women want*.

One of the complaints men have when they go from dating multiple women in a non-monogamous fashion, to moving to the commitment phase of a relationship (where he gives her full exclusivity), is that her sexual desire and overall enthusiasm declines, and she often doesn't treat him as well, and feels less-useful in your life as time passes.

This is because she feels like she has you locked down, and therefore any competition anxiety she had (over other women being around you, trying to take you away from her), is reduced so dramatically, that she begins to stop doing the things she first did to get you to commit to her.

Men stuck in this cycle often find themselves in the position of giving more over time, while - far more often than not - getting far less value back in return.

He loves her, so he naturally does more for her, but because she has his full commitment, and pledge to her, she often ends up doing less for him over time. This is compounded further if he wasn't her first choice.

A wise woman (who truly values what she has) will continue doing the things that got her foot in the door, and into his personal life, long after he has committed to her - but few women ever follow this advice. It's extremely unwise, and disrespectful for a woman to dupe a top-shelf man with a bait and switch maneuver. But, today, many average men find themselves in this position wondering what the hell happened to the woman he was with before he fully committed to her.

There is part of the process of "betatization through a thousand concessions" that your average man goes through, where he becomes a plow horse, which I described in detail in my first book.

The last thing a man wants is to be in a relationship with a woman that really isn't worth it, but because we are always told to "do what's right," many men often stay in an unsatisfactory relationship purely out of some perceived duty.

A smart woman *does not* make this mistake with a man they want to keep around.

Despite what women like to tell men, they don't value what they have, as much as they want us to believe. But, we do know (by watching how they respond to pre-selection), that they always value what *other* women want.

What's Good for the Goose, Isn't Good for the Gander

With all of that in mind, it'd be prudent to point out the fact that *many* top-shelf men can openly sleep with other women (and some do), as long as he doesn't bring any shame, STDs, or drama back to his committed relationship, or her family. However, pulling off this arrangement isn't exactly intuitive for many men, nor is it easy because he must be very attractive and valuable to women.

Most women will use insults ("you're not a real man"), or try using shame tactics ("a real man would…") to try and persuade you otherwise. Men need to understand that *regardless* of what the female first primary social order tells us, you CAN give a woman your most valuable commitment (your resources, your time, and your love), but not limit your sexual exclusivity to just her 100% of the time.

I should also point out, especially in the liberal world of "ethical non monogamy" (or whatever version of polyamory you want to call it), *she* should be fully committed to *you* **on all levels**. You **do not** want another man "poisoning the well" by sleeping with your woman. If she genuinely sees you as her very best, then she'll be *significantly* more inclined to "look the other way." She won't like it, and you certainly don't want to rub her nose in it, but it absolutely IS possible (and it happens more often than you think).

However, cultivating such optionality on your part doesn't necessarily mean that you *should* indulge in it (although I'm sure some men will). It just means that you need to be honest and upfront about the level of commitment you *are* providing her. Clearly stating that she has 100% of your commitment, but 99% of your sexual exclusivity is blanketed by the caveat that, if exercised, it would be **safe**, **very discreet,** and **responsible**.

That's really all that needs to be said on the subject.

Women will often try to set rules like "only when you are traveling" or, "no overnights together", but agreeing to additional terms will only complicate the matter further and restrict your optionality. The point of this exercise is to create true optionality. She may ask for details, disclosure, or try to limit the locations or demographics where you can exercise your sexual optionality in, but validating her concerns, then repeating to her **safe, discreet and responsible**, should be the extent of your compromise.

What that means is she shouldn't need to worry about another woman knocking on her door, announcing she is pregnant with your child, that you bring home a STD, or you make an "option" a priority by taking her to a restaurant or place (specifically "her place") that you would frequent with your woman. For the most part she just wants to know that you are safe, aren't in love with an option, and won't embarrass her in front of her family, friends, and co-workers.

Remember, when a man cheats, the first thing she wants to know is: "Did you love her?" When a woman cheats, the first thing men want to know is: "Did you have sex with him?"

Men and women are not the same and we get jealous for different reasons.

From an evolutionary psych perspective, men's jealousy is rooted in paternity fraud. A pregnant woman always has 100% assurance that she's the mother. Men don't. Women's jealousy is rooted in the loss of resources, time, and attention. If a man falls in love with another woman, she fears that he'll remove his care for her and re-allocate it to the "other woman."

Executing this asymmetrical arrangement offers men several benefits: first and foremost, women typically treat you better over the long run in the relationship when they know that you genuinely have options that you may - or may not - be exercising.

Second, as a man, we have been placed on this earth to "scatter seed." I have seen too many men painfully lament that they can't exercise options that they do have, over the fear of divorce rape, and the very real risk of being alienated from their own children by a vindictive woman.

So instead they sneak around scratching that itch with porn, rub-and-tugs, or prostitutes - which most women still count as cheating. Pledging monogamy while secretly acting adulterous? Cowardly in my book. But that's the go-to for Plugged-In men today - especially in North America and the West. Outside those spots, the upfront approach to open options gets way more acceptance.

Giving a woman sexual exclusivity is *very* expensive for men and is counter to their own sexual strategy. You should understand that once you give her your sexual exclusivity, it's *very* difficult to take it back, and remain in the same relationship (without completely breaking it down and restructuring it - which takes a **significant** amount of time, effort, and frame to even pull off).

The best time to have this conversation is when she is asking for your commitment at the "where do we stand" phase of the relationship.

Women: The Gatekeepers of Sex

Despite the narrative telling women that their car, home, pets, children from prior relationships, career, accomplishments, degrees, and decoration skills are all attractive to men, the truth of the matter is: no man has *ever* looked at a woman's degree on the wall, framed in the finest mahogany, (or any of the aforementioned items) and thought to himself: "Damn, check out the degrees on her!"

As I pointed out in my first book: ***Women are primarily beauty and sex objects to men, and men are primarily success objects to women.***

Sex, and the subsequent ability to bring a man his own children, is the primary value that most men seek in women. Make no mistake, there is an exchange of value between the sexes.

To put it more bluntly, men exchange resources for sexual opportunities with women.

A frustrating component of this exchange is that men also value purity, and chastity.

This can be frustrating for women to accept, but the value of this cannot be understated. I can safely say that no man, throughout history, has *ever* recited the words: "I wish my wife had sex with 50 more men before I married her." For women, a man's sexual past is background noise; for men, a woman's past is often a dealbreaker.

Women prioritize a man's future abilities to provide resources, and not his sexual past, but men evaluate things the other way around.

To illustrate this further, I ran a survey on my Unplugged Alpha Podcast YouTube channel to determine how men viewed promiscuity. To be more specific, I wanted to establish what was more undesirable to men: a single, childless woman that was promiscuous or, a single divorced mother that wasn't sleeping around.

I asked my audience this question: "Men, there are identical 30 year old twin sisters, who chose two different paths in life, who would you rather be in a relationship with? A divorced single mom of three with a notch count of two, OR her single twin who spent her 20s partying, and traveling racking up a notch count of 100+?"

It turned out that a promiscuous woman was *significantly* less desirable than a divorced woman with children - which I found surprising.

Sexual purity can only be exchanged once, and like the value of a new car as it drives off the lot, its value goes down, as the miles, number of owners, and the amount of wear and tear goes up.

Not sharing her body with many men should be taken seriously by women.

But, as today's modern version of toxic feminism keeps telling women, they can be promiscuous without consequence, which we know isn't true.

It's not that women with a promiscuous past *can't* find a man (they almost always do, and can do so with ease). It's just that they often can't find a man that they're **attracted** to.

Women are the gatekeepers to sex, and to when sex happens.

I'm often asked what my advice is to women, given that men are encouraged to cultivate optionality.

Truthfully, it's not complicated. Men must create value in the world. Women must preserve their value. The conversations you have with your sons, versus your daughters should be *very* different.

Men are born inherently worthless to themselves, women, and to society as a whole. It's only men that have done the work on themselves, and who have created value for themselves and for others that are admired by women and respected by society.

Women, on the other hand, are inherently born with the value that they must then work hard to preserve. It's those women who preserve their value and their purity that are admired by high-value men, and are respected by society.

Regardless of what I tell men, it would be wise for younger women to preserve their value, and not be promiscuous.

Yes, I understand it's very frustrating for women to hear, but men and women's sexual strategies are opposite.

Men in their 20s or younger rarely value her purity - all guys prioritize sexual access first. So women must gatekeep their purity wisely, especially around those men in her prime years.

Unfortunately, young women today in their 20s prioritize their career, travel, and indulging in short-term sexual experiences with multiple men *precisely* when they should be focused on finding a high-value man, therefore capitalizing on their SMV when they are younger.

Study after study has revealed that men, regardless of age, culture, religion or continent, all prefer women at the peak of their SMV, which is around 23-years old. But, as I've mentioned already, women often very unwisely squander away this opportunity in the wrong pursuits.

It's one part a lack of guidance from family, one part a lack of obedience if said good guidance is offered, and one (very strong) part societal, with Western societies pressurizing women to be promiscuous.

Unfortunately, I've learned from my Ladies Night podcasts on YouTube that most women never grasp this reality. And, if they do, it's usually *way* too late - they're now in their 30s or 40s. Women hitting "the wall" is legit, but most slam it twice: first in their early 20s as their looks start fading, then later on when life's forcing them to face the facts.

Their Biological Clock Is *Always* Ticking

Most women will ultimately love to have a family with their high-value "prince charming," but the window for that opportunity is smaller than it is for men. A man can have children *well* into the autumn years of his life, whereas for women, her fertility declines rapidly after her early 30s. Most medical professionals label pregnancies over 35 as "high risk" for the mother and child, although with IVF and other innovations, successful pregnancies over 35 are possible, but they're still unwise for many reasons (such as complications at birth, and a **much** higher risk of birth defects).

The high-value men that nearly all women are seeking for are **not** in nightclubs, backpacking around Europe, or dancing at a music festival. Because men's attractiveness, and especially their value, takes time to build through effort, dedication, and focus; men's SMV peaks in his mid 30s - 40s, so these particular men are in boardrooms, on their boats, in supercar rallies, golf clubs, and happy hours in the expensive urban jungle financial districts.

However, while high-value men are naturally attracted to younger women, they *aren't* particularly interested in inviting a party girl, or career-focused women into their lives to start a family with, although many plugged-in men do.

But... a woman that is beautiful, kind, useful, respectful, joyful, and pure in chastity, is a **very** attractive proposition to a man that has created value for himself and his loved ones.

With that being said, and with knowing what high-value men really want (especially when her value is at its highest), women would be wise to prioritize finding such a high-value man in her 20s for marriage and family instead of wasting those years on other pursuits.

The problem is that women typically don't become bothered with guarding their sexual value until it's too late, which is usually right around the age of 30 when they discover their biological clock is ticking (i.e. the "Epiphany Phase"), and they see their loved ones around them getting married. Only then do they start guarding their sexuality more, by asking prospective men "what are you looking for" before they will go out with them on a date.

It's usually at this point, when women have had plenty of sexual experiences that they mistakenly create rules that make a man wait several dates, or even three months for *any* kind of intimacy. This is a big mistake, because - as I explained in my first book - women *always* make rules for men they see as beta, and they'll **gladly** break them for men they see as alphas.

The problem with that approach is that no man (with any level of self-respect) wants to wait for something that was given away immediately (with enthusiasm no less) to lots of other men in her youth.

Manufacturing hoops for men to jump through is an unwise strategy for women to use with high-value men. This strategy *does* work, but only on the plugged-in men that she doesn't have GBD for. Even in her 30s and onward, the men she has GBD for, will have that rule broken ***immediately***.

In Conclusion

His game is different from her game - and that's okay. Men and women are still better together than they are apart, and they can (and should) complement one another in life, but only if we can openly accept these differences between our sexual strategies.

Men would be wise to take the time to level-up and make themselves as physically attractive as possible, build their value (solve problems, make money, etc.), cultivate sexual options, and then - when their value has peaked during his 30s - be discerning in who they offer their commitment to, and to what degree. Men should also **always** continue to chase excellence, and be on a purpose in life. That should *never* stop.

Likewise, women who *truly* want to be with such a sought-after man, would be very wise to preserve their sexual value, avoid being promiscuous, and prioritize finding a high-value man to have a family with when her value (sexual value and fertility) is at its greatest in her 20s. If she can do this and gain this commitment from such a man, then she **must** continue to do all the things he liked into perpetuity in exchange for his love, time, resources, and anything else that she values.

Until women quit seeing men as success objects and guys stop viewing women as beauty, or sex objects - both **very** unlikely - then this is how unplugged men who've grinded to level-up snag what they want in life. And pull in the kind of woman who *truly* complements his world.

The Cold, Hard Truth

Never forget:

- **Men view women as beauty objects; women view men as success objects:** This has *always* been the case. Learn to accept this for what it is, and use it to your advantage to live your best life.
- **The Gatekeepers:** Men are the ones to decide if they're in a relationship or not, this is why it usually is (and always should be) the woman asking for commitment. Likewise, women get to decide who they share their bodies with. **Never** give her your commitment if she's trying to make you wait for sex.
- **Choose women who choose you:** Women will *dramatically* lower the "price" to have sex with them the higher her GBD level is for you. Women with 10/10 GBD for you **will make it as easy as possible** for you to sleep with them. These women will willingly jump through *your* hoops instead! Conversely, the lower her attraction for you, the more hoops she'll start to throw out for you to jump through. Leave these women be.

9

The Truth About Long-Term Relationships (LTRs)

A long-term relationship with a woman - whether it's marriage or not - has always been a key goal for most men. After all, we're just a higher form of primate. It's wired into our DNA to want a beautiful woman by our side as we chase that drive to spread our seed and have children.

However, I've now talked to *thousands* of men that have struggled to attract and - more importantly - keep a woman in their frame over the long-term. This chapter isn't about the attraction part, *it's the retention part*, which arguably for many men, is very difficult.

For a start, keeping an LTR in your frame is certainly harder than dating or spinning plates, and while most men abandon variety in an LTR (over time), they often frustratingly find they are putting in more work, while getting less back in return.

In this chapter, I'm going to reveal all the little things sitting in your blind spots you are doing that are slowly removing her attraction, and interest in you and how to fix them.

Contrary to what women (and simps) say to me, I *truly* care about men, their challenges, and finding peace and happiness with a woman. There are no guarantees in life, but I can confidently say this: being aware, unplugging from the comforting lies, and adopting many of these suggestions below, will be your best bet at finding something loving, and maybe - just maybe - even blissful.

To preface this, I am *well* aware that many critics will argue that my opinions are void because I am not married. They are correct that I am not married, nor would I ever marry again where family law hates men. The reason for why you should consider the following is because I am a seasoned man, and have experienced *a lot*. I have been promiscuous, spun plates, had FWBs, been in many long-term relationships, and I've been married (and divorced).

I've seen it all and coached thousands of men, and *that's* why you should pay attention here. It's always wiser to learn from the mistakes of others, than to make them all yourselves. I wish someone had sat me down at twenty and explained everything I am about to dispense below.

Don't Be a Nice Guy

> ***Note:*** *While I also talk about this concept in more depth in the "His Game, Her Game" chapter, I wanted to make sure that you really understand the importance of not being this kind of guy, by exploring it in this chapter as well (it really is **that** important to fully understand).*

I wish that being kind, considerate, thoughtful, and respectful of a woman's wishes created Genuine Burning Desire (i.e. GBD), enthusiastic sexual intimacy, and a long life of happiness. But, unfortunately, it doesn't. In fact, it usually does *the exact opposite*.

Women will routinely tell men that they want a "nice guy," a "kind soul," and a "best friend," but then go off and do the complete opposite by enthusiastically fucking Mr. Exciting.

I've been the quintessential "nice guy" many times when dealing with women, and when a man genuinely loves, and cares for a woman, he naturally wants to do things that make her happy. Being somewhat "nice" is one ingredient in creating attraction, but it's got to be dispensed in **much** smaller controlled doses than men think.

Also, it's better to be a kind man, than a nice guy.

They may sound similar, but there *is* a difference. Kindness is defined as the quality of being friendly, generous, and considerate towards others (with nothing expected in return), whereas "Niceness" is more surface-level and is focused on social expectations like being overly polite and being a "people pleaser."

It's important to understand that you can be nice (without being kind), or kind (without being nice). It's the "pleasing her part" that men make the biggest mistake when it comes to this.

"Nice guys" make up their own unspoken "covert contracts" in their head that they think women also agreed to. It usually goes something like:

"If I am nice and pleasing to her, she will see me for who I am and offer me love and sex in return."

Eventually most guys learn the hard way that this simply doesn't work. Dr. Robert Glover has a classic book called "No more Mr. Nice Guy" on this topic which I think **every** man should read at least once.

This reminds me of a funny entry once on a blog run by women called: "Don't date him." It read:

"He had several "lady friends" who stayed the night at his house and he claimed they were "Just friends". He frequently forgot important details about me, such as the fact that I had a sister, my birthday and what sorts of hobbies I had. He blew me off constantly, would return calls a week later

with the excuse of "I was busy." I often spoiled him with gifts, rides and sex only to receive a bag of Skittles in return. (I don't even like skittles!) That was the only gift I ever received from him! I met a new friend and we were bonding over "worst ex-boyfriend stories" and suddenly we realized "boy, a lot of these sound the same... Was his name...?" IT WAS THE SAME GUY!!!

I've been around a lot of women from all walks of life. I know the sound of a woman pining for a guy they found really attractive, and it usually sounds like the woman in the Skittles story, then they complain about him being an "asshole."

The Skittles guy probably did everything to her in the bedroom, whereas she now tells the nice guy: "I don't do that!" or, "I'm not that kind of girl..." but the quiet part she leaves out at the end of that is: "With you." Because she **will** do it enthusiastically with the Skittles man.

I hate to say it, but being nice doesn't work, so learn how to say no, and stop trying to please women - they never respond positively to nice guys that give them everything they want. Be kind, and a good man, but not a people pleaser. It's been said that "nice guys finish last in divorce court" whereas bad boys "finish on her face." I think most men start out as the "nice guy" (because that's what society has been drumming into them since they were young), only to feel frustrated and let down when it gets them nowhere. Those that have observed how being nice didn't work, or for those who've been the Skittles man, will agree with that statement.

Anger

Most men will become angry with a woman at some point, they may even resort to calling her disparaging names. I've been told in the past that I have a temper, but I've preferred to see it as a swift reaction to bullshit. I've learned to save funny lines like that for my friends, because it doesn't work with women.

Likewise, there might be a place for anger in business, especially if I am in a position of authority, or a better bargaining position. A degree of anger *might* be useful, but with women, anger really isn't that productive (and, with the wrong woman, could land you in **serious** trouble with the law).

Believe it or not, it's actually more frustrating and cruel to them if you simply remain calm and cool. Women would rather have you angry, than neutral or disinterested. They *love* to see you fired-up over something. Women are much more neurotic than men, and respond well to emotions.

Also, once you get angry with a woman, you can never take back those words, they will remain in her mind **forever**. Sometimes angrily calling her names is one of the best things that can happen in a relationship for her, but only because the balance of power now shifts to her because she can hold that over your head and use your own words against you, for example: "It's like that time you called me a whore seven years ago."

I'll put it this way, it could take a hundred years of research and development to build the perfect exotic car, and one second to blow it all up into tiny pieces by hitting a wall. **Do not** let the precise work you put into a relationship blow up over your inability to control your emotions. Don't let women (who are literally afraid of tiny spiders) push your buttons and get under your skin. You **must** keep control of your emotions (and therefore your frame) in check - at **all** times.

I recall hearing someone once saying the reason women try to push your buttons, and throw a hissy fit is because: "They got no hands." In other words, they can't physically fight you. So, instead, they will rely on doing things that will anger you or manipulate your emotional state in general.

Do not lose your cool. Instead, take a deep breath, turn around 180 degrees, and then proceed to walk in that direction if you think you are about to blow your lid and start shouting at her. Come back when cooler heads prevail. The absence of your presence, and the lack of an angry response may well infuriate them, and they may well try to escalate things, but *never* match that energy, and always remain calm and stoic.

Just accept that all women will make a mountain out of a molehill at some point. I remember a funny meme I saw once of a stunning picture of a 10/10 woman, with the caption "somewhere, some guy is tired of her bullshit too."

And, when it comes to LTRs, there's also a higher chance of them becoming "bored" over time, which increases the odds of them looking to stir up some drama to "liven things up a little." As much as it might drive you crazy, accepting that women **need** to feel *something* at all times, and then finding ways to make her feel lots of different emotions, will curb her desire to manufacture bullshit drama that won't help your relationship one bit.

Look, anger is a legitimate response in the face of an injustice, and women will do many things during the course of your relationship that you will view as unjust, but the mark of a good man is being able to maintain his composure, and this is *especially* true with women. Anger rarely ever works to your benefit with women, it's your job to be the unflinching rock that a stormy ocean crashes up against.

Water is wet, the sun is hot, and women *will* be women. Learn to accept it, understand it, and then navigate it with poise and competency.

Caging the Wild Animal

When men fall in love with a woman, they tend to do things to please them, and that can lead to a man making concessions, abandoning his interests, opinions, or hobbies that they wouldn't normally stop pursuing if they were single.

I was in the gym changing room once shaving my head after a shower. A guy about my age - out of shape and balding - complimented the look and asked about the process. He had a fading barbed wire tattoo around his bicep that was bleeding out. Back in my 20s these were common among tough guys and alphas. Women *loved* them. But today this dude was pear-shaped and clearly a shell of his former self.

After I answered his question, I said "You should shave your head, you'd really look a lot younger, and better." He replied, hanging his head low, and with a very clear look of years of nagging "I would, but my wife won't let me."

Oof, I was standing before a man that had gone through betatization through a thousand concessions. I'm certain that he was once an animal, but now he's just a caged pussy cat.

Men often do this to themselves. Your opinions, hobbies, friends, and interests should **thrive** in an LTR. Over the longer-term, shared values matter (as I've noted elsewhere in this book). They keep your relationship peaceful. She should encourage you to pursue them - as long as it doesn't majorly disrupt raising your kids together.

One of the things I've seen pulled on me, and I know this happens to other men, is a woman will try to separate you from a friend, or certain friends. It's usually not because they are bad people, but because she sees them as a threat to her authority, or control over you.

Unless they are trash friends, you should never abandon friendships for a woman. Your network is your net worth, and I have seen far too many great men henpecked and isolated from their friends and hobbies, only to be left in the cold one day when she leaves you. Stay wild, and keep doing what you always did before you met her, it's the wild animal she fell in love with.

You need to have your own life outside of your relationship. Since I've fully unplugged, I've *never* once asked for permission to go anywhere, or do anything, it's always been a statement, I.e. "On these dates, I'll be hunting with the boys." Men that say: "Let me check with the boss" are already lost. ***Don't be that guy***.

Abandoning Sexual Options

This part is going to be very difficult for some men to consider (and I cover it again from a different angle in the chapter on the three "ity's"), but I want you to sit with the discomfort, and really marinate on this section. It's especially important for single men, or men just starting to date - those already in a committed relationship are usually in too challenging a position to do much to change it.

Women love a man that other women want, but they still prefer that he doesn't actually exercise those options. Note the choice of the word "prefer." In the second edition of my first book you heard Steve from Accounting's testimonials about his asymmetrical relationship where he may exercise the option to sleep with other women, and how surprisingly successful he found it, and her continued, and strong display of GBD - in spite of this knowledge.

> ***Editor's Note:*** *This is one aspect that you never really believe is true and possible until you experience it first-hand yourself. When a woman's GBD for you is a genuine 10/10, then you'll be absolutely gobsmacked at what rules she's not only willing to break, but she'll happily rewrite her own rule book for you. But only if you continue to chase excellence, be her hypergamous best, be upfront and honest with her, and then choose to bring her along for the ride.*

Just because a woman doesn't like something, it doesn't mean you don't do it. There must be some competition - whether it's real or imagined - if you want her to feel a strong pull to you. Women don't usually want a man unless other women desire him and quite often those things she doesn't like are actually good for her, and the relationship.

I wish it wasn't that way, but deep inside, even the most Plugged-In Beta knows this to be true. Several clinical psychologists have also expressed to me that they find this to be true with the women they work with.

Competition anxiety (aka: Dread), is a powerful and misunderstood aphrodisiac with women. It correlates very closely with pre-selection and why a woman will date a successful, fit, competent, influential, and married man, over a broke, fat, insignificant, loser who's still living in his mom's basement. At some point, every man sees a version of this type of relationship and realizes they've been lied to. I don't make the rules here, I am just a mirror reflecting back facts.

Also, commitment and sexual exclusivity are not the same thing; you can be committed without being sexually exclusive, and you can be sexually exclusive, without having a commitment. Believe it or not, there are many men (quietly) living in an asymmetrical relationship where she is fully committed, and sexually exclusive to him, and he is committed but not sexually exclusive with her.

I've only seen top-shelf men, or those in close proximity to that level pull this off. She must view you as her hypergamous best option with strong attraction - anything below a 9/10 on the Net Promoter Score won't cut it (check the chapter on GBD in my first book for details). If she pegs you as a Plugged-In Beta, then *no* woman will sign up for that setup.

I've certainly had a few women early on dating, not wanting to rock the boat, say something along the lines of: "If you are with other women, I don't want to know about it, just be safe please."

You don't necessarily need to act on sexual variety or explore those other options, but keeping the legal loophole open clearly keeps the balance of power in the relationship in your favor, and despite her voiced request for sexual exclusivity it absolutely creates more interest in you in most women.

There are an awful lot of women out there sharing men today. Surveys have been conducted among men and women, and they routinely come back with the same data when asked if they are in a relationship. Around 2/3 of women say they are "in a relationship," while only 1/3 of men report being in a relationship. The numbers don't quite add up there...

And when asked about sexlessness, about 1/3 of men report having no sex, while less than 20% of women are sexless. When it comes to fathering children, about half of men throughout history, never pass down their genes, whereas only 1-in-4 women remain childless. On dating apps, women only see the top 20% of men as attractive, with the top 5% of those men being seen as "twice as desirable"
as the top 20% men; whereas men deem at least half the women on dating apps attractive enough to sleep with.

Clearly, women are sharing most of the same high-value and attractive men at the top.

From my own anecdotal evidence from coaching thousands of men, and from my own personal experiences, women do start to lose attraction for a man once he gives up exercising the option of seeing other women, and this accelerates further when they live together, or get married.

Again, I wish this wasn't the case, but this is how women are hardwired. I recall sitting at an event with Esther Perel, a psychotherapist known as an expert on relationships, sexuality, and infidelity. The topic of "interest in your partner" over time came up. For men, it's a steady decline over time; but for women, it sharply drops off early (which looks like the shape of a hockey stick on a chart) and it remains lower than a man's, for the vast majority of the relationship.

I had a chat with a top-shelf friend of mine who lives in an asymmetrical setup with his woman. She knows he could exercise options if he chooses. He laid out the best approach for guys in this spot.

Date for a bit while spinning plates - exercising options - like I covered in my first book. Her interest spikes especially if she suspects you're sharing time with other women. Intimate or not doesn't matter. Soon she'll ask if you're seeing anyone else. Then she'll drop hints about not wanting to share you or claiming you as hers alone.

That's when you call her bluff. Acknowledge and validate her concerns and say "Yeah I get why you'd want that. I totally understand. But if it's not good enough for you there's the door." The calm, evenhanded vibe of that line from a man she strongly desires, will often make her pause and rethink her stance.

Tell her you'd rather end it now than drag both of you through a slow degrading mess. That keeps the power balance in your court. Once you surrender that edge it's damn near impossible to reclaim it.

Again, you don't necessarily need to act on the option to step out, but the fact that it exists on your end is what matters. She probably won't like it, but what women like, and what's good for her, and your relationship aren't always the same thing.

Finally, do not agree to an open relationship on both your ends, or give her the option to betray you. You do not want to poison the well! Men with options don't get *nearly* as emotionally attached to women after sex, men can "step out" many times during their relationship, and they can still come home to love and be present for their family just fine.

I'm not condoning the choice, but I know plenty of top-shelf men that have enjoyed the company of dozens and dozens of women while traveling on business from conferences, and events without any issues. Bottom line: men and women are built differently.

For women, there is a much deeper emotional connection being established when they have sex and allowing her to make that connection with another man won't be good for your relationship - trust me on this one. She needs to not only adore you, but also respect you and she sure as hell can't do that if she knows that you're OK with her sleeping with other men. Also consider the fact that women have an innate desire to feel safe, and you letting her go off to fuck some strange men will make her question how safe she feels with you.

It 100% needs to be an asymmetrical arrangement. Again, I wish this wasn't true, but this is what works very well.

She will probably try to negotiate some rules on you, which is normal, but generally speaking, the fewer the rules the better. Being discreet, safe, and not doing anything to embarrass her seems to be the top ask from most women when it comes to you "stepping out" on occasion.

Women don't want another woman knocking on their door and announcing they are pregnant with your baby. STDs are an obvious issue to avoid, and finally, taking her to "your" favorite restaurant (that you visit as a couple), or taking vacations with another woman will infuriate her. If you are going to do anything at all with other women, then it's probably best to keep it to casual hookups, Friends With Benefits (FWB) type of arrangement, or keep it to when you're traveling by yourself.

Of course, some men in this arrangement will not even be tempted to step out if she is expressing GBD, is genuinely useful in his life, offering him frequent mind-blowing sex, and is completely respectful of him as the man whose lead she follows without question. Some men start to lose interest in other women when the one we love ticks off all our boxes, i.e. The grass is greenest where you water it and take care of it.

Ultimately, you are the man, so it's up to you to decide what kind of relationship you want, and how you want to run it. But, if you enjoy true GBD from her, as outlined in my first book, then at the very least, she should have the distinct impression that you genuinely have other options, even if you do not exercise them.

Women & Embarrassment (Moff's Tale)

Women will tolerate a lot in dating and relationships if he is That Guy/her hypergamous best.

They will look the other way if a high enough value guy steps out, come over to Chad's house at 3 AM for some bedroom fun then be promptly shown the door, and lie to her friends about it to avoid judgment.

That last point is key - women can't *stand* to be embarrassed, *especially* in front of the sisterhood. They are naturally averse to criticism from the majority of the tribe, because in Hunter and Gatherer times, this type of criticism would have led to ostracism, exile, and eventually death.

Quick Story

In my cohabiting LTR a few years ago, we invited about a dozen friends over to our place to hang out. This was in NYC in the middle of COVID so having people over was really our only option to have any sort of social interaction outside of just each other.

Lockdowns started in March, and this get together was in July. Over the stressful months of lockdown, both working from home, trying to raise a new puppy, and trying to keep an already failing relationship going - things were starting to take a toll.

I had gone from unequivocally wanting to marry this girl, to being completely unsure in just a span of months. To be honest, I probably would have continued marching towards the slaughterhouse even though I knew deep down that I was making the wrong choice.

These subconscious feelings bubbled to the surface during this get together while we were playing a card game. The point of the game was to draw a card, and then you would have three seconds to answer the prompt written on the card. My prompt was "Name Three Things You Do on Your Wedding Night".

I had been drinking a bit so my internal filter didn't do its job on this one, and I ended up blurting out "Yeah like I'm ever getting married." *The whole room fell silent.*

In front of my ex's closest friends, the girls she told all the stories about our plans to get married, have kids, the McMansion, white picket fence - just heard her boyfriend say that all of that was bullshit and not happening.

A few hours later they all left and the bomb went off. The screaming, crying, wailing, you name it. She eventually tired herself out and went to bed. I followed soon after.

The next morning she sat me down and said she never felt so embarrassed and unloved in her life and that she needed space.

I couldn't really believe what I was hearing. I told her that while it wasn't the right time to say something about not getting married and make a joke out of it, I wasn't sorry for having those thoughts because they were the truth, and it wasn't something we could work on.

She wanted to part and I decided to drive to Virginia for a week to give her the space she asked for. We tried rekindling things, going on a vacation or two, but I'm convinced that the moment during the card game was the nail in the coffin for that relationship.

There was no way she could stay with me after that, and have to live with the embarrassment of continuing to stay with a guy who told all of her friends he's never going to marry her. She gave it enough "effort" and time over the next few months to give everyone the *illusion* that she was trying to make it work, but it eventually came to an inevitable end.

REMEMBER! Don't bore women, and don't embarrass them. Once your business becomes the world's business, or the business of your family and friends - *especially* if it's business that makes her look bad in any way - you can bet that the clock has started ticking down to the end of the relationship.

Jealousy vs Managing Risk

In the past, I've also been jealous, and I've also experienced *biblical* levels of jealousy which involved the use of highly complex monitoring systems, keeping track of my behavior and my whereabouts on a daily basis. Jealousy is an ugly emotion, and unattractive to *both* sexes.

It needs to be said that being attentive to situations that could lead to a woman cheating on you (like bachelorette parties), and feeling jealous are absolutely **not** the same thing.

Being jealous, and constantly questioning her in an insecure manner, **will** make you *very* unattractive to her, and in some sense push her away.

This is why I can't stress enough the importance of only **choosing women that choose you**. It *always* starts here in the selection process.

In the dating phase you should hear soundbites like: "Did you eat?," "Be naked when I get there," "I saw these boxers at the store and bought them for you," "Let me know when you are home safe," " I'm proud of you," Etc. Again, she MUST be the one that asks for your commitment in a relationship. This ensures there's a healthy power dynamic where she enjoys being with her (hypergamous) perceived best option, and she is looking up to you.

Far too many men chase after women (of the same, or higher value), ask her for her commitment, and then become extremely jealous because they fear losing what they - in their mind - worked so hard to get. I know I've personally done this before in my 20s. For a relationship to operate in a healthy fashion, you need to be of higher value than her (especially in her own mind), and then *maintain* that position of looking like a success object to her. *Do not rob a woman of her innate need to feel admiration for you.*

This power dynamic will leave you in a comfortable place, and it's unlikely to create any unattractive levels of jealousy on your part - IF you manage it correctly.

However, some women do have a very insecure attachment style, and will resort to using surveillance methods that look like extreme jealousy, and competition anxiety is generally good (as long as it's not excessive). As I've said before, some of the things that women really don't like are actually good for her, and for the relationship as a whole.

The Importance of Having Her Respect

When it comes to having a woman genuinely look up to you and ***truly*** listen to what you have to say, you **need** her respect.

If a woman doesn't respect you, she **cannot** love you. Her respect for you **must** come *before* her love.

This is *essential* to understand because, as you're about to see in the next part of this chapter, a woman who cannot respect your leadership *will not* follow your guidance, or willingly accept any boundaries that you set that's for the benefit of the relationship.

Being able to - unapologetically - set the standards for how you wish to live your life (which includes defining what you will - and will not - tolerate, without worrying about how that's going to make her "feel") is *critical*.

You don't need to be a dick about it either. For example simply state that you "don't find XYZ situation appropriate while she's in a relationship." If she gently pushes back - usually by asking what you'd do if she did it anyway - treat it as a mild competency or frame test. Remind her it's your role to keep her and the relationship safe. However, make it **crystal** clear to her that, if she ignores your wishes, she'd be doing that activity as a single woman and you **will** replace her.

Being *very* calm, firm, and affirmative in such a response (while looking them straight in the eyes) will **greatly** increase the likelihood that she'll take your standards seriously. They'll quickly pick up the subtext that you *aren't* fucking around and that you're serious, without you needing to raise your voice once.

Setting Healthy Boundaries

One of the biggest mistakes I see men make is not setting, or reinforcing, healthy boundaries around how *they* want to lead the relationship. High-risk activities such as: Bachelorette parties, weekend trips to places like Vegas, hanging out with male "friends," playing in co-ed sports, hiring a male personal trainer, going out salsa dancing for the night, taking work trips with male co-workers, having a "work husband," etc. they're *all* activities that **greatly** increase the odds of something happening that won't be good for your relationship.

If you truly love and care for a woman, you won't passively tolerate behavior that threatens the integrity of the relationship. Instead, you'll clearly communicate your boundaries and expectations - leaving the choice up to her to either align with them or not, while being fully aware of the consequences beforehand. It just makes logical sense. Look, I trust the locks on my supercar, but I'm not parking it in a terrible neighborhood overnight.

I've had two male strippers on my podcast over the years, and they revealed that about 80% of women that attend a bachelorette party, indulge in some sexual act with them. It's not just the guests either. Brides-to-be, have also indulged in sexual acts with the male strippers, while the other women cheer them on like it's a sporting event.

Imagine how many men today took wedding vows before their church, while their bride to be is wearing a white gown (which is supposed to portray purity/virginity), but there she was, indulging in sexual acts just a few days before at her bachelorette party?

Now knowing this insider information from male strippers, I would never allow a woman I loved to attend a bachelorette party. That's not jealousy, that's just me setting a healthy boundary around protecting our relationship, and a woman that *truly* loves and - most importantly - *respects* you will accept that boundary (even if they don't "like" it) and they'll take a pass on the invite to said bachelorette party. If you choose to marry a woman, do not permit a bachelorette party.

Male personal trainers that work with women have also reported to me that they sleep with more than half of their attractive female clients, with many of them being in a relationship. If you think letting your girl get trained by an athletic young stud is a good idea, then you're being a gullible fool. If she needs a personal trainer, then there are plenty of good female ones out there - or lead by example and get her to join you at the gym. Otherwise, it's as dumb as driving your nice car to a bad neighborhood, leaving it unlocked, and then leaving the keys on the seat. More often than not, something bad is going to happen.

A weekend girl's trip away to Vegas for her friend's birthday should be **completely off the table**. A woman that *truly* respects your relationship wouldn't even contemplate attending these types of events. Women literally invented the "what happens in Vegas, stays in Vegas" cliché to justify and dismiss their promiscuity. Nothing good for your relationship happens on these "girls trips."

Compare and contrast that to a weekend spa-retreat with her closest friends (who barely drink) and they're chilling out, going for nature walks, and bike rides. The odds of something happening that'll ruin your relationship are **significantly** higher on a Vegas trip...

Likewise, keeping male friends around, or playing co-ed sports are another area of risk. I remember a gal I dated in my 20s cheated on me with a guy from her co-ed baseball team, while I was away for a month in the summer visiting my family in Europe. You're the man, *you* set the boundaries.

"He's Just a Friend"

Remember, **nobody** fucks more girlfriends and wives than "He's just a friend." It's *always* the guy she tells you that you have "nothing to worry about," **that's** the guy that men *should* worry about. Again, if she has chosen you, and asked you for your commitment, then she should have no problem switching to an all-women's sports league, saying no to trips that aren't appropriate for a woman in an LTR, or even letting go of male friends.

This includes hanging out with old exes, her ex-fiancée, or any other male friends for dinner, coffee, or whatever. Women *aren't* stupid when it comes to this; they instinctively know that most (if not all) of her straight male "friends" would fuck them in an instant if asked. A woman with *true* GBD for you **will not** want to run the risk of fucking it all up if you're truly the best man she's ever likely to find and will cut them out of her life.

Men and women share little when it comes to social interests. We've seen what happens when men pretend to be women and compete in female sports - the women get *decimated*. It's simply not a level playing field. Staying fit is great and attractive. Just have her do it on an all-female team, or have her join you at the gym for workouts together.

The way to handle these issues is simple, and are best handled when she asks you for your commitment. Remember it's at this point she will be saying things like she really likes (or loves) you, wants to claim you, and doesn't want to see anyone else. If you have seen her doing any of the above, simply tell her something like: "I feel the same, but I can't take a woman seriously and invite her into my life if she is doing X, Y or Z, it's only going to lead to problems down the road if you choose to do those things, if that's what's important to you, then I'm not the right guy for you."

If she announces a couple of years into the relationship that she wants to take a girls trip to Miami, simply remind her of your boundary and that you don't want to put your love for one another at risk. Trips like these can be taken as couples.

Women will sometimes persist, perhaps calling you "controlling" or "insecure," but it's none of those things, it's just a healthy boundary you won't let her cross. Tell her you aren't going to stop her, but if that's her decision, tell her she can enjoy that activity as a single woman and the locks will be changed by the time she gets back.

If a woman *truly* adores you and views you as her best hypergamous match, then *anything* risking betrayal should feel downright unappealing to her.

However, sometimes a woman's biggest enemy is *other women* - often fueled by envy over what you two share. Plenty of women (especially those in unhappy relationships/marriages) will resent seeing her happy and will drop subtle digs, or try to stir up trouble to pull you two apart.

That said, those women aren't her real friends. Her true friends would thank you and tell you that they've never seen her so content and happy.

Also, don't be unreasonable; a relaxing girls trip to a cottage or lake house for the weekend with her all-girls book club is absolutely fine, and should be encouraged, but be sensible and attentive - just don't let her put herself in a bad position.

I think jealousy is a normal evolved firmware that both sexes require to ensure commitment, but it's for different reasons. Men want assurance of paternity, so they want to know she is sexually exclusive with him, while women are more concerned with love, protection and provisioning (because from an evolutionary perspective, without that, it would spell certain death for her and her offspring). It's why, when men cheat, her first question is "did you love her?" When women do it, men ask, "did you fuck him." Nothing has changed with this firmware, it's been hardwired into our DNA.

Don't let jealousy sneak in on your end. Handle the relationship from day one by unapologetically laying out your standards and expectations. And **never** tolerate extreme jealousy from her. Plenty of women today wrestle with insecure attachment styles. Therapy can sort that out - but that's *her* job to fix, *not* yours.

Never - Ever - Be Her Second Choice

In my first book, there is a chapter that talks about the topic of Genuine Burning Desire (i.e. GBD), where I break women's interest in us into three categories: whether they're a "promoter," "indifferent", or a "detractor." I think one of the mistakes I've certainly made in the past was chasing a woman that expressed indifference for me, and working hard trying to get her to see my virtues and value.

You look like a lost puppy dog wanting its owner to acknowledge you, but for the most part, get ignored.

You could call this simping, which is essentially an unequal exchange of value between a man and a woman. He showers her with attention, love and resources, while she returns breadcrumbs to him.

However, it's *critical* to understand that you **cannot negotiate desire in a woman**. She either naturally has it for you, or it's not there and, as stated earlier in this chapter, you can't ever motivate her to GBD by trying to be a "nice guy."

The best way to have GBD, and maintain it, is a two-step process:

1. Be attractive and valuable.
2. Don't be unattractive and have no value.

I appreciate that this soundbite sounds trite, but one of *the* most valuable benefits of doing the work is becoming naturally more attractive. Many, *many* men who're in my community have shown me the receipts of what's possible in every area of their life once they've begun to do the work to fix their weak areas. And, seeing as so few men these days step-up to do the work, you'll *significantly* increase the odds of finding someone who digs your vibe *so* much that they can't get enough of you.

Desire isn't a permanent state though (even for those women who're a 10 on the scale). They may change their opinion of you over time (e.g. constantly complain about problems and watch her GBD for you start to take a significant hit), and their desire for you can also go up as your value increases.

I've certainly had my share of women that passed on my advances earlier in life only to come around later when they see my increased wealth, popular videos, and influence trying to worm their way into my life, and say things like they "made a mistake" and would "like to see you." I even had an ex who was married and shameless enough try this approach once.

Over the long-term, I'd rather have an agreeable seven with very high GBD, than a disagreeable 10 with a lower level of attraction to me.

The "Alpha Widow"

This brings me to my next point of being her second (or third, fourth, etc.) choice. A lot of the time, women will pine for a man that they absolutely *adore* (he "ticks all of her boxes") - but he won't offer her any commitment, and will happily keep her as a casual hookup, or FWB *at best*.

This man is usually sitting on the top-shelf and is out of her reach; he's some combination of being very attractive looking, rich, visibly competent, socially influential (i.e. high-status), is very resourceful, etc. He may sleep with her (when no other options are available), or be the "skittles man" and give her little breadcrumbs of his time (as outlined earlier in this chapter), but he makes *very* little investment in her, and he *certainly* wouldn't marry her, let alone be exclusive with her.

In some cases, there may be several men ahead of you that she chose, but *they didn't choose her*, and so you become the guy that she "settled for." I'd argue most marriages today are born out of a woman settling for a man she could get (i.e. would commit to her), and so - by default - he isn't her first, or even second choice. Personally, I think one of the reasons so many wives dislike their husbands today is because they didn't marry their first choice.

The great danger with being her second choice is that, when she's got the children she wants from you and becomes bored, you either become one of those "dead bedroom" statistics (where there's no intimacy - of any kind) or, she starts listening to her single friends, starts working out, and thinks she can do better by entering the sexual marketplace as a single mom, so she decides to divorce you, take half your stuff, and alienate you from your kids by drip-feeding them a poisonous BS narrative about you.

I'll say it again (and I'll keep repeating it as often as it takes): *only choose women that choose you*! It will make your life, relationships, and sexual intimacy with a woman *so* much better than having a relationship with a woman who felt like she "settled" for you.

Dealing With Disrespect

I **firmly** believe that the mindset women need to constantly have to keep a good, high-value man around is as follows:

1. Being useful in his life,
2. Enthusiastically give him the mind-bending sex that she's *never* given any other guy, and
3. **Always** give him their utmost respect.

Earlier on in this chapter I mentioned just *how* important it is for a woman to openly respect her man. Shows of disrespect should *never* be allowed. I've previously allowed it in my life, but by accepting it and not calling her out on it, you are training her to see you as less and you have now - unwittingly - negotiated a new dynamic of how the relationship works going forwards. Ultimately, you have granted her permission to treat you like garbage both in private, and in public.

You will get out of life what you tolerate and, if you tolerate disrespect, you will only ever get more of it - not less.

A good friend of mine mentioned to me once that he rarely dealt with disrespect, but if he did, he would use harsh humor e.g: "It'll be a long walk home in those heels."

It's also been said that contempt (which is a *very* close relative of disrespect) is the clock that ticks down to the end of the relationship; so a disrespectful woman is a woman who already has one foot out the door.

Never get angry or name-call. As I've stated elsewhere in this chapter, it's far more impactful and cruel to remain cool, calm, and sincere in your tone.

Simply state something like: "Don't **ever** talk to me in that disrespectful way again. Because, if you do, I'll know you don't want to be with me anymore," then turn around 180-degrees and proceed to walk in that direction.

Nothing else needs to be said, and the ideal response from a well-calibrated woman, will be to take some time to self-reflect (rather than just immediately become defensive) and quickly realize she was out of order and apologize for crossing that boundary. You **need** to draw a line in the sand, point to it, and let her know she should never cross it again.

It's also worth remembering that being willing to call her out on her BS is actually an *attractive* trait to women. Most women are accustomed to men being spineless and supplicating. A man straight-up telling his woman that she's out of line (in a calm and cool manner) is a man that has *immediately* sub-communicated to her that he has enough self-respect, still has his balls *firmly* attached, and that he has the confidence in himself to immediately put her in her place (versus saying nothing and letting it fester).

Do note though, that you **must** call her out on her disrespect **immediately** after it occurs. Whether you tell her to her face, or tell her that "we'll talk about this later," you need to let her know that she royally fucked up. Leaving it to fester and then calling her out on it long after the event has occurred, is a Plugged-In Beta male move that will only be seen by her as you being too worried about how she'd react in the moment.

Also, don't draw a boundary that you aren't willing to take action on. Setting a boundary that will "end the relationship" (and then *not* ending the relationship if she does it again) is actually far worse, as she now knows she's got the power in the relationship, and she'll take that and run with it. *Women must understand they* **are** *replaceable.*

Say what you mean, but mean what you say.

On the flip side, a woman that shows respect outwardly is *very* attractive and memorable. Years ago someone in a group setting made a joke about "dick in a box" (from a stand-up comedy skit). My girlfriend at the time responded "Rich's wouldn't fit in that box. That box is too small."

So, I'll say it again, **DO NOT TOLERATE DISRESPECT - EVER!** - if you do, you are literally training her to see you as less. And, again, if she can't respect you as a man, she cannot love you. Never forget that.

Trying Too Hard

I think when a man truly loves a woman, he will usually do anything to keep her happy. I've certainly tried to reason my way through conflict, make concessions, offer more to her to placate her, and it never seems to work. In fact, the harder you try the *worse* it seems to get.

Treating her better never seems to fix bad behavior - all it does is train her to initiate *more* bad behavior and throw even bigger hissy fits to get more out of you. Remember, women would rather have you angry than in a stoic or disinterested state - they thrive off of emotions (both good **and** bad). This is why it's significantly more effective to remain calm with your emotions.

Trying too hard leads you down the path of one of those "nice guys" that gladly regurgitates that ridiculous line I always hear from plugged in betas: "Happy wife, happy life!"

Being Her Number One

The only way you will be the number one most important thing in her life, is if you make sure that she's **not** the number one most important thing in *your* life (this is why I urge men to chase excellence over women).

To put it another way: all women want a man with a sparkle in his eye, but she doesn't want to **be** that sparkle.

Egalitarian (equal) style relationships are often pushed by those that want us plugged-in. The most obvious form of this is when I hear someone refer to their wife, husband, boyfriend, or girlfriend as their "partner."

You aren't running a law firm and you aren't partners. This blurring of the gender lines is one of the things that doesn't work, and that leads to two people fighting for the driver's seat. As I mentioned in my first book, one of the red flags is a woman trying to compete with you. If she is trying to compete with you, then she sees herself as better than you; otherwise, why would she try to one-up you?

In the chapter that covered marriage as a sweet spot, a common theme to enjoying success in marriage was the man leading, and the woman naturally following his lead.

Truly equal (i.e. "50/50") relationships don't generally work very well, or for very long - there's *always* an exchange of value and power in each relationship. Truthfully, men and women that complement each other's lives are *far* better together, than they are apart.

Since we know and accept that women are hypergamous by nature, then that means there must be an adorer, and adored role. You **never** want to be the adorer, because it deprives her of satisfying her hypergamy and of her feeling like she's with her number one.

Betatization by 1,000 Concessions

I've mentioned a version of this concept in other parts of my writing and my videos over the years. However, it needs its own place in the world of mistakes that men commonly make in long-term relationships. It's not a question *if* a man will go through the process of betatization, it's a question of "to what extent." Quite simply, the longer you're together with her, the more opportunities there are for making said concessions.

It's always a sequence of making lots of small concessions that you make as a man to please her, that ultimately lead to a small dent in your perceived value to her, each dent impacting her GBD level for you. It's like the age-old saying: "death from a 1,000 paper cuts."

Allow me to share an example.

I remember during the COVID scamdemic I had a coaching client sharing the following frustration. Remember when masks were mandated for entrance *everywhere*? People were *so* indoctrinated, they would drive in their cars (alone with the windows up), **while still wearing a mask**. During Christmas at my client's girlfriend's family's house, they all wanted to take a large group family picture together, wearing Christmassy COVID masks they had made.

By this point it was very apparent that masks simply didn't do anything *at all*, and they were just used as a mechanism to control us. Basically, they were a public symbol of oppression. Naturally, on his principles, he refused to wear the mask for that picture. They didn't like it, but had he made that concession, it would have been another paper cut in the process.

It may seem trivial, and some might say it was unreasonable of him to opt-out (and I'm sure he certainly got some dirty looks for holding his ground), but his values are more important than his need to fit in, especially with the way they were trying to control us at the time.

It's the collection of such small concessions that add up over time to make us men look like less in their eyes.

Look, a long-term relationship will require *some* concessions (it's inevitable if a relationship between two people is to last any substantial length of time), that's why you must understand that you *will* go through this process, and that's also why I think men should be *very* choosy and intentional with the concessions he makes. However, how much of the process you go through is *entirely* on you - and you alone.

Little Indignities

These little indignities are often small things (like sniping remarks) that make a person feel embarrassed or even unimportant, and they really start to pile up over time. It's like death by a thousand paper cuts. She will do them to you, and you will do them to her.

Remember that time she sent you a message early on, telling you how important you are, how much she loves your kid, and if you ever need help to call upon her? Then, when you do, she is cold - or worse - unresponsive. That's a little indignity.

Conversely, she'll remember the time you let her down over a promise, or lashed out verbally, or when you physically pointed a finger at her and called her a name out of anger.

These "times" of small indignities all start to add up, and it's not any one item that becomes the breaking point, but at some point, it will be the one (time) straw that broke the camel's back.

It might seem reasonable at the time to be indignant to something that annoys or frustrates you, but just know that nobody dies from a single, small paper-cut, but several thousand small paper cuts in relatively quick succession may well do the trick.

If you are attentive early on, and you start to frequently spot such indignities during the honeymoon phase, then it's probably a good idea to cut your losses early, and walk away because they will only increase over time.

You should understand that you **can't** have it all in the same person; she *will* frustrate you from time-to-time and she *will* let you down on occasions. So, when it comes to LTRs, learn to pick your battles, make *some* small concessions (that you can genuinely live with), and then do the work to maintain your composure when tested, and stay focused on your mission.

Indignities are often just little annoying shit tests designed to test you and your resolve. You'll start to notice them increase in frequency if her GBD levels ever start to take a hit, so be aware of that, and check yourself to make sure you're not unintentionally doing something to kill her attraction to you (like complaining about anything).

When it comes to maintaining an LTR, it's also *incredibly* important to choose a woman who has as few faults as possible (which can only ever be discerned over time), and be sure that the faults that she does have (because no-one is perfect), are the ones you can live with and don't impact your life.

The Importance of Remaining Attractive

I've often summarized how men and women view each other as: "Men are success objects to women, and women are beauty objects to men." But that's not the *entire* picture because being attractive to a woman is more than just being "handsome."

Women have the expectation that you are not only handsome (to them), but also: masculine, visibly competent (e.g. working hard to being recognized as "world-class" in your field of expertise), resourceful (i.e. can solve real problems quickly), loving, kind, a good man, generous, remain successful, physically strong, be a good father, emotionally resilient, etc.

The list is long (and it's also not something that's exclusive to "modern women" either - previous generations of women have *always* had a checklist of boxes that they'd want their "ideal" man to tick off), but the point here is - when it comes to attracting a woman - we as men can't ever relax, and many men do tend to get very lazy when they're in a long-term relationship.

Guys who wake up at the same time every day just to punch a clock never seek advancement. They're content with the same dead-end job they landed 22 years ago - as long as it funds their weekend beers. They let themselves pack on the pounds then plop their saggy asses on the couch nightly for sports with food crumbs collecting on their ever-expanding beer belly. Those dudes can't expect prime results with women.

At best, she might stick around if she lacks better options (which means she either has self-esteem issues, or got fat and lazy herself), but there's no fun being in a relationship with a woman that doesn't find you even remotely attractive. You're basically roommates at that point.

However, even if you've let yourself get to this point, the good news for men is, we generally reach our absolute peak later in life, into our thirties (potentially into your forties if you step-up quickly enough); we also age a little bit better as men have thicker skin and tend to lose collagen at a slower rate than women do (which can be slowed down even further with the right workouts and nutrition).

And while men typically lose their testosterone at the rate of one percent per year after the age of 30, there are *plenty* of supplements, activities, and even testosterone replacement clinics that can be very useful in your efforts to delay the aging process.

I covered this in a chapter in my first book, but I can categorically tell you that I do *not* want to be the average sedentary 75-year old that's sitting in a chair, staring out into the world in a care home. Fuck that. I'm going to enjoy my life to the fullest until my dying breath, going out knowing that I gave this one life my all. So should you.

Conversely, because women are primarily seen as beauty objects to men, they universally peak in their early twenties, so it's not until our thirties where the tables turn in the sexual marketplace, and so the men that have done the work to improve their lives, have *naturally* become more valuable.

The key here is that if you want to maintain a really good experience with women over the long-term, then you can't ever get lazy, boring, *or* predictable.

Editor's Note: *One thing I'd like to personally add in here, is that it's easier to prevent such boredom from becoming an issue in an LTR when you continue to invite her to enter into your world (where you're - hopefully - doing fun things with your downtime). The reasons for this are that you:*

1. *Keep the frame of the interaction by making her willingly enter it. She's joining you to do something that you enjoy and are - hopefully - naturally good at (i.e. displaying competence).*
2. *If her GBD is a solid 9-10/10, then she should trust your leadership without question. If that's the case, help her to step out of her comfort zone more often. That may look like taking her to a gun range to shoot some guns, taking her out dancing, or anything that you two can enjoy together (but that she's never "seen herself doing" before). This opens her up to experiencing many, many more "firsts" with you, anchoring those memories and experiences firmly to you.*
3. *If you need to travel for business (and you know she might like it/has never been there before), then ask her if she's free that week(end), and when she says yes, book her a seat on the plane and then straight-up tell her to "pack [insert your favorite outfits here] and your passport as you're joining me at [insert destination] I'll pick you up at [insert date and time], see you then." You don't need to do this often (maybe once or twice a year), but the spontaneity of the surprise (and the submission implied that you're **telling her** she's coming with you (you didn't ask her)) is a **very** potent combination. Again, save this sort of surprise for the LTR **that's earned it!** Women without a 9 or 10 GBD level **do not** get this treatment.*

When I was married, I didn't understand the importance of any *of this chapter - and my kids have paid the price dearly for my mistakes. Now? Things remain effortless because my LTR has no option* but *to enter into my world/frame, so I'm always doing something that I* genuinely *enjoy (which I now enjoy mixing up to keep her guessing). A woman with true GBD for you* **loves** *to see you "in your element" and that'll only enhance her feelings for you.*

As men we need to expect our ROI in the relationship to dip over time. A decade in and you might be with a woman who started at a solid 10/10 GBD early on, but now sits at an 8/10 - even as you've continued to stack more wealth and success. Your value goes up, but you will experience less GBD in return.

Unfortunately, as per my "Proximity, Familiarity, and Exclusivity" chapter in this book, these areas breed comfort, safety, and - for some - even contempt. It's just a reality of the game of relationships (even more-so with LTRs).

So, what's the solution?

From my own experience, the best way to offset this inevitable risk is to remove both some certainty *and* your proximity out of the relationship. A close friend of mine has been happily married for 30-years now, and he *still* reports having enthusiastic sex with his wife on a *very* frequent basis. One of the things that he believes is a strong contributor to this success is that he is usually out of the house on business for half of the month.

Esther Perel is - in my opinion - one of the ***very*** few women who has any real insights on male-female relationship dynamics (she's the author of "Mating in Captivity," a book I recommend you read). Her 2013, 20-minute Ted talk titled "The secret to desire in a long-term relationship" is worth a watch:

▶ The secret to desire in a long-term relationship

Scan Me →

▶ https://youtu.be/sa0RUmGTCYY

In this talk she confirms that my friend is right to give his marriage some breathing space by being away as "absence and longing can fuel the imagination." She also talks about how letting your woman see you in your element is a major attraction trigger and can often remind them what they first found attractive in you all those years ago.

The key to retention and GBD with women will always remain men maximizing their attractiveness, and value.

Overlooking Red Flags

Men, especially those lower in attractiveness in the sexual marketplace know they have fewer options, and so tend to overlook serious red flags in a woman (due to their scarcity mentality). The notion of the "fixer upper" might make sense when renovating a house, but it rarely translates into a good idea when it comes to women. These men are often mocked and called "captain save a hoe," or a "white knight."

In my first book, I covered 21 of the biggest Red Flags in great detail, but to summarize them they are:

1. Daddy issues,
2. Feminists,
3. The unhappy and unlucky,
4. She competes with you,
5. Keeps men from her past around,
6. Poor with money,

7. Violent women,
8. Extreme jealousy,
9. Party girls,
10. Heavily tattooed & pierced women,
11. Big notch counts,
12. Single mothers,
13. Women seeking validation,
14. She was a sugar baby, on OnlyFans, or a sex worker,
15. Pathological liars,
16. Baby rabies,
17. Hissy fits,
18. Be in control of the birth,
19. Drama queens,
20. Addictions, and
21. She can't follow your lead.

Since my first book came out I've heard plenty of guys gripe that most women they meet carry a ton of red flags. And honestly, I'm not shocked. The older we get the more we'll bump into women hauling unresolved baggage. Fathers and seasoned men ought to drill this into younger guys' heads. If the men in your circle are hunting for a committed woman or a family start early - snag them in their early 20s before those flags begin to pile up.

Now, some red flags aren't as big a deal as others, and you can work with a woman willing to change her bad choices. For example, if you are dating a woman with a shopping addiction, and she is constantly buying and returning clothes, accessories, decorations, or furniture, when she asks for your commitment, you tell her "I like you too, but I can't invite a woman into my life with a shopping addiction." That's easier to resolve than dealing with a single mom of three young kids from three different fathers, who is covered in huge tattoos, who also had a stint as a stripper.

The older you get as a man, and the older the women get that you can reasonably date, the more likely you will need to make concessions in what you will and won't tolerate. This is why I **strongly** advocate for spinning plates as long as it takes for the cream to rise to the top (i.e. the best woman **will** come out top given enough time). You **will** need to sift through an *awful* lot of women who won't want to compliment your life in the way that you need her to - there's no way around that.

As the old saying goes: "You'll need to sift through a lot of dirt to find the gold."

Remove (Some) Certainty

There has to be *some* mystery in a long-term relationship, certainty (i.e. being predictable) **cannot exist;** with certainty comes too much safety, and too much safety breeds complacency. There has to be *some* level of uncertainty for her to maintain a strong attraction to you.

For example, this can happen when it falls into patterns and schedules - certain nights of the week become "your night" together. In my case there was a scheduled night that my girl would normally arrive after work by 5pm, but she announced that she'd be late due to a work conflict, and wouldn't arrive until 8pm. I decided to make other plans with some friends, so I told her to not worry about it tonight and that I'd look forward to seeing her again at the weekend.

I proceeded to go do my thing with my friends and came home around 9pm to find her waiting for me at my house. Such sudden changes in weekly plans can cause a woman's imagination to run riot.

You **must** be somewhat unpredictable with a woman. If she knows your every move and you become *too* predictable and certain in what you're doing (and why), it'll eventually be one of the contributing factors that lead to a loss of attraction.

I really wish it didn't work this way, but displaying certain commitment always *crushes* the critical element of desire in women; it's always the stable, perfectly punctual and reliable guy that gets screwed.

Remember, you can do *anything* to a woman - **except** bore her (even if she doesn't like it).

Ultimately, she **has** to know that she is 100% replaceable and that you **won't** tolerate disrespect. Sometimes leaving a woman is one of **the** strongest power moves you can make, but you **must** have the mental fortitude to walk away from her.

It's definitely counter-intuitive, but the moment a woman believes you are **100%** committed, is the moment her desire begins to drop for you and the moment her complacency in the relationship starts to rise.

As a general rule, the more stable, and nice you are, the more you **will** be punished. The more you care - the less sex you will get. Again, it's important to note that you must be **VERY** attractive to her if you are going to successfully dispense some version of your inner cocky asshole. However, even for the less attractive men, it's still much better to lean towards being an "asshole," than being a "nice guy."

Be a - Playful - "Asshole"

Women don't want a nice guy, they don't turn her on; women always have (and always will) respond *much* more positively to a man that is a *bit* of an asshole, isn't always agreeable (he'll stand by his beliefs), and who has an edge to them.

Whether we like it or not, both men and women inherently know that it's assholes that get things done in the world. For some further insight on this, look into *Steve Jobs'* biography.

Now, there's some nuance required to understand and pull-off this part correctly. Don't just be a straight-up asshole. Instead, think of it as being somewhat cocky (which is the playful part), but mix it in with some well-placed confidence. Again, don't be an ass for the sake of being an ass.

So, what does being a "playful asshole" look like? Well, the "Skittles man" from earlier in the chapter is a good example, but it's essentially a guy that will say or do things that *make her smile to herself* and think: "He's a bit of an asshole."

The nuance is required because this is more of an art than a science, so there's no exact recipe to follow giving us the right amount of asshole to put into the relationship, it's something you got to figure out on your own from trying. If you apply *too much* asshole (and if you're lower on the attractive scale) you're going to get into problems more often than not. As a general rule, the more attractive you are to her, the more asshole you can dispense.

A good test is to see whether or not your idea of being playful is landing correctly, is whether or not she gives you a slap on the arm with a smile as she calls you an asshole. Pairing a glint in your eye and a wry smile as you're being a playful asshole sets the tone and lets her know that you're not being overly serious.

Briffault's Law

Relationship equity means *absolutely nothing* to a woman, and *Robert Briffault*, a French Surgeon, figured this out in the early 1900s.

Briffault's Law states:

> *"The female, not the male, determines all the conditions of the animal family. Where the female can derive no benefit from association with the male, no such association takes place."*
>
> — Robert Briffault

What this means today, is that everything you bought for her to enjoy: the house, the car, the vacations, or the social events you attended for her, the puppy that you agreed to (but didn't really want), the in-law suite you built for her parents at her request, the expensive kitchen renovations, and ***everything*** that you've done for her in the past, **has no meaning to her because she has already enjoyed that benefit.**

Let me say that again so it's **crystal clear**:

You DO NOT earn *any* "points" or "equity" for *anything* you ever do for her. None what-so-ever. Nada. Zilch. Any value you provide to a woman is on a single-use basis only and provides you with zero leverage in the relationship (either now, or in the future).

So, no, **none** of those sacrifices you have ever made to "make her happy" create **any** sort of equity in the relationship. Therefore, your value to her is *entirely* dependent on the *future* value you provide. Again, I wish it wasn't this way, but that's how women operate (even if they aren't conscious of the fact).

It used to really bother me when I was in a relationship where the woman would start to take for granted the things I would do for them. In some cases, they took credit for things, or the travel that I had paid for. That's just how women are wired. They are solipsistic, and have a difficult time seeing past their own nose, so it's completely understandable that their focus is on what future value you can provide (which is why many women will get with a guy based on his "future potential").

When I think of a man and a woman a thousand years ago, I'm reminded of the fact that if he didn't continue to bring home food for the family, and also maintain the home so it was warm and watertight, what use would she have for him in the future? Again, this is a feature of survival, not a bug in women's firmware. It's the very reason why your countless generations of ancestors lived long enough for you to be born. Only the strongest survived in the harshest of times.

Don't Be a Beta

After I got divorced around 39, I dated a lot of women who were also in the same boat. I can't tell you how many of them had negative things to say about their ex-husband. He was: "weak," "a beta," "a loser," "couldn't hold down a job," "didn't do anything with the kids," "incompetent," "couldn't change a flat tire," "let the house fall apart," and so on.

Again, women **want** to look up to a giant, and if *you* aren't going to fulfill her hypergamous needs, then she *will* eventually start looking to get them met elsewhere. Women simply do not keep around weak men they can't look up to, respect, or even rely on.

Don't become a beta.

Apologizing

Men today apologize for *everything*. We all grew up on a steady diet of marketing, Hollywood, sitcoms, and popular culture mocking men, showing men apologizing frequently, and making men the butt of all jokes.

It's important to understand that most apologies aren't necessary, and that the more you apologize for insignificant things, the more you **will** weaken your position in the relationship.

You are also training her to see you in the wrong all the time, so expect her to want more of those placating apologies to come from you.

Apologize when you actually make a *real* mistake, but never because of societal pressure, or if she doesn't like something. Also, if you *do* mess up, you own up, but only ever make that apology **once**! DO NOT repeatedly say "sorry" for the same mistake. Own it, don't make it again, and move on.

Know When She Is "Checking Out"

There will be subtle signals that she is beginning to "check out" of the relationship (which is when she starts to withdraw from you emotionally to begin with, then physically), so you **must** be aware of them, and plan accordingly. She will start to: become colder, more distant, less conversational, be less enthusiastic about sex, maybe she'll even start to withhold sex, she'll bicker/nag at you more, and of course, start to become condescending towards you and express contempt for you.

It's critical to know that this is **not** the time to chase after her, cry, sulk, or look weak (or needy) in any way, shape, or form whatsoever; you *must* remain strong and vigilant. Sulk to a friend if you *really* need an outlet - but **never** in front of her.

In general, over time (and when left unchecked), women tend to get away with getting lazy in a relationship, taking more (while giving back less), all while still expecting their man to stick around for longer than he should. Men seem to do this out of a sense of duty.

You get out of life what you tolerate.

She must continue to be attracted to you, to see you as her very best option, so she must want to be there with you in an organic way. **GBD *cannot be manufactured.***

She cannot perceive your commitment to be free; the more expensive she sees it being, the more valuable she'll perceive it. Men today make *far* too many concessions. It's these concessions that move the balance of power and control into her court. Most of the time you don't even notice this, because it's that super-slow process of betatization through a thousand concessions in effect.

That's why it's super important to learn how to say "no," when it's appropriate; no is a complete sentence and it shouldn't lead to an argument or a long debate. For example, if she tries to hand you her purse in a store and says "hold this" while she attends to something else, this is an appropriate moment to say "no." (it's only miserable looking Plugged-In Beta males who comply with this).

But, if she's slammed with a work deadline, if you're free, and if the kids need a ride - then this probably *isn't* the time to dig in your heels. In this scenario, she's not testing or disrespecting you like in that first scenario. So, learn to navigate these situations by first taking a step back and assessing the nuances of the current circumstances. Does this make sense?

The more power and control she assumes, the more masculine she becomes and the more men give up, the more *he* becomes feminine in response. So, how do you fix this?

By being as attractive as you can to as many women as possible, by having options available, and by leaning into your inner cocky, playful asshole just that little bit more often.

Likewise, women also respond very well to pre-selection (being the man that other women *clearly* want. It's a strong driver of attraction - even in an LTR, as it's a reminder that *you* really are the prize and that you'll be snapped up if she screws up.

"Why Do You Still Have a Boat?!"

The stand-up comic, Patrice O'Neil, has an excellent bit on fishing and how it compares to dating. If you search YouTube for his name + fishing, I guarantee you you'll find it. The analogy goes something like this (and he obviously isn't talking about fish): Men like to fish for sport, so we'll catch a fish, we'll then take pictures of the fish we caught, to let our friends - and other "fish" (i.e. women) know that we can catch lots of different fish. Then we let it go. Sometimes a fish will willingly jump *back* onto your boat, preferring it (and its amenities), to the cold dark ocean.

Sometimes men will take this particular fish back home, invite it into his life, and care for it. But, at some point, the fish will ask why you "still have a boat." You see, they're concerned that if you keep fishing, then you may find other fish more appealing than them.

So, the moral of the story is that, as a man, you *always* need to "have a boat," (i.e. stay attractive) and you always need to know how to catch fish (i.e. have game). Likewise, she also needs to know you can still catch fish, and so, to some degree you must smell a little bit like fish.

This means that you need to periodically practice "catch and release," meaning it's okay to occasionally flirt with other women, so you don't lose touch with the skills required to attract women to you. In the pick up community, "catch and release" refers to approaching, cultivating attraction, getting a number, and then throwing that number away.

Any muscle will begin to waste away if you don't use it. Constantly practicing the art of seduction and attraction is something that most men lose sight of in an LTR. I can't count how many men tell me that after 20-years of marriage, they have **no** idea how to date, or even attract other women because they lost that skill in the marriage. The worst part of this, is that they often sulk about her moving on so quickly to a new man, while he's like a lost puppy dog wondering what his next move should be while she's already our banging new guys, or has a new boyfriend

If you're chasing excellence to stay as attractive as possible and you **know** you could still snag - and release - other women (and hell, you even smell a bit like fish), but she *still* drags her feet in the effort to keep you around? Her GBD is gone. She doesn't really want to be there anymore. And that means it's probably not worth your time either.

Don't Cry (or Even Complain) to Your Woman

As a man, the only acceptable times to cry to your woman is if a pet, friend, or family member dies - that's it. I know, I know, we've all heard for years that women want us to be "more emotional," and "share our feelings," but as I've mentioned many times before, what women say they want, and what they *actually respond to*, are often two **very** different things.

Whenever I dated a divorced woman I'd always ask why she split. More often than not, they'd spill *everything* - sing like canaries. One told me her ex was "a total loser who couldn't hold a job." He'd whine to her about his mean boss then quit time after time. She found it all *massively* unattractive and she bailed because of it.

She wants to know that you can figure it out, that you've "got this," so **stop** dumping every one of your problems on her!

Look fella's, I'm not saying be stone cold, but don't cry to your woman about your day-to-day struggles. I'll say it again:

> ***Women do not care about your struggles***, they hang out at the finish line, and pick the winner.
>
> — Richard Cooper

If you've got a problem to solve, then figure it out on your own or, better yet, you should have a group of men that you can trust to act like a board of advisors. Whenever I have troubles, I ping one or a few of them, we hop on a call, and run the issue up the flagpole to get a good look at it with my peers, and see if it deserves a salute, or needs looking at from another angle.

Always use other men in your tribe to help you resolve problems; you want a rational approach, and even if women want to hear your problems, (and they don't), they are too emotional for it. If you lack a tribe of good men that are *also good at being men*, then I strongly suggest that you visit my community , select the right one for you, and get involved, we are a global organization filled with men who are also good at being men.

On a final note on this topic, women **will** come to you to dump their problems on you, but just know they aren't *always* looking for a solution (which is important to know when we're problem-solvers by nature). Especially when we love a woman, we want to look out for her best interests. However, she doesn't always want a solution; most times, she's just looking for someone to vent to. When she is done, if she doesn't ask for your opinion, you may want to say something like: "Would you like a solution to this issue?" If not, be her rock (by not trying to give her solutions), and let her waves of emotions bounce off of you like they're nothing, hug her tight, and then go about your day if she's done. You'll find that she'll respond to that approach a whole lot more positively than trying to force-feed her a solution that she never asked for.

In Conclusion

Dealing with women over the long-term is still most men's goal (even in the hostile sexual marketplace men must navigate today). However, most men aren't told the uncomfortable truth about the numerous mistakes they constantly make with women (and how to avoid them for a better life). We're sold comforting lies instead.

This chapter is a collection of some of the most important issues that can cause havoc in your relationship, that you must be aware of in advance ***before*** inviting a woman into your life on a longer-term basis. Take it all in and, if you have any questions, feel free to call in on one of my podcasts on The Unplugged Alpha YouTube channel, it's totally free when subscribed to the channel, or ask me directly in my community.

The Cold, Hard Truth

Never forget:

- **Stay *exactly* who you are - don't change**: Don't abandon your hobbies, friends, or your personality to please her. Women are naturally drawn to the untamed man when they first meet, not the empty shell-of-you version broken down by 1,000 concessions. By simply **not changing**, you can increase the odds of the relationship working out - with the minimal amount of hassle too.
- **Keep your options open, real *or* perceived**: Women's desire *thrives* on competition anxiety. So, maintain the impression you could easily attract other women, even if you don't act on it. Closing that door kills her GBD for you faster than getting married *ever* will.
- **Set boundaries, don't chase her approval**: Say "no" to risky behaviors like bachelorette parties or male "friends," not out of jealousy but to protect your relationship. A woman who adores you *will* respect these lines (even if she doesn't like them), and make the right choice.
- **Deal with disrespect *immediately***: Call out *all* disrespect the moment it happens. Keep cool, calm and collected when doing so. Only set boundaries that you're 100% willing to enforce if she steps over that particular line again. Not following through if she steps over the line is worse than not addressing it at all. If she still respects you enough, she'll come and apologize. Tell her you appreciate that, and then move on (don't bring it back up).
- **Be attractive and kind, *not* a "nice guy:**" "Sneaky Fucker" nice guys give women the "ick" and get given divorce papers for their trouble; cocky assholes with confidence and humor get her passion and loyalty. Lean into your inner edge, stay fit, dress well, and keep growing in every sense - women don't stay with men who stagnate on the couch with their crumb-covered beer belly.

10

The Three Ity's: Proximity, Familiarity, and Exclusivity

These three "ity's" are killers of most modern long-term relationships today.

Society pushes women to demand these, and men cave - even when it tanks the relationship. I think we as men often do this because we - naturally - want the women we love to be happy.

But, as stated elsewhere in this book, just because women *want* something (or want you to stop doing something) *doesn't* mean that you should do it. Sometimes, the *very* things she is asking you to change are actually bad for her long-term attraction, and cohesion in the relationship.

Great marriages, with Genuine Burning Desire (i.e. GBD) for one another, that last decades are a real rarity today. That 3% bliss stat? Straight from Acevedo and Aron's 2009 study - romantic love tanks for most after eight years.

If you want to avoid the misfortune of having a relationship you care about fall apart, then managing the balancing act of proximity, familiarity, *and* exclusivity **must** be front-and-center in your mind.

Before we take a closer look at each of these three "ity's", I want to remind you that I realize that this chapter is outside of conventional thinking for most, and will violate a lot of strong feelings you might hold - especially around exclusivity - but, as I always say, facts don't care about feelings.

When unplugging, we must be willing to simultaneously dislike an idea, but also see the truth in it.

Proximity

I've seen *very* few relationships that have lasted decades where men have a great relationship with a woman. But, when I do, I always ask them the question:

"What do you think has been the contributing factor to the success of your relationship with your woman?"

The answer is always some version of "time apart" or, "discomfort."

It seems clear to me that absence does, in fact, make the heart grow fonder.

One of my best friends from a business forum traveled half the year for his toy company, leaving his wife to handle home base. Result? Decades of solid marriage - absence breeds desire.

It seems what I have been saying for years now is true: men and women do best when men resign to their natural masculine role doing blue jobs, and women in their natural feminine role, doing pink jobs.

The point here is that he attributed the long-term success he enjoyed in his relationship to time apart from one another and I think this was natural for human beings and sexual relationships throughout the 2.6 million years we lived as nomadic hunter gatherers. For perspective, we moved away from this lifestyle only 10,000 to 12,000 years ago with the advent of agriculture when we would move around less, and more or less stay put with everyone we loved in close proximity.

Men would go out to hunt and conquer, and women would take care of the kids, gather resources locally, and work with other women to take care of the village.

But, in today's modern era, we are often *far* too quick to move in together, and be as close as we can with each other.

We also love to find excuses to do it, like saving on rent, traveling less to see one another, or just being in each other's presence more. Oftentimes, society at-large applies significant pressure on couples to move in together as it's "the done thing." Ultimately though, humans in general are masters of complicating their lives, and then justifying why they do it afterwards.

I can't say for certain where this idea of being in close proximity originated from, but it seems to be a new phenomenon, and constantly being in close proximity to one another *clearly* doesn't work if you want to sustain that *essential* GBD from a woman over the long-haul.

It's my assertion that there should be some distance in your schedule from a woman. How you structure that distance is entirely up to you, but it seems crystal clear to me that seeing her daily for months (and years) on-end is a *sure fire* way to erode her desire for you, and yours for her.

Believe it or not, you can love a woman, and not live under the same roof as her.

Being Together, but Living Apart

Aside from the obvious risk of inviting the government into your home to decide what happens to your assets if you break up after a common law period has passed, too much proximity and familiarity is another reason why I advocate for men to put off living with a woman for as long as possible.

If a woman is 100% in your frame, is genuinely attracted to you, and she truly sees you as her hypergamous best option, then she **will** (far more likely) accept this boundary. She may not like it, but as stated elsewhere, sometimes the very things women don't like are actually good for her and the relationship. It's your job as a man to draw the line, and hold firm on it.

Editor's Note: *I just wanted to back this up with the fact that if a woman's GBD is 10/10 for you, then she will not only accept this framework, but she'll even advocate for it with others that are close to her. For example, I'm still seeing the woman I talked about in my Field Reports from the 2nd Edition of TUA, and she's openly advocated this approach of "being together, but living apart" to her friends and family. They don't get it (societal programming at play), but for those of her friends who've tried it, they have immediately seen the benefits for themselves. However, the onus is on men to keep a frame strong enough that helps keep the fire of desire strong in her - for the **entire** *duration of that relationship. Here's a copy and paste of a message that my LTR sent to me earlier in the year:*

Fuck Yeah!!! High 5 to that! Literally our journey is so unique. I'm loving the fact that you continue to drive me wild nearly 3 years on! I just cannot get bored of you! I want to taste you... Eat you... Touch you... My pussy still now throbs on my journey to reunite with you week in and week out... Let's not lose that... *Please.*

— SFA's LTR

So, you see, you must understand and accept the fact you need to keep things fresh, fun, and surprising. Because, you must also understand and accept the fact that you can do **anything** to a woman - *except* bore her.

Familiarity

Familiarity? It's that ease from repeated exposure, but as the old line goes, it breeds contempt - flaws surface, mystery dies. I've seen guys reveal insecurities too soon; she loses respect - fast.

"Familiarity breeds contempt"

This is an old saying for a reason, it means that when you know someone *very* well, you may start to notice their flaws, imperfections, or negative qualities more clearly (this is when the limerence for you/her starts to wane). Over time, this acute awareness of such flaws can erode the admiration or affection you both once felt, potentially replacing it with the much more negative feelings of disrespect or dislike.

When you first meet someone, you might be impressed by their charm or kindness. However, as you spend more time together and become familiar with them (especially in situations where either of you are under stress), you'll notice their bad habits, or you'll get so familiar with their repetitive schedule that it'll eventually begin to annoy you.

The issue here is that there's a loss of mystery when she becomes *too* familiar with you. It's common for a woman to see your confidence, and competence early on, but as she spends more and more time around you, then your insecurities will often reveal themselves, and *regardless* of how competent you are as a man, as that familiarity grows, she will discover things you are either incompetent at, or she'll see a side of you that she may not like as much.

Familiarity reveals emotional shortcomings, annoying habits, and differences in lifestyle that didn't matter before you started spending more time around each other.

I *really* can't stress this enough. You've got to remain somewhat of a mystery to her, don't become too predictable, *or* too available.

Women will push for more of your time, and that's to placate their own needs or anxieties. But, again, just because a woman *wants* something, it doesn't mean that you *should* give it to her, sometimes the very things women don't like are actually *good* for the relationship and keeping her attraction strong for you (which will more often than not be at a subconscious level for her).

Giving Her What She Needs

There's nothing wrong with occasionally rewarding her with something that she wants (again, assuming she's genuinely earned it), but I prefer to give her far more of what she *needs*. That, to me, means she **needs** some space and time apart from me (which naturally breeds mystery as she wonders what I'm doing). She **needs** to know that I'm her hypergamous best, she **needs** to want to be in my frame (which allows her to feel safe when she's in my presence), she **needs** to feel those "tingles" when we catch-up together again.

Women don't inherently dislike men when they become too familiar. It's more about what that familiarity reveals: if it's flaws, stagnation, or a loss of intrigue without enough redeeming qualities, then contempt can follow - just as it can for anyone. The key is whether both people adapt and value what's beneath the surface once the honeymoon phase fades (and it will fade, whether it's three months, or three years from when you meet).

Exclusivity

This "ity" is the toughest one for men to understand and accept, but until giving a woman what she wants all the time leads to much lower divorce rates, endless respect, and fantastic long-term relationships, I'm going to tell you how it is.

So, with this "ity", a key ingredient is how attractive, and valuable a man happens to be and the more attractive and valuable he is, the more likely it is he will have success with this approach.

This is especially true in North America, UK, Australia, and New Zealand because we overtly operate under the declaration of strict monogamy (yet 1-in-4 admit that they operate with clandestine adultery). However, the numbers are likely *much* higher due to the social shame associated with cheating in a relationship.

In most other parts of the world, sexual exclusivity isn't usually expected (or even enforced) from women dating high-value men.

When men reach a position near, or on, the top shelf, giving a woman sexual exclusivity is often a *very* expensive proposition to these men since one of the most appealing byproducts of leveling up, and becoming a high-value man, is naturally gaining access to more women that are more attractive.

Doing all that work to abandon the optionality that you can enjoy, is the equivalent of building a multi-car storage facility, stocking it full of beautiful, high-performance exotic cars, and then never visiting your facility or driving any of them, instead choosing to drive the same car for the rest of your life.

Look, I "get it," when you build a life of success and purpose, attractive women will *naturally* want in, but the *real* game is staying true to your mission, not focusing on chasing the perks.

Most women, when they have been seeing a high-value man for a while, will eventually try to claim him for herself, and lock him down. This is natural and to be expected. Women aren't stupid, and they know when they're in the company of a man who naturally "ticks all of their boxes," so they'll be keen to lock that guy down as best as they can, as early as they feel they can.

It's not uncommon for women in the earlier stages of dating, especially when she isn't in a position to make demands (because she knows you're the kind of man that'd tick the boxes of *many* women), to make a statement along the lines of "If you are seeing anyone else, please be safe," or something similar.

She's saying she "gets it," that you're truly attractive and she *knows* that other women want you. She knows these women might spend time with you and that you might be sleeping with them. Bottom line: she may not like it, but during this time she can "look the other way" and live with it. Just as long as you don't jeopardize her health or reputation - and are being *very* discreet.

It's not that women don't care about you having sex with other women, it's that she just doesn't care *quite* as much as she makes you think. That's why, when men cheat, the first thing she wants to know is "Did you love her?" The act of sexual intimacy for women often leads to love, and she knows that when a man falls in love with a woman, that woman gets the lion's share of his financial resources. If that happened a thousand years ago, then that often spelled doom for a mother *and* her children.

In the early stages of dating women are very likely to put up with things they don't like, so they don't scare you off, or push you away (and the higher her GBD for you is, the more she'll put up with - even if she doesn't like it). In many cases, she is also likely aroused by the fact that other women want you, and are spending time with you.

This doesn't even have to be at a conscious level either. Women naturally want what other women want, and this is often especially true of her and her closest friends. If *they* signal to her that she's with a man that they also find very attractive, then that sub-communicates to her that "she's found a winner" and that social validation from her closest-friends will help reinforce the fact that she's with her hypergamous best.

But unless her GBD for you is starting to wane, at some point she will probably try to claim you as her own with "the talk."

She will likely try to pull on your emotional heart strings with language that suggests that she is hurt or sad, that she has to share you, or that she is a "one man kind of woman" and is "strictly monogamous," wants commitment, and sexual exclusivity from you.

This talk is the pivotal point in most relationships, and men often make the mistake of yielding to her request.

I'm of the opinion that we make this mistake as men, because we love her, and truly want to make her happy.

However, there are several mistakes with giving her what she wants (versus what she actually *needs*). When you search for definitions of "monogamy" you get something resembling:

"A monogamous relationship is one where two people commit to being exclusively romantically and sexually involved with each other, meaning they are not romantically or sexually involved with anyone else."

A defining element of this definition of monogamy is: "they're not romantically or sexually involved with anyone else." If you add "right now" to the end of that definition, *then* her statement about monogamy is accurate, and it also makes it clear that monogamy in humans isn't lifelong, but more-or-less serial in nature.

Unless she was a virgin when you engaged in your intimate relationship, then she has - by definition - shared her body with other men. I don't think it's possible for her to call herself *strictly* monogamous.

Strictly monogamous relationships do exist in the animal kingdom, but it's *exceptionally* rare with gibbons, swans, and albatrosses being the most common examples. So, if one of the bonded pairs dies before the other, they almost never take on a new mate.

That's the definition of "strictly monogamous" which is how women often put a label on what they are looking for. Women today are more "monogamish," and have serial sexual relationships with men (i.e. are natural "plate spinners").

Diving Down the Rabbit Hole

The following graph summarizes researcher *J. Teachman's* body of work on women, and the effect of premarital sex partners on marriage:

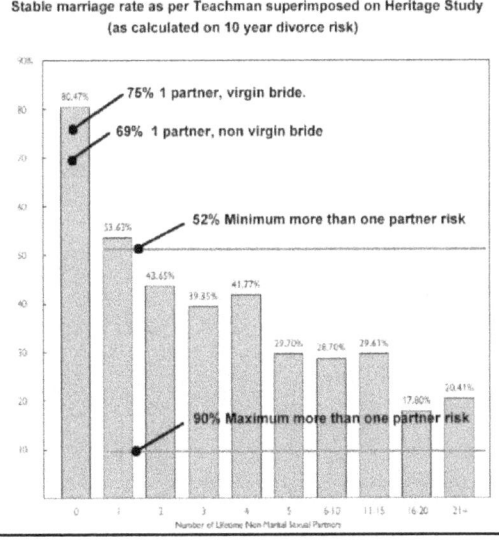

Teachman's Heritage study shows: higher pre-marriage partners = higher divorce risk.

My consults confirm: more exes means more cheating with "He's just a friend." Remember: **Nobody** bangs more girlfriends and wives, than "He's just a friend."

Bottom line: the higher her body count is prior to your relationship with her, the greater the risk she'll get restless and you'll wind up leaving you, or getting divorced.

Personally, I don't think that I've ever been with a virgin in my life. If you find a pure woman, great, but with so many women today already carrying baggage from not just one guy (but a string of them), it raises a fair question. Why would you - if you are a high-value man who's put in the work - ditch your options for a woman that's shared her body with dozens upon dozens of men? You know damn well that keeping those options open and around is what keeps her hooked on you.

As stated earlier, you don't necessarily need to indulge in said options, but you shouldn't *fully* close the door on them either. That loophole - for you (and only you) - should exist if you want her to have genuine desire for you over the long haul.

Ultimately, women are drawn to men who other women desire. So, Unplugged Alphas know this and they may choose to leverage this pre-selection and competition anxiety to intentionally fuel her genuine desire for him.

So, I don't buy that she can be "strictly monogamous" with you just because she says so, and as I dedicated a chapter in my last book to the topic of humans and monogamy. I must restate that sexual monogamy shouldn't be enforced upon you, by her or culture, rather it should be a conscious and well-educated choice a man makes for himself.

Keep in mind that commitment, and sexual exclusivity are *not* the same thing, and plenty of men do give a woman their commitment, but *not* their full sexual exclusivity.

It's this type of relationship that an Unplugged Alpha may structure for himself should he so desire.

To recently unplugged guys or those still plugged in this might sound totally alien. But I've seen plenty of high-value men with a wife and kids pour all their love into the family, provide solidly, hit those key events - and still snag a bit of extracurricular fun on the side.

As long as it's very discrete, responsible, safe and doesn't take anything financially away from the core relationship, women - throughout history - *do* have a propensity for looking the other way. All women love a man that has options and can cheat, most prefer it if he doesn't exercise those options though.

Believe it or not, you can give a woman 100% of your commitment, with 99% of your sexual exclusivity.

If she puts up with it during the dating phase of the relationship, she will also (more than likely) do the same during the committed phase of the relationship if it's safe, responsible and discreet. When you ignore women's rants, but watch who they are strongly committed to long enough, you will notice that they are more likely to stay with a top-shelf man that cheats occasionally (with discretion), than a faithful man that bores them.

By all means, you can give her 100% sexual exclusivity if she's offering you effortless peace and she's a genuine compliment to your life, but the more of these three "ity's" you give a woman as time goes by, the more likely it is that you will see her move away from you as a result.

A big complaint I hear from men is they end up giving more to a woman, while they're getting less in return from their efforts. I've found balancing these "ity's" is absolutely *key* if you want a good long-term relationship to last as long as possible.

In Conclusion

If you want to maintain true GBD from a woman, as I described in my first book, it's my **very** strong opinion that you should **always** manage these three GBD killers over the long-haul better.

Look, I've spelled it out very clearly for you in this chapter, so it's now up to you to decide how you want to execute and manage your relationships with women who chose you over the long-term.

If you date multiple women, you'll never fall in love (or, at the very least, the cream will inevitably rise to the top). Date only one woman and, not only do you develop the real risk of developing "oneitis" for her, you'll also ultimately lose faith in love and you unintentionally begin pushing her away by being too close, becoming far too familiar, and - worst of all - make it clear to her that "she's the only one for you." Whether she likes it or not, knowing subconsciously that other women would snap you up in an instant if she wasn't there, **keeps her there**! Social-proof (even with her closest friends) is the subtle-dread that keeps her on her toes.

The Cold, Hard Truth

Never forget:

- **Women want what other women want:** The more you stand out as a man, the more optionality you will **naturally** enjoy. As long as the woman/women you're with know other women also find you very attractive (preferably subconsciously via social cues that women **will** pick up on), the easier it will be to keep her GBD for you up, and her in your frame.
- **Provide space and air for desire to breathe:** If you're around each other *all* the time, then she'll never need to wonder what you're doing (killing that all-important mystery factor). Make time for her, *but on **your** schedule*. If her GBD is truly high, she'll *gladly* mold her schedule around yours.
- **Don't become predictable:** While there's *some* positives to having something of a routine, it's super important to mix that up with some genuine surprises. Keep mixing things up *and keep her on her toes*. Remember, you can do **anything** to a woman - *except* bore her!
- **Unexclusively exclusive:** Socially, women *don't* want you sleeping around as you're inviting risk into provision of time and resources into her. Historically however, men who've done the work to become attractive and successful have often enjoyed exercising their optionality in a super discreet, safe, and quiet way. Whether or not you choose to exercise those rights is your call. But she at least, on some level, needs to understand that you *could*.

11

Hypergamy, a Puzzle With a Thousand Pieces

Hypergamy is one of the most hotly debated, and misunderstood drivers of female mate selection, and it's often very confusing for both men and women to understand. In this chapter, I'll explain what hypergamy is, and how men and women can leverage hypergamy to get what they want.

If you Google "hypergamy" this is how it's defined as a term:

"Hypergamy is the practice or tendency of marrying someone of higher social, economic, or educational status, often associated with seeking upward mobility or security. Historically, it's linked to women marrying "up" due to societal structures, but it can apply to any gender. The term comes from Greek: "hyper" (above) and "gamos" (marriage)."

This definition is the most commonly accepted version. But as the title of this chapter suggests, hypergamy is a multi-piece puzzle. It can move to include a man's looks or his sex appeal to her. Or how influential he is and so-on. And to complicate matters further, a woman's hypergamy prioritizes different things depending on her own age or her current financial status. Or even where she is in her menstrual cycle in any given month.

Yes, hypergamy is fickle, and therefore often difficult to navigate.

I've heard women accuse men of being hypergamous too. And while men sometimes date or marry up to women, it's usually short-lived. Or, it's because the woman has very low Sexual Market Value (SMV). For example, a rich old obese widow that a young man is trying to extract resources from - aka a sugar momma.

No woman wakes up in the morning dreaming of financially taking care of a man.

Women very rarely exchange financial resources for sexual opportunity with men (one of the only exceptions that springs to mind are the hyper-successful business women paying male escorts for their time and sexual experience).

Short-Term vs Long-Term (and the Overlaps)

A woman's choice in men changes depending on what kind of man she is looking for, and - more importantly - what she needs at a given point in her life. Sometimes her filter is tuned for short-term excitement: raw attraction, physical chemistry, the kind of man who can light her up in minutes. Other times her filter shifts toward long-term stability: provision, loyalty, leadership, and the qualities that build a family or sustain a household.

These two strategies aren't mutually exclusive either; women can swing between them, or even try to secure both at the same time. That's where the overlaps happen, and where confusion for men usually begins. Understanding this split is key to decoding female behavior, because it explains why the same woman can chase one man recklessly on Friday night, then demand commitment and caution from another by Sunday morning.

Short-Term Requirements

If it's short-term mating, like hookups, a Friend With Benefits (an FWB), or something just sexual, then women prioritize men with high testosterone cues, such as: a more chiseled jawline, someone who's taller, who has a deep voice, and displays a very masculine frame with a body type approximating the "1.62 golden ratio" (i.e. broad shoulders and narrow waist), which I discussed in my first book. For short-term dating, he doesn't need to be rich, influential, have immaculate grooming habits, or even know the difference between "your and you're." She just needs to find him hot.

It's *these* men that women break the rules for when it comes to sex (see the chapter in my first book: "Women's Rules - Who They Make Them and Break Them For" for more detail on this).

They won't make these men jump through hoops, or make them wait eight expensive dates for sex. They have true Genuine Burning Desire (or, GBD) for them, and they'll become intimate with them *very* quickly. In the club bathroom, in the dark alley, or 20 minutes after meeting them in the foam cannon party in Cancun during Spring Break. It doesn't matter: they don't need a home, a job, or a high school diploma, they just need to be hot and good to go.

Long-Term Requirements

As women age and they start looking to "settle down" for a long-term relationship, women start adding more requirements for men to meet (i.e. "boxes to tick"). He still needs to be attractive, but she will - eventually - settle for a less attractive option, or a man that slots into the indifference category that I discussed in my first book (see the Chapter on "Why Genuine Burning Desire Matters"). He also needs to be successful, competent, resourceful, funny, loving, caring, generous, a good father, protective, and so - much more but interestingly - he doesn't need to be the "super hot guy" that she immediately broke her rules for.

If she wants children, he also needs to meet the bare requirements of genetic requirements. He doesn't need to be 6'2", but he can't be too short either (the taller, the better). He doesn't need to be devilishly handsome, but he needs to be handsome enough that her children won't be judged for being ugly.

He will also have rules made for him that the man she was sexually enthusiastic for short-term dating didn't need to meet (like waiting several dates before she sleeps with him).

These two types of dating strategies sometimes overlap, and are often described as "alpha seed and beta need," so in some cases, women will act duplicitous and take on the seed of an alpha she has a strong sexual attraction for, while telling the beta cuckold, who has more in the way of resources, that *he* is the father of that child. Hence the increasingly common issue of paternity fraud that has always plagued men. This is also why you see so many single mothers on dating apps looking to "settle down" because she's "had her fun" and wants a "serious relationship."

This is a much less duplicitous form of cuckoldry. But make no mistake, men without better options *will* still willingly volunteer to raise the seed of another man.

Hypergamy, Mate Choices, and Age

When women are younger and their SMV peaks, they often lean toward short-term mate choices. We call a woman's 20s her "party years" - a phase of promiscuity. But short-term dating isn't just for the young. *Plenty* of women marry early, raise kids, and divorce in their 30s. Then they dive back into the party scene as adult single mothers to catch up on lost time.

Not *all* women have a promiscuous phase (especially those who've always had a strong, masculine father figure present in their life that she respected and valued), but given the opportunity to indulge in hot men with "no strings attached" sex, women always have, and always will, "look to discover themselves."

A frustrating component of hypergamy for unplugged men to accept, is that a 30+ year old woman that is now finished with her "party years" and is looking to settle down and start a family all of a sudden, has more rules and requirements for men - once she hears her biological clock ticking loudly.

She has learned by this point that the men she has had short-term dating experiences with, that she has also been **strongly** sexually attracted to, haven't been willing to "settle down" *with her*, and so she felt that she was "forced" to relax her standards, just so she can attract a long-term relationship with someone.

But, as her standards for men relax, her rules also go up, and - more specifically - the generosity and enthusiasm with which she offers her body to less handsome men, goes down.

This is when men usually meet women on dating apps, and go through a flurry of interrogating questions. "What do you do for a living?", "Where do you live?", "What kind of car do you have?", "What are your hobbies?", "Do you like children?", "Do you have any children?", "Were you married before?", "Do you smoke?", "Do you drink?", and so on.

These are all questions that none of her short-term dating encounters needed to answer and, while he is working hard at jumping through all the hoops answering these questions, she is also looking to make him wait for intimacy because she learned that giving it away too quickly was associated with not getting a long-term commitment from any of the prior men that she had true GBD for.

Men need to understand that her "clock is ticking," and that she doesn't have "time to waste" with men that aren't suitable to satisfy her long-term hypergamous relationship needs.

Unfortunately women need to understand that this is also precisely the time to be less stringent with gatekeeping her sexual intimacy. Whether it's overtly stated or not, men inherently don't want to wait longer or pay more for something that was given away immediately for less to another man. The amount of men that I've coached that discover that their now "asexual" wife had done some seriously filthy acts - with much enthusiasm - in the past that they point blank refuse to do with them now is so common it's practically a cliché now.

Unless she has strategically been gatekeeping her virginity her *entire* life, making a man that she is trying to court for marriage wait very patiently for sexual intimacy is *exactly* the wrong thing to do. Many of the higher-value men she is trying to set rules for (who understand their value), will simply move on, or become disinterested in the waiting game and pursue women who either don't play such games, or have a higher level of GBD for him.

Post-Divorce Return to Party Years

Plenty of women hit their 30s or 40s after checking off the family box. They married young, popped out kids, and leaned on a reliable beta provider for years. But once the nest starts emptying or the marriage sours, hypergamy kicks back in with a *vengeance*. Now that the provisioning side is sorted - often through a fat divorce settlement that strips the ex of half his assets and slaps him with child support - she circles back to those alpha thrills she craves.

Take Becky for example. She's your average suburban wife who locked down a steady-earning husband in her mid-20s. He worked overtime to fund the house, the minivan, and the kids' soccer leagues while she handled the home front. Fast forward a decade: the kids are older, Becky's bored, and she's eyeing the exit. She files for divorce, cashes in on the family court windfall, and suddenly rediscovers her "wild side." Out come the dating apps, the girls' nights, and the hookups with tattooed bad boys or gym-rat alphas who wouldn't have committed to her back in the day.

The cold reality? She's trading long-term security for short-term excitement, convinced her SMV hasn't dipped. But, post-wall and with baggage in tow, those alphas see her as easy fun - not wife material. Meanwhile, her ex is left rebuilding from scratch, often googling "how to recover from divorce." Guys, if you're in this spot, focus on leveling up your own value. Chase excellence, rebuild your frame, and spin plates with women who add to your life - not subtract. Hypergamy doesn't sleep, so neither should your game.

Hypergamy and "That Time of the Month"

A woman's ovulatory shift (menstrual, follicular, ovulatory, luteal) changes her hypergamous preferences within a monthly cycle. Both the woman, and especially the man she has committed to over a long-term basis, should be aware of these shifts in her menstrual cycle.

When a woman is approaching, or is at ovulation, she is far more outgoing, sociable, energetic, she looks for stronger, and more alpha traits in a man. Whereas when she is at her menstrual phase, she is more fatigued, introspective, and emotionally sensitive, so her preference for men shifts to the more softer, and therefore beta/comforting traits in a man.

Women also dress and act differently during these phases of her cycle. During ovulation, she will show more skin, wear brighter lipstick, has a much stronger libido (due to her increased testosterone levels) and she also has increased interest in flirtation and romantic pursuits.

Men should be aware of this because, if a woman that has asked for his commitment isn't expressing much in the way of sexual interest in him, but routinely goes out with her friends for "girls night out" - **_especially_** during her ovulatory phase of her cycle - then she is _far_ more likely to cheat on him in that relationship during that phase.

This is why, if you can track her cycle naturally (especially in an LTR), you can feed into the cycle directly by ramping up your dominant teasing and vigorous role-playing side when she's ovulating, and then slowly dialing that side down a bit and providing her with some more calibrated comfort when she's menstruating.

Hypergamy and Birth Control

Hormonal Birth Control (HBC) works by putting women in a perpetual state of imagined pregnancy, and that often shifts her preference for men _dramatically_. Women on HBC show less preference for hyper-masculine traits, as the hormonal cues driving these preferences are muted, and there is a shift towards stability-oriented partners.

These women favor men with traits associated with nurturing behavior, emotional warmth, or financial security, over traits linked to short-term mating. HBC can also lower the libido in some women by reducing free testosterone and stabilizing the hormones that drive her libido. This may dampen overall mate-seeking behavior, or shift her focus away from physical attraction, towards emotional or practical partner qualities.

While she's on HBC, her preference is basically for beta men.

Quite often, women spend their 20s or 30s on HBC for the duration of the relationship, and when she gets married, and comes off HBC to start a family, she surprisingly finds herself no longer as attracted to the man she married when her menstrual cycle returns. I believe this is a strong contributor to the high divorce rate we see today in the West (along with the man letting himself becoming a shell of his former-self as he succumbs to "Betatization through a thousand Concessions.")

HBC at a glance might *seem* like a good idea to men, because they can have plenty of sex, with a very low chance of pregnancy; but I believe it's better for a long-term relationship with a woman to keep her off HBC, and let her cycle run naturally - *especially* if you are considering children or marriage.

A better alternative to hormonal birth control is non-hormonal methods. They're healthier for her and your relationship. Consult a doctor about options like copper IUDs - non-hormonal and 99% effective at preventing unwanted pregnancies. Or try apps like Natural Cycles paired with an Oura ring - FDA-approved and highly effective when used correctly.

Hypergamy and Fame

Hypergamy isn't all about looks or wealth. A lot of what drives a woman's mate selection choices can also be tied into fame. Fame often signals high social status, which is historically correlated with abundant access to both resources and protection.

Women, certainly from an evolutionary standpoint, are drawn to men who display traits associated with success and dominance, as these traits could ensure better survival for any future offspring. Famous individuals, by virtue of their visibility and influence, often embody this high-status archetype.

Fame implies that many people admire or value an individual, which can create a "halo effect." Women may find famous people attractive because their popularity serves as social validation, signaling desirability, and we know that women want what other women want.

The - Odd - Case of Tom Brady and Gisele Bündchen

Tom Brady is a world-class NFL athlete, who was married to Brazilian supermodel Gisele Bündchen, but their 13-year marriage ended in October 2022, a year after meeting her Brazilian Jiu Jitsu instructor, Joaquim Valente.

This left many men, who understand hypergamy, somewhat confused. Why would Gisele leave a handsome, famous, and influential 6'4" world-class professional athlete worth over $300 Million, for an unknown, less attractive, 5' 11" BJJ instructor who was worth only $2 Million in comparison?

To fuel the controversy further, 44-year old Gisele had Joaquim's child approximately two years after the divorce from Tom.

When Gisele was probed about why she left the marriage, she indicated contempt for Tom returning to his football career for another season, Tom's supposed "lack of involvement" in their children, and the apparent "sacrifices" that she made for the benefit of Tom's career.

Men should be aware that contempt is the clock that always ticks down to the end of a relationship, it's one of the key indicators that a relationship is beyond saving as the respect required has vanished completely.

As I stated earlier, hypergamy is a puzzle with many pieces. In this case, Giselle arguably had the best man she could ever get in Tom, and by using the conventional definition of hypergamy, she appears to have downgraded when starting a romantic relationship with Joaquim.

Personally, I think because Giselle already had three beautiful children, a greater net worth than Tom, and more fame from her modeling career, the wealth and prestige of Tom Brady wasn't significant enough to keep her glued to the marriage.

She didn't really "marry up" per-se, but for a woman of her status and beauty, it would be nearly impossible for her to find a man to marry up to, especially in her 40s as her beauty and sexual market value is on a rapid decline.

Joaquim would have been unfamiliar, and therefore "new" to her. But, another underlying element of hypergamy is "hybristophilia" - which is a paraphilia (which is where a woman experiences sexual attraction toward men who have the capacity for extreme violence). This condition is often associated with an interest in "dangerous" individuals and it's why we see women chase after incarcerated convicted murderers with their frequent jail visits and love letters.

Women *love* men with a capacity for violence, and in the setting of Joaquim's BJJ dojo (while Gisele was experiencing her relationship-ending contempt for Tom), Joaquim seemed to catch Gisele's eye.

It's an odd outcome to be sure, but if I was in Tom's shoes and cared about the marriage and the family unit, I wouldn't even have let my wife train with a male BJJ instructor in the first place.

No good could come from a woman you love rolling around on the ground with another man - even if it is in a combat training setting. He could have easily prohibited it, and recommended that she find a female BJJ instructor as an alternative if she was truly *that* passionate about the sport. They certainly could have afforded it, so it wasn't about the money.

In Conclusion

An entire book could be dedicated to the topic of hypergamy, and exploring all the many different nuanced ways it plays a role in women's mate choices with men. It is a puzzle with many pieces that goes down many different rabbit holes.

As a man, understand that women want the best she can get, and usually when she has it, other men become less visible to her.

Satisfying her hypergamous nature will also ensure you are on the receiving end of her all-important Genuine Burning Desire (as described in my first book).

If you want to retain a woman over the long haul, then you must surrender to the fact that you won't be getting a woman of higher value than you. She might be more attractive physically, but she'll likely come with burdensome liabilities (hidden debt, a high notch count, children from prior relationships, etc.). On the flip-side, she might be less attractive, but she may bring less burdensome liabilities to the table in return.

It's unlikely that you will engage in an LTR with a woman, and retain her, if she believes that she's of higher overall value; and, even if you do, she'll probably be *far* more indifferent to you than you are to her, so it likely won't be worth the long-term effort and work to retain her.

Ultimately, to maximize dating options (and relationship satisfaction), a man would be wise to do everything he can to increase his physical appearance, status, wealth, competence, influence, and success. It's one of the many reasons I keep telling men, chase excellence, not women.

The Cold, Hard Truth

Never forget:

- **Alpha seed; Beta need:** Women chase alpha thrills for short-term flings but demand beta stability for long-term bonds - where she is in her life will often dictate what she's looking for.
- **Age shifts the target:** Young women prioritize looks and status; older women hunt for security and resources - your value must match her shifting checklist or she'll eventually trade-up.
- **Cycle-driven cravings:** Her cycle amps up her hypergamous radar, craving peak masculinity at ovulation - miss the mark, and you run the risk that she'll eye the stronger option across the room.
- **Fame's pull:** Fame rockets your perceived value, making you *far* more attractive as your social status rises in unison.
- **It's a feature, not a bug:** Her hypergamy is evolutionarily hard-wired into her to test you over the longer-term, to reassure her that she's "with the best that she can get." Learn to accept it for what it is, and you'll find that navigating its - many - rabbit holes will be a *lot* easier and *far* less frustrating.

12

How Marriage can be the Sweet Spot for the Average Man

In my first book, I talked about why smart men avoid marriage today. When I wrote that, I approached it from the perspective of a successful male, living in the West.

    I didn't want to disparage marriage, or shatter the ideal with that chapter, I just wanted to point to the facts and let you see them for what they are. I've had a lot of questions since then, but the one that comes up most often is something that sounds like: "Yeah Rich, I get it, but I want a family, so what's the best way to navigate this?"

In this chapter, I'm going to reveal some interesting insights I think will help make a more informed decision, if they choose this path.

In November 2024 I asked my audience:

"Married men only. A lot of men today seek marriage as a goal. What makes your marriage a relationship "sweet spot" for you?"

Here Are Some of the Top Responses

"My wife and I share the same beliefs and religion, and she agreed to the Biblically submissive role of wifehood when we got married. Our relationship is largely trouble free because even with her feminine mood swings and hormones, she remembers the agreement and genuinely believes she is called by God to serve and aid me in any way possible. In return I do everything I possibly can for her and try to lead the family as unselfishly as possible. She was a virgin when we married and is completely faithful, and now we have five children who are happy and healthy. She minds her diet and her weight and strives to do what she believes is right. She doesn't try to usurp authority or take over."

— Edward

"Been married for 8 years and have 2 kids. My way or the highway. Can't expect a woman to respect you if you don't respect yourself to set boundaries. If you don't like certain shit, SAY NO! Even the nicest woman will take advantage of you if you let her. The women I see now, are totally fked, Good luck, guys!"

— Amin

"Married to my amazing wife for 14 years and counting. Before her, I dated single moms, broken women, etc. I was exhausted and was driven crazy. I was also in the military at the time. When I got out in 09, I not only left the military, but also decided to have a ZERO tolerance policy on bad behavior. I met a younger woman who was optimistic, positive, friendly, and just a great person. And F-ing HOT!! To this day, we are each other's peace and we work great."

— Chris

My wife: follows my lead, doesn't get in the way of my career path, seeks my council first, knows appearance matters, is fit with a six pack, doesn't bring negativity home, is appreciative, is 42 and looks better than the whale moms, didn't bring baggage like debt (and I make the financial decisions). brings me caffeine upon waking up and meal preps my food based on calories daily, takes care of our home, knows i won't tolerate BS attitudes. Sometimes I wake up thinking maybe I'm dead and it's all a dream.

— Mike

She listens to my instructions, always asks me about various things (what I want), whether it's buying something, going out, fixing things etc. She isn't afraid to get her hands dirty (outdoor work). She loves being physical. We share the same beliefs and values. She grew up with a great Dad which really helped her understand what a man wants. She doesn't raise her voice at me or acts crazy – and is soft spoken and uses reason to some extent.

— Charles

I've been with the same woman for twenty-two years, with four years dating and eighteen years married. Overall, it's been great. She has none of the 21 red flags as described in your book. Both of our families are traditional when it comes to gender roles and there is no history of divorce My wife is religious, I am not, but both of our families see marriage as a traditional institution in an unstable world. This view can be traced to her Lebanese and Orthodox Christian descent. Her Dad is one of my favorite people in the world - someone who everyone looks up to and is the Don of the family routinely displaying strength and virtue. The same could be said of my father. My wife has a deep respect for her father and I think that carries over for my role as a husband. Our sweet spot is that we get along very well despite not having any common interests. We do, however, share common values on money, family, gender roles, politics, education, etc. I have never lost respect or trust for my wife and she has never disrespected me. Additionally, she follows my lead. I found your site after coming to the realization that I know nothing about dating. With a set of twins (boy-girl twins) who are about to be teenagers, I thought I should brush up on the topic before their interest in the opposite sex took off. I will say that if anything ever happened to my wife I would not get remarried. The risk is too great now that I am older.

— Barry

These are just a handful of the replies I read through, but a common theme arose from the men that indicated that their marriage was a place of happiness, refuge, and peace in their life. I got the impression that these responses came from the average man, so I think this feedback is a good representation; let's unpack that now.

Shared Beliefs

Sharing beliefs around politics, religion, diet, parenting, education and roles in the relationship clearly has a very positive impact on the experience shared above. It would seem that sharing beliefs *significantly* reduces disagreements, and arguments in a long-term relationship.

Imagine trying to be in a relationship with a vegan, when you are a meat eater. Shopping for groceries, meal preparation, and cooking would effectively require double the effort, and that doesn't take into consideration some of the other differences that may exist around beliefs on animal welfare that would also likely add stress to the relationship.

Submissive and Traditional Wife

Many of the commenters reflected that a woman that could "follow their lead" in the relationship also added a sense of peace and added to their happiness. A good friend of mine has a simple way of explaining marital roles as blue jobs for him, and pink jobs for her.

He identifies, and assigns the tasks, and he happily takes on the typical blue roles like disciplining the kids, setting boundaries, making the lion's share of the money, snow removal in the winter, lawn care in the summer, and she happily takes on the typical pink roles like grocery shopping, cooking, cleaning, decorating, and helping with homework.

Clearly men and women are built differently, and rather than fighting over who wears the pants, both parties seem to be happier when they take on their traditional masculine and feminine roles.

If men are expected to have responsibility to the family, to preside, provide for, love, and protect it, then it should come with authority, because responsibility, without authority, is essentially slavery.

It becomes clear that having a submissive woman that trusts her man can positively add to the equation. Working together, and taking advantage of each other's respective strengths and interests appears to be very good for a long-term relationship.

Lack of Prior Promiscuity

A number of studies have been conducted over the years that all seem to conclude that female promiscuity has a negative effect on Long-Term Relationships (or, LTRs), happiness, and increased divorce rates.

Data from the National Survey of Family Growth indicated that "women who are sexually active prior to marriage faced considerably higher risk of marital disruption than women who were virgin brides." These scholars explain that even when controlling for various differentials between virginal and non-virginal groups - such as socio-economics, family background as well as differences in attitude and values - non-virgins still face a much higher risk of divorce than virgins."

Additionally:

> Those who marry as non-virgins are also more likely - all other things being equal - to be unfaithful over the remainder of their life compared with those spouses who do marry as virgins." "Those who are virgins at marriage are those who go to greater lengths to avoid divorce.
>
> — Laumann, 1994, p. 505

In 2003 Sociologist Jay Teachmen found that: "[i]t remains the case, however, that women with more than one intimate relationship prior to marriage have an elevated risk of marital disruption."

In 2011 Anthony Paik (University of Iowa) also found that females who first had sex in their teens had roughly *double the* risk of divorce later in life compared to women who had their first unmarried sexual experience in their adult years.

Science has shown what our grandmothers, and pastors have always known. Female promiscuity damages the cohesion of an LTR. The anecdotal evidence above and my own personal experience reinforces my beliefs with this.

From the studies I've read above, they seem to focus on the effects of female promiscuity over males, because women seem to have a harder time than men forming a long term monogamous pair bond when they've been promiscuous.

Also I've noticed from my Ladies Night podcast, a man's notch count doesn't seem to matter to women, and in many cases it appears preferable that the man has experience because it demonstrates pre-selection from the opposite sex. Women really do want what other women want. It's why women will date a successful married man, but a broke loser is invisible to them.

For men on the other hand, I don't think we'll ever hear a man say: "Gee, I wish my wife had slept with 50 more guys before I married her."

It seems reasonable that if a woman has had a significant amount of prior sexual relationships, then when things get difficult, it's more comfortable and easy to move on to the next man than the virgin bride who seems to be *far* more willing to work on the marriage.

(Dis)Respect

It's been said that contempt, or disrespect, is the clock that ticks down to the end of the relationship. In an LTR men seem to want three things from a woman:

1. A useful complement to his life,
2. Access to enthusiastic, frequent and mind blowing sex, and
3. Respect.

Disrespect is hard for a man to take from a woman, especially when he has maxed out on the seven spokes of a high-value man as I describe in my first book. High-value, unplugged men are rare, and they tend to experience more attention and interest from women in their day to day lives, so respect is big for them.

In the previous men's responses, respect for his boundaries, and listening to him showed up in many comments. There is also an element of carry over from the father to the husband. I've often said that if a woman couldn't respect her father's boundaries, what chance do you think you have.

Unfortunately we live in a culture today with weak, or absent fathers, where single motherhood is all too common. I covered "daddy issues" in my first book in the red flag chapter and have seen plenty of genuinely good men, that are good at being a man, suffer at the hands of a woman that couldn't respect her father, because he was absent or otherwise, and it transcends their own relationships.

Zero Tolerance for Bad Behavior

In reading all these comments, some version of "It's got to be my way or the highway" showed up. This is expected from a strong man that wants to lead his relationship. Some might say that's over the top, excessive, or even abusive. I don't think it is if you are a highly-competent man.

We all know women want to be with a giant, their hypergamous best option, and a highly-competent winner. Therefore, it's not reasonable for a man that *has* the capacity to put a small dent in the universe outside of the home, to yield to all of her requests to become a plow horse at home.

If a woman (who's in a long-term relationship of any type) *truly* loves a man, then she will follow his boundaries and carry out his instructions. I frequently coach men on how to do this. I'll use a prior client as an example, who's a public figure with a large audience. He would instruct his woman to never post or tag him on her social media. He would explain that there are haters, and unhinged internet weirdos that would love to know who the apple of his eye is, and make her life difficult. This instruction was for the benefit and sanctity of the relationship and he prefers to keep who he's with protected from such people.

His girlfriend would routinely breach this boundary and post, and often tag him on social media during something like his birthday because she wanted to mark her territory, and let other women know that he's claimed. This insecurity infuriated him, as it created risk, and blatantly disobeyed a loving boundary he put in place for them.

You might think that's unreasonable, but I always tell men that their woman has three options if you provide her with clear instructions:

1. Carry out the instructions,
2. Ask for clarity or,
3. Come back with a better solution.

Throwing a hissy fit, or expressing blatant disregard and violating a boundary is not one of the options. Needless to say, this bad behavior can take years to correct, and even when it does stop, other ways of protesting reasonable boundaries can replace it, so be vigilant.

Clearly one of the contributing factors to men's happiness in a marriage is a good woman that follows his leadership. It eliminates unnecessary conflict and adds to the peace a man seeks at home. A woman that can't follow your lead will rob you of your joy, and only adds stress to your life.

Stays Fit and Feminine

As I've said many times already, men are success objects to women, and women are beauty objects to men. It seems clear by the responses that men value their marriage far more if their wife maintains an attractive, and feminine presence in his life.

I don't think I've ever heard a man say: "Gee, I wish my wife was a landwhale" or, "I wish my wife was less feminine, and more of a feminist."

Bottom line, maintaining attraction, and looks matter. For both of you.

Stuck Through Thick and Thin

Men love a "ride or die woman." Not only are they supportive when things get tough, but they show commitment to the cause with actions, and words, by being by his side when making passage on stormy seas. You want a woman that has your back, and is on your plan. One of the most underappreciated elements of a LTR is a woman that has your back when you aren't around, or involved in a conversation about you. She should *always* speak highly of you, and your purpose.

I can recall several times in my life when a woman, who had my commitment didn't defend me or support my mission when the opportunity presented itself to her and I found myself very disappointed, especially if I had invested in her, and the relationship. Your woman has an obligation to make you look good with her presence, conversation, grace and her behavior when she is in public with you and even when you aren't around.

I think a good man has the right to expect his woman to make him look good, and have his back and clearly by the replies from the survey, men calling their marriage a "sweet spot" seem to be enjoying a woman supporting his mission.

Alternatives to Tying the Knot

Marriage feels rigged and - for most men today - it is. However, you *don't* have to play by those rules. You can build a family with her commitment without inviting the state into your life. I've seen unplugged alphas structure setups that keep the fire burning while dodging divorce traps. Here's a few ways on how to flip the script.

First off, you can have a relationship with a woman, love a woman, and not live with her. I've explained throughout my work that if you want to eliminate the risks of common law or marriage, you shouldn't live in a way that the state will interpret as marriage especially with women prone to elevate these risks (red flags, promiscuous past, etc).

A lot of plugged-in men get angry when I say this, but you can also have children and not live with a woman. My hour-long private Tristan Tate interview (which I only send out to my email list), clearly shows how he and his brother manage multiple relationships with several women who don't live with him, and who are also the mothers of his children, while they remain 100% loyal to him (I appreciate they're an extreme example, but they are pulling this off successfully).

Granted, it takes being **very** valuable, and *highly* attractive as a man to pull this off and, if I am being honest, no matter *how* good your frame is in the relationship, you will always have more relationship issues when you choose to deal with multiple women at once. But, as an upside, the risk is spread out more, and you enjoy more variety *if* you can manage it successfully.

For example, there's the harem dynamic for top-shelf men - multiple women/wives for one man. That's not some fantasy either - I know real dudes pulling this off discreetly, but it I also know (from their stories) that it can also be a super-complex arrangement to set-up and then maintain over any length of time (for example, look up Tony Huge in Thailand). History's *full* of kings doing this; modern alphas also do it, but now it's with apps, networks, and a cast-iron frame. For more information on other such alternatives, be sure to check out the Nuance chapter at the *very* end of this book.

Remember, women would rather be the King's mistress than the peasant's wife. Like you I wish none of this was true, but until buying her chocolates, flowers, gifts, and treating her nice all the time begins to work on women long-term, we have to observe, and adjust accordingly.

Then there's being together but living apart. Get rid of proximity-related problems by keeping separate residences. Again, you can love a woman, build a life together, even raise kids - *without* merging roofs and exposing yourself to unnecessary risk under family laws. I've coached guys through this: she molds to your schedule, mystery stays alive, desire doesn't tank. Society pushes cohabiting for "progress" - screw that. If her GBD's real, she'll buy into this and she should willingly adopt your boundaries. She won't love it, but again, it's often the very things she doesn't like that are good for her and the relationship long-term.

Guidelines? Start with vetting for women with a low number of red flags (but a high number of green flags - see my chapter on these), who has a "ride-or-die" vibe, and has shared values (minus the baggage). Be comfortable communicating your unapologetic boundaries upfront - she needs to know that - ultimately - it's your way or the highway. Keep leveling up so your options increase naturally, and finally, keep in mind that subtle dread works wonders, so she knows deep down that she's replaceable, which helps keep her invested.

But here's the caveat: these kind of setups aren't foolproof and *plenty* of guys crash and burn trying. It can take a **significant** amount of time, energy, and money to maintain such arrangements and manage a woman over the long haul. Slip on your frame *even once* and all sorts can go wrong: harems can implode, separate pads breed resentment, and you're back to square one. Ego trips blind vetting, so you rush in without solid 9/10 GBD and you end up with low-interest women who make your life difficult.

If you mismanage your relationship, then drama can erupt there's: health risks, reputation damage (which is a **big** deal for women), or even legal headaches that can ruin it all in an instant.

In Conclusion

Marriage, or living in a way that looks like marriage, is an incredibly risky proposition today for men. Because women are hypergamous, they tend to marry up on the socio-economic scale, and with 50% of marriages ending in divorce, and less than 13% of people reporting being in love after eight years, it's a very high-risk and low reward choice for most men, but a very high reward and low-risk choice for women.

For the most part, family law still **strongly** favors the mother.

From what I've seen, marrying young boosts the odds of a solid marriage. Pair that with a woman with: zero body count, real submission and respect, a tight bond with her dad, sticking to your boundaries, shared values, keeping herself fit and feminine, and her being a true ride-or-die partner for the best odds of success.

I think few men today fully understand the risks of marriage, and since the average age of marriage is around 30 now, men aren't getting virgins anymore. Instead, most are finding disagreeable "Becky's" that have accumulated baggage from prior relationships, are disrespectful and have been told their entire life to never rely on a man.

Marriage is still the route most men take because they want a family, with children at the core of this decision. Done right, it can become a true sweet spot in life: a stable home, shared resources, and a clear mission that ties everything together. But the risks are *very* real, especially when a breakup drags the state into your wallet and reduces your time with your kids. That's why it pays to hedge your bets before you commit, because the jurisdiction you live in often matters more than the relationship itself.

This means doing the boring work up front. Plant yourself in a state where shared parenting is the default and where courts begin with the assumption that both parents matter. The National Parenting Organization makes this easy with their annual report card; at the time of writing, Florida, Michigan, Kentucky, and California all rank well for fathers. Knowing the rules and choosing your ground first gives you a **much** stronger position to build from later.

It's also important to understand the cultural shift you're walking into. In your grandparents' era, marriage was the point where sex began. Today, entering into a relationship is the point where you're expected to stop having sex with anyone else. The word is the same, but the incentives are *very* different, and it means that your frame and your boundaries have to carry the load, not the social pressure around you.

That's why marriage <u>**has**</u> to be treated as *the single most important decision of your life*. Who you choose as your wife will shape **everything** that follows. Pick a woman who respects your mission, aligns with your values, and demonstrates consistent stability. Avoid the 21 red flags I outlined in my first book. Protect your position with smart geography, clean paperwork, and a clear head. Then, and only then, lead with confidence.

The Cold, Hard Truth

Never forget:

- **Shared beliefs lock in peace:** When you align on politics, religion, values, and roles, you cut out 90% of the arguments other couples drown in. A house divided collapses; a house aligned stands.
- **Submission isn't a dirty word:** A woman who trusts your lead and plays her role brings calm, not conflict. Responsibility without authority is slavery; authority with responsibility is leadership. Take the lead or lose it.
- **Her past matters:** The numbers don't lie - promiscuity wrecks pair-bonding. Virgins or low-notch count women stick around, high-notch count women leave. Don't buy into modern lies; if you want longevity, pick purity.
- **Respect is oxygen:** Without it, love suffocates. Contempt is the slow countdown to divorce. A wife who respects your frame, your mission, and your boundaries is a wife who fuels your peace.
- **Zero-tolerance works:** Boundaries only mean something if they're enforced. A woman who violates them, tests them, or mocks them will drain you. A woman who honors them strengthens you.
- **She stays fit and feminine:** Men are judged by results; women are judged by beauty. She doesn't need to be a model, but she must value her health and femininity.
- **Ride-or-die is rare, but priceless:** Storms and trials come for **every** man. The sweet spot is a wife who has your back when you're not in the room, who makes you look good in public and private, and who stays solid when things get ugly.

- **Vet well and protect yourself:** The odds tilt against you the longer you wait. If you choose marriage, choose wisely; set your frame, and protect your assets. Location matters, law matters, and your vetting matters most of all.

Part Three

Steve From Accounting's Guides

13

Steve's "How To" Guides Preface

Rich was kind enough to give me space at the back of this book to share a few key lessons of my own. Think of these chapters as an expansion of the field reports I wrote for the 2nd Edition of TUA. Back then, I closed each chapter with my own take; what I applied, how I tested it in real life, and the results I got.

This time, the reports have grown into full chapters. I've pulled from my 30 years experience as a non-fiction guide author to create practical "How To" guides that you can actually use. They're not theory; they're lessons I've lived, broken down step-by-step so you can apply them in your own life.

My writing style is a little different from Rich's. That's intentional. These chapters are meant to complement his framework with tactical tools and field-proven approaches in areas he doesn't cover. While there's a strong AI theme in many of them, I've kept everything as straightforward and accessible as possible.

I used every one of these lessons to level up my own life. And back then, I didn't even have the benefits of AI or automation to help me. You do.

I hope you find these chapters as useful as I've found the lessons behind them.

Keep at it, savages.

Note: None of this book was written with AI. Both Rich and I wrote our chapters ourselves. Members of Rich's community donated their time to give feedback on early drafts. AI was used only for editorial tightening at the end, translations into other languages, and as the test-bed for building my custom content publishing tool.

14

How to: Leverage Generative AI in Both Life and Business

Look, generative AI isn't some savior that's going to fix your problems or business overnight. But if you're a man serious about leveling up - whether that's reclaiming your time, sharpening your edge in business, or just cutting through the daily bullshit - then this tool can be a game-changer.

I've been using it to handle everything from drafting responses in high-conflict situations to streamlining workflows that used to eat up hours. Done right, it frees you to focus on what matters: building your empire, staying sharp, and living on your terms. Done wrong, it's just another distraction. Let's get into how you make it work for you.

> **Note:** *A deeper technical breakdown (covering context windows, token costs, chaining strategies, and more) is available in the resource download linked at the start of the book. This chapter focuses on how to use AI effectively, rather than digging into the technical weeds of how it works.*

Cut Through the AI Noise

Generative AI isn't magic. It's a toolbox, and like any toolbox, each tool is built for a different job. Text models like ChatGPT handle writing. Image models like Midjourney (or Gemini's "nano banana" update) are your digital artists. Claude is built for coding and data tasks, and Grok is tuned for cutting through complexity without the usual censorship.

Think of it this way: you wouldn't pick up a hammer to fix a watch. The same rule applies here. Don't waste resources using a heavyweight model for a simple job. Small, cheap models are like everyday tools, they're fast, efficient, and reliable. Bigger models are more like specialist consultants - they're far more powerful (as they've been trained on a lot more data) but they're also more expensive to use, so you save them for the complex work. Then there are the multi-format tools, like GPT-5, which can handle text, images, and audio in one place. They do a bit of everything, but they're a jack-of-all-trades, master of none.

Here's where most guys go wrong: they dive in blind, pile everything into one giant prompt, and then complain when the output is garbage. You wouldn't hand a new employee a week's worth of work on day one and expect flawless results. AI is no different. Respect the strengths of each model, break the job down into clear steps, and feed the model exactly what it needs - no more, no less. Do that, and AI becomes a tool that lets you operate at a much higher level.

It's like sculpting. Give the same block of marble and the same set of tools to a beginner and a master, and the difference in results is obvious. Using AI works exactly the same way - the tools at hand are powerful on their own, but it's your skill with knowing what tool to use when is what makes *all* the difference.

Trust, But Verify

AI can speed up your work dramatically, but don't ***ever*** make the mistake of trusting it blindly. Think of it like any other powerful tool: it amplifies your ability, but it isn't perfect (it's *far* from it). The cheaper and faster models, in particular, have a habit of spitting out answers that sound convincing but turn out to be completely wrong - what we call "hallucinations." Sometimes they also miss the mark because their training data is too old to include what you need.

One lesson I learned the hard way: AI models only know what they were trained on. When I asked for coding help, the model usually gave me exactly what I asked for, but it often over-engineered the problem. Unlike a human, it never paused to ask, "Is there a simpler way to do this?" More than once, I showed the model a much cleaner solution myself, and it instantly agreed with me. I'm not even a coder, and yet the AI needed me to tell it when it was over-complicating things.

That's the point: you have to enforce simplicity and logic. The model won't do it for you.

Your job is to verify *everything*. That means double-checking translations, running test cases on code snippets, cross-checking market insights, and sanity-testing strategic advice. If something feels off, trust your gut and dig deeper.

Bottom line: AI can make you faster, sharper, and more efficient, but the final responsibility for accuracy always sits on your shoulders.

Context Is King

Every text model comes with a hard limit on how much information it can juggle at once. Think of it like short-term memory. This limit is called the context window, and it's measured in tokens - the chunks of text the model processes. As a rule of thumb: 100 tokens is about 75 words, 1,000 tokens is about 750 words, and so on.

If you try to cram too much into that window (by asking the model to brainstorm, outline, write, edit, and optimize all in a single go), it'll start to lose track of key details. Push it further, and it won't just forget. It'll begin to make things up, stacking errors as the conversation goes on, and once this starts happening, the output quality nosedives off a cliff.

This is why you need to break tasks down. Keep each request clear, use the smallest and cheapest model that can get the job done, and then chain outputs together step-by-step. That approach keeps your workflow lean, efficient, and focused. It also stops you from chasing every shiny new model that gets released, thinking it'll magically solve all your problems.

And here's something worth remembering: newer and larger models aren't always better. They're often slower and more expensive because they're designed to handle immense complexity. Older or smaller models are sometimes far more effective for basic jobs like formatting or summarizing. They're leaner, faster, and cost next to nothing to run in comparison.

A Perfect Example

Back in 2023, when I translated the second edition of The Unplugged Alpha into Spanish, I made the rookie mistake of feeding the entire book into DeepL all at once. The result was predictable: half of it came out fine, a quarter turned into gibberish, and the last quarter was literally just squiggles.

When I switched to translating one chapter at a time, the results jumped to over 90% accuracy, verified by a human translator, and the process was both faster and cheaper. Today, DeepL can translate the whole book in about five minutes for around $15. And ChatGPT's 4o-mini model can do the same job in about ten minutes for just twenty cents, with the help of a few custom scripts.

Note: Context windows are a limitation unique to text models. Image and audio models work differently; their limits are usually based on resolution or length instead of tokens. But the principle still applies: tailor your input to the model's strengths, and keep it within its optimal range for best results.

Assign the AI a Persona

One of the simplest ways to get better results from an AI is to tell it exactly who to be before it answers you. Think of it like giving clear role instructions to a new team member.

Instead of just asking a question cold, start with something like: "Act as an expert financial advisor," or "You're a concise assistant who summarizes dense reports into bullet points." By giving it a persona, you tighten its focus and steer the style of its response right from the start.

And you don't have to stop there. You can chain multiple models together, each with their own role. Imagine having one model that drafts, another that fact-checks, and a third that edits for tone. That's like building a dedicated team on steroids, and all it takes is clear instructions at the start of each step.

The Importance of Prompt Iteration

Your first prompt is never the final word - it's just a draft. Don't expect perfection straight away. If the output misses the mark, adjust your instructions, add an example, or ask it to approach the problem from a different angle.

Getting the most out of AI is all about iteration. You refine the input, the model refines the output. It's no different from training a new hire. You don't just dump work on their desk and hope for the best. You give them clear nudges, correct mistakes, and keep shaping their performance until they deliver what you actually need.

The process is the same here: guide, test, refine, repeat. That's how you turn average answers into results that actually move the needle.

How to Actually Use AI in Your Daily Life

AI shines when you hand it the low-value, time-sucking tasks that drain your energy. That frees you up to focus on the work that actually builds strength and momentum. The trick is not to over-complicate things. Start small, test the outputs, and adjust as you go. That way, you build it into your routine without turning into a tech-dependent zombie.

Get Shit Done (Productivity)

Routine tasks are energy vampires. They eat up time and attention that could be spent on higher-impact work. This is where AI earns its keep.

Calendar and Reminders

Feed it your schedule, your priorities, and your habits, then ask it to flag conflicts or suggest optimizations. For example: "Based on my meetings at 10am and 2pm, plus gym at 6pm, remind me of key prep steps and block focus time." The model turns that into a clean plan, so you no longer have to juggle it all in your head.

Mundane Comms

Drafting emails or messages that used to take twenty minutes can now take two. The rule is simple: one prompt, one task. Something like: "Draft a neutral reply to this client complaint about delays, sticking to facts and offering a fix." Review the draft, tweak it to sound like you, and send. During my divorce, this saved me hours, turning emotional rants into watertight, fact-focused responses.

 Pro tip: Use a basic model like OpenAI's 4o-mini for these jobs. It's fast, cheap, and accurate enough when the task is simple. If you need to handle a large pile of messages at once, split them up: summarize one batch, then the next.

Stop Staring at a Blank Page (Creativity)

Writer's block doesn't stand a chance when you have AI to give you a starting point. It won't write the final product for you, but it will give you something to work with so you're never stuck looking at an empty screen.

Outlines and Drafts

If you're stuck on a book chapter or a business pitch, try: "Outline a no-BS guide on building frame in relationships, key sections only." The model gives you structure, and you fill in the substance with your own edge.

Phrasing and Ideas

Or: "Generate three punchy ways to explain why men should master violence, conversational tone." You then pick the best option and refine it. Instead of wasting an hour hunting for the perfect opening line, you start with workable drafts in seconds.

Chain Models Here If You're Advanced

Once you're more confident, you can chain models together. For example: use a text model for the outline, pass it to an image generator like GPT-4o for visuals, then send those visuals back to a text model for captions. With APIs, this hand-off happens instantly, turning hours of work into minutes. But always start manual until you've dialed in what works.

Fast-Track Your Learning

Knowledge gaps slow you down, and AI is a tutor that never gets tired. The catch is you have to prompt it smartly. During my own family court prep, I used AI to parse through over a dozen child-maintenance documents, each one more than 100 pages long, and summarize them section-by-section in *seconds*. That beat paying a consultant, and it gave me page-referenced insights I could act on right away.

Skill Acquisition

If you want to learn something new, you can ask: "Explain testosterone optimization like I'm a beginner: key factors, simple steps, no jargon." It lays out the basics, and you apply them. For languages: "Translate this paragraph to Spanish, explain grammar changes." It teaches and tests you at the same time.

Close Gaps Quickly

When you're researching a market, try: "Summarize the top five trends in EV tech from 2025 sources, pros and cons." Then, in a second step, ask it to analyze. Splitting the tasks keeps it sharp. For reliability, sometimes older models like ChatGPT 4o are better, they stick closer to the facts and are less likely to hallucinate when you learn to stay within their smaller limits.

GPTs as Permanent Prompts

Some platforms, like ChatGPT, let you create custom GPTs. Think of them as permanent prompts on steroids. You define the instructions once, upload any supporting documents, like your style guide or reference material, and then reuse them without starting from scratch each time.

You can keep these private or share them with your team. They're perfect for testing ideas or creating proof of concept tools before you invest in coding full-blown tools/apps. No re-pasting, no hunting down old prompts - it's all ready to go with one click.

Straightforward AI for Your Business

Business is war, and AI is your tireless junior worker. Use it to automate repetitive tasks, sharpen your marketing, and improve your decision-making. But always remember: no tool replaces your gut. Verification and final judgment stays with you and remains *your* responsibility.

Security and Privacy

Never upload sensitive client data or business details to free-tier AI tools. That's a rookie mistake. Remember the Tea App fiasco? User data leaked all over the internet because people trusted a free platform with critical information. If privacy matters, and it **always** does, pay for the tiers that have strict data policies, or better yet, stick to offline, local models. That's how you keep your work secure.

And if you're building your own tool, don't "vibe code" your way through security. As an absolute **minimum**, run different AI models (set up with security-specific personas) against your own code to look for vulnerabilities. You'll be surprised at how often one model spots issues the others miss. Two or three cross-checked security gap reviews are usually enough to strengthen your tool's security setup. However, this may well be one area where you're best setting aside the money for a professional software security specialist to review your code. It's your budget and your ass on the line, so it's your choice, just don't ignore it.

Legal Risk & Real-World Gotchas

Governments aren't asleep at the wheel. Regulation is ramping up fast, and ignoring it could hit your business harder than a bitter ex-wife in divorce court.

US Legal Landscape

Right now, there's no federal AI Act in the US, but over 45 states have proposed more than 500 AI-related bills - most of them are focused on privacy, misinformation, and bias. In January 2025, President Trump signed an Executive Order shifting national policy toward "less regulation = more innovation." That leaves enforcement largely up to state laws, which are all over the map.

EU AI Act (in Force 1 August 2024, Fully Phased in by August 2026)

The EU takes a stricter approach. Its rules are risk-based, and they cover almost every AI function. If your system falls into the "high-risk" category (think: hiring, lending, credit scoring, or legal tools), you're facing heavy oversight. Violations can cost up to 7% of your global annual turnover. Transparency and human oversight aren't optional; they're baked into the law, even for general-purpose models like GPT.

Global AI Treaty

In September 2024, over 50 nations (including the US, UK, and EU), signed the Council of Europe Framework Convention on AI. It requires human rights protections, transparency, and risk assessments from the development stage onward.

Why This Matters to You

If you're operating in the EU, or even touching EU markets, the AI Act applies to you whether you like it or not. Compliance isn't optional, and ignorance won't save you. Depending on how you use AI, the risks range from fines and bans to forced transparency and public audits.

Key Business Impacts

If you're running AI in sensitive areas like hiring, lending, law, or healthcare, you're going to need proper governance, audits, and documentation ready to show regulators. The EU's code of practice also puts pressure on businesses worldwide, enforcing things like transparency, copyright compliance, and secure design - *even if you're not in Europe*. Meanwhile, US laws are fragmented and state-driven, but some are already strict: California has rules on chatbots, New York requires bias audits. Expect more of this.

Quick Reality Check

By 2026, pretending AI is the Wild West with no rules will be professional suicide. Regulation is rising, and the penalties are real. That means you need guardrails in place now: audits, approvals, and fallback human oversight. Building with compliance in mind protects you, your business, and your clients, without slowing you down.

Bottom line: The legal landscape is shifting constantly, just like AI itself. It's on you to keep up with how these changes affect your business. No one else is going to do that for you.

Automate Your Workflow

Stop micromanaging. If a task is repetitive, hand it off to AI and free up your time for bigger moves.

Docs and Training

AI is great at turning rough notes into clean, structured documents. For example: "Draft a simple Standard Operating Procedure for onboarding new hires, based on these bullet points." It spits out a clear, modular SOP that you can review and roll out. Instead of hours wrestling with formatting, you get a ready-to-use draft in minutes.

Code and Tech

The same applies to technical work. Ask it: "Review this Python script for bugs, suggest fixes." Or: "Generate modular code for a basic API chain." By modular, I mean code built in small, reusable chunks, they're easier to update and are far less likely to break the whole system when you make changes, or update functions in your code.

For more complex workflows, you can chain libraries, scripts, and AI models together. In my own setup, I use Python libraries and scripts to extract data, then feed the raw text into GPT-4o-mini for formatting. That combination - code plus model - gives me greater accuracy in significantly less time.

This approach has turned weeks of debugging into days. It's faster, cleaner, and far less painful than grinding through every issue manually.

Scripts Over Models for Data Consistency

For data wrangling - think parsing CSV files, or converting formats - scripts beat using AI every time. AI is consistent at being inconsistent; which means that they're really good for nuanced stuff like email replies (where understanding context is paramount), but if you need identical outputs run after run (e.g. converting Markdown to HTML, or a .csv file to .json), then using AI models for those types of tasks are a complete crapshoot.

Use AI to code the script itself. For example: "Draft a Python function to strip tokens from Markdown, make it modular for re-use, and create a log file for any errors found." Then chain these different, modular scripts into as many workflows as needed. They're predictable, small, quick, reliable, and they don't suffer from "hallucinations" or similar issues you can find with AI.

A Quick Note on Coding Environments

If you're using AI to generate or run scripts, learn how to use virtual environments (often called venvs in Python). It sounds boring, but it will save you *massive* headaches down the line.

I learned this the hard way. I built a CMS on Windows, only to find none of my code would run on my MacBook because the Python libraries were tied to my Windows install. Schoolboy error on my part.

A venv solves that. It keeps all your project's libraries bundled together in one place, separate from the system. That means you can move your project to another machine, recreate the environment in seconds, and everything just works.

Bottom line: If you're going to code even a little, use venvs from the start. It keeps your projects portable, consistent, and pain-free.

Resource Management (Cost & Scalability)

AI feels cheap at first glance. A few cents here, a few cents there - until something goes wrong. One careless script looped against GPT-5 or Claude Opus overnight can torch $500+ before you even wake up. I've seen it happen to lots of developers. Lesson learned.

The fix is simple: watch your spend. Set limits, rate-cap your calls, and put budgets in place. Don't *ever* assume the system will look out for you - because it won't. Stress-test your workflows before you go live. Otherwise, the "cheap" advantage of AI turns into a very expensive lesson.

Maintenance and Long-Term Sustainability

AI workflows aren't "set and forget." A single model update can wreck your entire pipeline overnight. I've seen it happen - OpenAI dropped GPT-5 as I was working on this chapter and, without warning, killed off every older model. Plenty of people woke up to broken systems they relied on (they've brought some back, but only for a short while).

The only way to protect yourself is to plan for it. Build your workflows like Lego, not Jenga. Keep tasks modular so you can swap out one piece without collapsing the whole structure. Always have fallback options ready.

If you don't, you'll end up scrambling every time a provider decides to pull the rug out from under you.

Version Control (Practical Reality Check)

If you're using AI to build serious code or custom workflows, version control isn't optional - it's mandatory. Tools like GitHub or GitLab track your changes, let you roll back when things break, and keep your projects organized. Think of it as an insurance policy for your work.

That said, not every situation calls for it. If you're mainly working with text documents, blog drafts, or book chapters, then simple backups or a cloud service like Dropbox or Google Drive will usually cover you. Don't overcomplicate what doesn't need to be complicated.

Bottom line: If you're experimenting with code or "vibe coding" your way through projects, version control is the safety net that saves you when things inevitably go sideways. If you're not coding, stick to simpler backup systems and keep moving.

Ethical Considerations

AI can scale your reach faster than anything else, but if you use it to fake results, you'll torch your credibility. Deepfakes, fake testimonials, and fabricated case studies aren't shortcuts - they're landmines.

Use AI to amplify what's real: your ideas, your work, your expertise. Let it handle the heavy lifting on drafts, visuals, or automation, but keep the integrity intact. Authenticity scales. Bullshit doesn't.

Elevate Your Marketing Game

Content is still king, and AI can turn you into a content factory. It helps you produce material quickly and consistently, keeping your presence strong. The danger is overdoing it, which makes everything sound robotic. That's why you should always run it through your own filter and edit for your voice.

Targeted Copy

For example, you might say: "Write a LinkedIn post on why men avoid marriage, keep it punchy, around 200 words, and finish with a call to action for my book." The model will give you a few options, and then you choose the one that fits best and adjust it to sound like you.

Social Strategy

Or take social media planning. A simple prompt like: "Plan a week's Instagram content for a men's coaching brand: themes, captions, and hashtags." The AI lays out the framework, and then you automate the posting with tools. But don't just set it and forget it - you still need to curate, trim, and make sure it feels authentic.

Make Smarter Decisions

When you're dealing with more data than you can realistically sift through, AI can step in and make sense of it for you.

Insights

You can ask: "Analyze this sales data CSV: highlight the top trends, outliers, and give me recommendations." It will boil the mess down into something clear and actionable.

Trends

Or: "Predict Q4 risks in real estate based on 2025 news summaries." Hook that up with a search tool API for live data, and you get a forward-looking snapshot you can act on.

I've used this exact approach to spot market shifts early and avoid bad investments. The caveat is obvious: always check the sources. AI can hallucinate if the context window is exceeded or if the training data doesn't cover what you're asking..

Practical Examples

To make it concrete, imagine you're building an app. First, you ask a coding model to write modular functions - one problem at a time. For instance: "Write a user authentication module in JavaScript." Once you have that, you chain it to a testing model with: "Test this auth code for vulnerabilities." The output flows into deployment. It's a process that feels like superhuman speed, without hitting the limits of a context window.

Or, on a smaller, everyday scale: AI can summarize your ex's rant in one step, and then draft a neutral Yellow Rock reply in the next. Two tasks, clean outputs, no overload.

Modular Code: Clear and Effective

Keep both code and prompts modular - small, focused units that do one job well. That way they're easier to maintain and reuse. For example: "Update this email module for GDPR compliance." Because it's modular, you tweak just that piece without breaking the rest of the system. In collaboration, modular design also keeps everyone working consistently, without stepping on each other's toes.

Responsible AI Use (Don't Screw This Up)

AI is your wing-man, not your pilot. You still have to oversee the process: edit outputs, fact-check results, and keep your privacy tight. That means sticking to secure platforms and paying for the higher tiers online, so your data isn't shoveled into training sets.

And don't chase trends for the sake of it. Chain models together where it makes sense, but keep your choices deliberate. In fact, older, lighter models often beat newer ones for small, highly specific jobs. Test them, compare them, and use what works.

Online vs Offline AI Models (the Pros/Cons)

You've got a choice. If you want simplicity, speed, and instant access to the latest models, then online platforms - ChatGPT, Grok, Claude, Gemini, etc. - are attractive. If privacy and long-term stability matter more, offline models may be the better play, even if they demand more investment upfront.

Let's take a closer look at some of the pros and cons of each approach:

Online Models (ChatGPT, Grok, Claude, Etc.)

Pros:

- Fast, with low hardware requirements.
- Pay-as-you-go: cheap, flexible, no huge upfront spend.
- Easy access anywhere, great for teamwork and prototyping.
- Maintenance and updates handled for you.

Cons:

- Unannounced updates can wreck workflows overnight (see GPT-5's launch).
- Privacy risks if sensitive data leaks.
- Dependent on the internet - no connection, no workflow.
- API costs can quickly spiral out of control if you're careless.

Offline Models (DeepSeek, Qwen, Etc.)

Pros:

- Total control and security, your data stays local.
- Long-term savings, so once it's set up, you can run models indefinitely.
- Zero latency, no waiting on servers to be available.
- Perfect for secure or remote environments.

Cons:

- High upfront cost for capable hardware.
- Setup complexity - either you learn it, or you pay someone who already has that experience you need.
- Performance limited by your hardware specs.
- Maintenance is on you, so no vendor support and no automatic patches or upgrades to more efficient models.

Advanced Use-Cases: The Hybrid Approach

A third option is a hybrid setup, where you mix online and offline models. You might run offline as a backup when cloud services go down, or split tasks across offline models in parallel when they don't need to share data. That's the approach I use in my own custom-built tool. It gives me maximum flexibility, but it comes at the price of more complexity and programming work.

Advanced Use-Cases: Fine-Tuning and RAG

Once the basics are solid, you can push further. Fine-tuning lets you train a model on your own material (whether that's your writing style, your coaching scripts, or your business docs), so the output comes back sounding like you.

RAG, or Retrieval-Augmented Generation, layers in external data. Instead of the model guessing, it pulls facts from your sources to ground its answers. Use them together, and you can create outputs that feel personal while also being verifiable.

This isn't beginner territory though. Nail the fundamentals first, *then* test these methods on small projects. The payoff is big: responses that carry your voice and your accuracy.

Lessons From Building My Own AI-Powered CMS

Over the last year, I built a custom CMS from scratch, powered by different AI models. I used it to edit, produce, and even translate this very book - along with several others. It wasn't easy. I learned plenty of lessons the hard way. But here's the truth: AI made the whole thing possible for a fraction of what it would have cost to hire a senior developer.

I started small. One problem at a time. Importing documents. Adding images. Exporting to PDF. Each step became its own function, heavily commented and fully documented. Over time, those functions stacked up into a solid, reusable toolkit, like an ever-expanding Swiss Army Knife. I could mix and match these scripts, functions, and AI models together to solve new problems.

Take my translation tool. With two clicks, I can send a book - chapter by chapter - to whichever translation model I choose. Or my custom export tool: one drop-down menu lets me change the *entire* style of a book, then generate both a print-ready PDF and an ePub at the click of a button.

I've chained libraries, scripts, and AI models into workflows where one parses data, another converts it, and the AI ties it all together. That setup feels superhuman. My CMS can transcribe a two-hour YouTube podcast into fully formatted text in under three minutes. And if it fails? I hit a button to re-run the exact same prompt through Gemini 2.5 Pro, or I switch to the offline Whisper model. Redundancy built in.

Bottom line: building this tool taught me how powerful AI can be when you use it to amplify your strengths. It let me focus on delivering quality while pushing all the repetitive, routine work onto scripts and models. The details of my system don't matter as much as the lesson: understanding the trade-offs of each model — and how to chain them together — is critical if you want to stay ahead.

The AI Models Starter Kit

There are hundreds of AI models out there, and it's impossible to cover them all. Instead of drowning in options, start with a short list you can actually test. Try them out, see which ones solve your problems, and get a feel for how they behave.

Many services let you access both the major online models and some of the heavier offline ones, without needing your own hardware. Just remember: the same trade-offs apply. If you're running them through a third-party site, you're still dealing with the risks that come with online models.

Here are a few online sites you can visit to see which model(s) work best for your specific use-case:

- https://poe.com

- https://deftgpt.com/en
- https://mammouth.ai
- https://teamai.com
- https://llm-stats.com (latest model analysis)

Note: Never test these platforms with sensitive data. Always use dummy files or a repeatable test scenario. That way you save time, keep your privacy intact, and make fair comparisons across different models.

In Conclusion

Generative AI isn't magic, and it isn't a shortcut to skip doing the work. What it *is* though, is a force multiplier. Used properly, it clears away the busywork so you can focus on what **actually** builds your life: your business, your health, your relationships, your mission. Used poorly, it just becomes another distraction that eats your time, burns your money, and leaves you weaker.

The rules are simple: respect the strengths and limits of each model, break big jobs into smaller steps, and always verify the outputs. Protect your privacy (with business terms or learn to use offline AI), control your costs, and keep backups ready because tools can fail and platforms (like ChatGPT) can change overnight - and without any warning. Treat AI like a junior employee on your team; it can handle repetitive tasks at superhuman speed, but it still needs your leadership, your judgment, and your final call.

Above all, remember that AI amplifies the man who uses it. If you bring discipline, focus, and high standards, the outputs will reflect that. If you bring laziness and wishful thinking, the outputs will reflect that too. Start small, master the basics, and scale up when you've proven the workflow. That's how you turn this technology into leverage rather than liability.

Done right, AI won't replace you; it'll simply free you to operate at a higher level. Ultimately, as always, the responsibility for results stays with you and you alone.

The Cold, Hard Truth:

Never forget:

- **AI is only a tool:** The quality of what comes out depends on the quality of what you put in. Garbage in equals garbage out. Use models intelligently, chain tasks step by step, and don't overload the context window.
- **AI amplifies you, it doesn't replace you:** Always verify what it produces and own the final decision. This tool is for men who deliver value, not for lazy guys looking for shortcuts.
- **Productivity spikes when you offload low-value work:** Automate routine tasks so you can put energy into the gym, business, or your relationships. But use AI with discipline, or you're just wasting its potential.
- **Your edge comes from decisions, not data dumps:** AI can surface insights, but you still have to act. If you hesitate, someone else will use the same tools and pass you by.
- **AI breaks. Keep backups:** Updates, outages, and model deprecations happen. Back up your workflows, scripts, and key data, or risk losing everything overnight.
- **Trust your gut when it matters:** AI is powerful, but it isn't human judgment. In high-stakes moments, your instinct beats the model.
- **Keep your security tight:** Paid tiers or offline models are the only safe bets for sensitive material. Free services leak - it's only a question of when.
- **You don't need to master every detail:** Learn just enough to solve the problem in front of you, then refine over time.
- **Models only know what they were trained on:** If the data didn't exist at the cutoff, the model can't magically invent it. Use RAG - retrieval from up-to-date databases - to bridge that gap.
- **Sanity checks save you headaches:** If an answer looks like bullshit, it probably is. Double-check before you act.

15

How To: Document Your Divorce Like a Pro

Preface from Rich: *I've consulted with thousands of men one-on-one as they navigate their divorce, and I put out a solid divorce course in my community. If you're approaching that pivotal moment of untying the knot, pay close attention to what "Steve From Accounting" has provided here and combine it with the advice I give in my course. Divorce isn't the time to be chivalrous or cut corners. Nice guys get destroyed by family law every day. Document consistently, remain stoic, and use every tool available to your advantage.*

By now you've seen how AI can supercharge your productivity and decision-making. Here's where it gets real: family court. This is where documentation becomes your weapon, and AI gives you an edge if you use it right.

Documenting your divorce isn't about drowning in endless paperwork. It's about arming yourself with proof that stands up in court, cuts down your legal costs, and keeps you one step ahead of the chaos that usually comes with it.

I've lived this process myself, and I used my 30 years experience as a documentation professional to build a system that's simple, effective, and designed to safeguard what *actually* matters.

That system didn't just help me come out on top financially in the UK courts - it even had the female judge presiding over my case making stronger arguments on my behalf than my own barrister. All I did was present clear, organized evidence, while my ex handed the court enough rope to hang herself with arrogance and hubris (including turning up late to both virtual hearings - **never, *ever* do that gents** - my ex-wife is *still* paying the price).

Judges don't care about your emotions or your story. They want facts. They want timestamps. They want evidence they can access and verify easily. Do this right, and you protect your assets, your sanity, and your frame. Do it wrong, and you'll be left scrambling - and scrambling never wins in court.

This approach shifts you from reactive chaos into proactive control. You're building a fortress of evidence that holds firm no matter what's thrown at you. I'll walk you through the same steps I used, focusing on the 80/20 that delivers maximum impact with minimal hassle. Keep it simple. Your time is far too valuable to waste on unnecessary complication.

Cautionary Note for All UK-Based Brothers

The UK Family Court system isn't interested in you "building a case." If you show up with diaries full of rants and emotional commentary, you'll look like you're attacking your ex instead of focusing on your child. That approach almost always backfires.

What the court *does* pay attention to are clean, neutral facts that show patterns over time, backed up with evidence.

The best way to build this is with a simple daily log. Nothing dramatic, just the basics: date, time, who was present, what happened, and how your child was affected. Stick to what you directly saw or heard, not what you think happened. If you've got evidence to support it - like a text, an email from school, a timestamped photo - then note that alongside the entry. Over time, this log becomes a record that speaks for itself.

From there, build a short chronology. Think of it as the highlights reel: key events listed in order, with exhibit IDs attached. That way, if your solicitor or the court asks, you can instantly produce the proof. Judges don't want to wade through noise, they want sharp, easy-to-follow material.

> **Note:** *If your child volunteers how they feel, write it down as a direct quote with the date and context. Keep it short, factual, and never prompted. Pair it with your neutral observation of their behavior. That way it's clear you're recording, not shaping, what happened.*

Just as important is what *not* to do. Don't write essays about how awful your ex is. Don't flood the court with hundreds of pages of petty incidents. And don't share anything publicly; family cases are private by law, and breaching that can land you in serious trouble.

Be very careful with recordings. Secretly taping someone may feel tempting, but it often backfires. Judges will ask why you did it, how you did it, and whether it damaged trust with your child or professionals. Even if the recording is admitted, it might carry little weight. If you believe it's necessary, keep it short, specific, and provide a transcript.

And if allegations of abuse come up, be ready with a clear schedule of incidents: dates, what happened, and the supporting evidence. Keep it factual, not emotional.

Here's the bottom line: give them facts over feelings. Present clean entries, tie them to evidence, and show the impact on your child. That's all the court wants to see, and it's the only way your documentation will work in your favor.

Why Metadata is Your Secret Weapon

Metadata - the hidden details embedded in files like timestamps, locations, and file origins - can turn an ordinary document or photo into rock-solid proof. It's often overlooked, but it's one of the cleanest ways to back up your story and quietly dismantle false claims without ever raising your voice.

Metadata creates a clear record of when and where events happened. That makes it very hard for your ex to spin an alternative narrative.

Take selfies with your kids as an example. With timestamps and GPS location attached, they don't just show you were there - they prove it. Over time, a series of simple photos like this can demonstrate consistent involvement as a parent.

To make this work, go into your phone's camera settings and enable location services. Take a test photo at the park with your kids, then check the file details to confirm the GPS coordinates and timestamp are included. Once you know it's working, make it a habit. Those small, consistent captures add up to an undeniable timeline.

Metadata Modification Caution

When you create a file (whether it's a document, photo, or recording), the system records the date and time it was created and, just as importantly, when it was last modified.

Here's the warning: if you plan to rely on metadata in court, **do not** modify the file after it's created. If the "last modified" date is miles apart from the "created" date, you hand the opposition an opening to argue that the file was tampered with. Even if it wasn't, the credibility is gone.

The solution is simple: once you've created an important file, lock it down. For example, if you're using Word or another text editor, set the document to "Read Only" as soon as it's saved. That prevents accidental edits and preserves the original metadata. Apply this rule file by file.

Handled properly, metadata is one of your sharpest weapons. Mishandled, it can undermine your entire case.

Scan and Stitch Docs Like a Boss

Scanning your paperwork turns messy stacks of paper into clean digital files. That makes them searchable, shareable, and secure - and ensures nothing important gets lost. Done right, it saves your lawyer hours of digging, reduces your bill, and shows the court you're organized and on top of things.

Take bank statements as an example. On paper, they're often scattered across multiple pages, half-folded, or missing context. Once scanned into a single PDF, they reveal clear financial patterns that go straight to the heart of a dispute.

Here's how to get started:

1. Download a free app like Adobe Scan, or use the document mode on your phone's camera.
2. Open the app, select "scan," and snap each page. The app will automatically straighten and combine them into a single PDF.
3. Name the file clearly, something like *2025-01-01_Bank_Stmt_v01.pdf*.
4. Upload it to your cloud storage immediately, so it's backed up and accessible.

Keep everything consistent. Over time, you'll have a digital archive that makes your side of the case fast to present and impossible to ignore.

Capturing Emails, Texts, and Audio

Capturing your communications locks in the full context (think: timestamps, conversation threads, even tone), so no-one can later twist what was said. It creates reliable timelines that expose broken promises, shifting stories, or outright lies.

Emails and texts are your strongest allies here. In Gmail or Outlook, use search filters (search for: dates, senders, or keywords like "kids" or "money"), to pull up old conversations. Export them in raw format (*.eml* or *.msg*) to preserve provenance, and save those to a folder called "*Originals*." Then convert them into PDFs for easy review, with clear filenames like *2025-08-08_Email_Thread_Ex_Custody_v01.pdf*.

For texts, use your phone's export features or apps like SMS Backup to create PDFs that capture entire conversations in order.

Audio can also be powerful, but tread *very* carefully. Laws on recording vary country-by-country, and even state-by-state in the US, so check with your lawyer first. If it's legal, use your phone's recorder, note the exact timestamp, and save the file with metadata intact. If it's not legal where you are, make a contemporaneous note instead, write your notes down **immediately** after the conversation, using something like Google Docs so it auto-saves and timestamps the entry. Contemporaneous notes carry far more weight than memories written down days or weeks later.

Social media chats fall into this same category. Backups preserve timestamps and make old messages searchable. During my divorce, backed-up WhatsApp threads helped prove contradictions in my ex's testimony, including her claims about how she was using money. Those messages undermined her story in court.

To set this up in WhatsApp, go to *Settings > Chats > Chat Backup* and connect it to your cloud storage. My backup ran over 11GB, mostly from pre-divorce history, but it was worth it. Search within the app for keywords, screenshot relevant threads with timestamps visible, and save them with clear filenames like *2025-08-08_WhatsApp_Thread_Ex_Pension_v01.jpg*.

For Messenger, Signal, or other apps, enable auto-backups or use their export options as early as possible. Historic chats can vanish, so preserve them before they're gone.

Leverage Cloud Services for Backup and Sharing

Cloud storage keeps all your files in one secure, accessible place. It backs them up automatically so nothing gets lost, and it lets you share view-only links instantly without bloated emails or the risk of someone editing your originals.

This setup was a game-changer during my own hearings. My lawyer could pull up documents on the spot, without delays or fumbling through piles of paper. It showed preparation, saved time, and cut down costs.

Here's how to set it up:

1. Pick a trusted service like Google Drive, OneDrive, or Dropbox.
2. Create a master folder called something like *Divorce_Docs_2025*.
3. Inside, make sub-folders for categories such as *Finances* or *Custody*.
4. Upload files, then set permissions to "*view only.*" Share links only with your lawyer, and restrict them to specific email addresses.
5. Turn on two-factor authentication to lock it down further.

Follow the 3-2-1 backup rule:

- Keep three copies of your data.
- Store them on two different types of media (for example, cloud + external drive).
- Keep one copy offsite.

Make it a routine to mirror your cloud contents to an external drive monthly. That extra step means you're covered even if a service fails or your account is compromised.

The "How to Use.txt" Efficiency Hack

A simple text file in the root of your cloud storage can save you hours of wasted effort. It acts as a quick guide that explains how your folder system is laid out, so your legal team doesn't have to waste billable time figuring it out.

In my own case, this one hack saved hours. Because everything was clearly explained, there was no fumbling around or confusion. My lawyer could dive straight into strategy instead of asking me how to find things.

Here's how to set it up:

- Open a basic text editor like Notepad.
- Write a short guide, for example: "Folder Guide: *Finances* contains bank documents, searchable by YYYY-MM-DD. Use Ctrl+F for keywords. All files are timestamped."
- Save the file as *How_to_Use.txt*.
- Place it in the main folder of your divorce documents.
- Update it any time your structure changes.
- It's simple, it's fast, and it makes you look professional and organized. Lawyers definitely notice (and appreciate) that. And it saves them time, saving you money.

Organize With Naming Conventions and Chronology

Consistent file names and a clear timeline make your documentation easy to follow. That alone boosts your credibility - judges can see patterns without you having to explain every detail.

Disorganized files create confusion. A chronological system does the opposite: it brings clarity. In one of my hearings, presenting a clean timeline of documents directly supported my position on asset division. The order and naming spoke louder than long explanations ever could.

Here's how to set it up:

1. Create and then use a standard format for every file (Example: *2025-01-01_Bank_Stmt_v01.pdf*).
2. Sort folders by date so the story unfolds naturally.
3. Once a week, review any new files. Rename them in batches to match your system.
4. Maintain a master timeline document that lists the key files in order.

That master timeline becomes your "map" of the case. It's easy to hand over, easy to follow, and it reinforces the impression that you're calm, organized, and credible.

Pick Your Battles: High-Value Proof That Wins the War

Not all evidence carries the same weight. If you try to present everything, you'll bury the points that matter. By focusing on high-value proof (especially around custody and finances), you protect what's most important while showing the court that you're reasonable and disciplined.

In my divorce, I gathered mortgage quotes from three different advisors. Those documents proved that I could afford a home with dedicated rooms for the kids, but *only* if I was to come out of the divorce completely debt-free. It showed the court I was focused on family needs, not ego or lifestyle and - more importantly - the courts place a **very** high priority on equality between homes. That one bundle of evidence carried *far* more weight than a dozen petty examples - and the mortgage quotes didn't cost me anything.

Your legal team should guide you on which fights are worth prioritizing. For example, my ex bought a £3k motorbike right before the first court date. My barrister advised that looking to divide the bike's value wasn't worth the hassle. But... what *was* worth arguing was what the purchase revealed; if she could afford the bike, the gear, the lessons, and the insurance, then she could afford to pay more of our kid's private school fees without struggling. *That* angle had *real* impact in court, **far** more than squabbling over the bike itself ever could have.

Here's how to apply it:

1. Ask your solicitor or barrister to help you rank which issues matter most in court.
2. Gather evidence that ties directly to those priorities.
3. Combine documents into single, well-named files, for example: *2025-01-01_Mortgage_Options_v01.pdf.*
4. In your timeline, note why each piece of evidence matters; not just what it shows, but what it proves about the bigger picture.

That's how you win: by focusing your firepower where it counts.

Leveraging the Power of AI

Once you've nailed the basics of documentation, you can step it up with AI tools that can scan, sort, and summarize documents at a speed no human can match. They're pattern-matching powerhouses.

But there's a knack to using them, and you need to be careful. Sensitive documents should ***never*** be uploaded blindly to online services. If you're using something like ChatGPT, make sure you're on a paid plan so your data isn't fed back into training. If security is critical, use an offline model. The trade-off is that the quality depends heavily on the size of the model and the hardware you're running. Bigger models demand serious power.

Here's how I'd approach it today:

- Set up a custom GPT as your "divorce doc coach."
- Give it clear instructions like: "Analyze for custody and finance relevance, summarize key points, suggest tags."
- Upload a file, review the output carefully, and then share the refined insights with your lawyer.
- Always verify what the AI produces. Treat it as a speed boost, not gospel truth.

Back in 2020, I didn't have access to these tools. If I had, scanning, compiling, and searching through the hundreds of documents I uploaded for my legal team would have been so much easier. Today, that process can take minutes instead of days.

In Conclusion

Building a solid documentation system is about making facts easy to find, easy to present, and impossible to ignore. When you, your lawyer, or even a judge can pull up proof instantly, you turn potential chaos into clean wins.

This isn't about being flashy, it's about leveling the field, cutting legal costs, and letting the truth do the work. Start making everything searchable from day one and you'll face the storm with steady control instead of panic.

It's not fun work, but with practice it becomes smooth and routine. My own solicitor (the MD of his firm, an ex-army sergeant with 25 years in family law), told me he had *never* seen such organized, searchable documents from any client before. He even adapted some of my methods for use by his junior team.

That's the level of clarity you want to hand your legal team. It keeps you credible, keeps them efficient, and makes the whole machine work in your favor.

Cautions and Nuances for Documenting Your Divorce

First off, a disclaimer: This isn't legal advice - it's based on what worked for me. Always run your setup by your solicitor, because laws vary and assumptions can backfire hard.

- **Privacy is crucial:** Encrypt sensitive files in your cloud storage. Revoke sharing links once they're no longer needed.
- **Avoid going overboard:** Stick to the 80/20 rule; focus on what actually impacts your case. Drowning the court in extras makes you look desperate or unfocused.
- **Test your setup early:** Do a mock share of your folders with your legal team. Do this ASAP so you can catch any access issues sooner rather than later.
- **Be cautious with metadata:** Remember it can be edited. If tampering is a risk, set files to "read-only" to lock integrity in place.
- **Watch for document quality loss:** In my case, junior staff sometimes printed my PDFs and re-scanned them, which degraded the evidence. Push for digital-only handoffs to keep files crisp.

The Cold, Hard Truth

Never forget:

- **Metadata locks in proof:** Embed timestamps and locations to timeline your involvement. Facts close gaps. Spin doesn't stand a chance.
- **Scan and centralize smart:** Upload digital files to the cloud storage, backed up with 3-2-1 redundancy.
- **Capture clean communications:** Export with provenance, check audio laws, back up chats like WhatsApp daily automatically in the app.
- **Guide your team:** A simple "How to Use.txt" saves them time and saves you money. Messy setups bleed billable hours.
- **Focus on the high-value battles:** Find out from your legal team which arguments hold the most weight in court, use these to protect your kids and assets.
- **AI boosts the basics:** Use it to tag and summarize, but always verify. It's a tool, not a crutch.

16

How to Deal With a High-Conflict Ex-Wife

> ***Preface from Rich:*** *Family law encourages women to behave very badly. She wants your stuff and the kids (ensuring she'll get paid well and keeps her in control), almost guaranteeing to make your divorce high conflict. Understand that no matter how bad things are, the pain will pass with time, and your own stoic resilience to her bullshit will increase. Sticking to what's good for the kids, and ignoring just about everything else she tries to distract you with is key. It may take a year or two for her to lighten up, and become more agreeable, but consistent, steadfast resilience to her BS is key. Steve's been dealing with a bitter ex-wife for years now and his following tips have already helped out numerous guys in my community to live more peaceful lives.*

You've learned how to build your AI toolkit and how to document your case like a pro. Now let's apply it to the most brutal battlefield of all: daily communication with a high-conflict ex.

Most men don't walk into divorce expecting to face an emotionally unstable, bitter ex-wife. But if you're the one who filed, or if you've got kids together, the odds go up fast. Sadly, that's the reality.

What usually follows are child-like tantrums and emotional outbursts whenever she isn't getting her own way. Most guys don't know how to handle that. They react emotionally, and that's *exactly* what she's baiting them into.

I've spent the last five years dealing with an ex like this, and I found an approach that not only made it *far* easier to handle her bullshit, but also stripped away the anxiety I used to feel every time her messages hit my inbox. My goal here is to show you how to do the same - and maybe even get to the point where handling her nonsense becomes, if not enjoyable, at least manageable.

The first rule is simple: if you've got kids together, ***never*** respond emotionally. No matter how angry you feel, don't let it bleed into your replies. In fact, the more her message bothers you, the longer you should wait before drafting an answer. That's the rule of thumb I used during the worst of my separation and divorce.

If you can't step back from inflammatory accusations or provocations, you'll make yourself look bad in front of a judge. Judges don't care about your temper; they care about calm, fact-based communication. Swear back, lash out, or match her tantrum, and it'll only be used against you in court.

So let's get into how to respond the right way.

Welcome to AI - The Ultimate BS Handling Tool

Believe it or not, I now use AI to process the accusational or tricky messages that come in from my ex-wife. The benefits are immediate, and they stack over time.

Benefit 1: Pattern Recognition

LLMs are trained on massive datasets, including forum threads and blog posts full of high-conflict conversations. They've seen tens of thousands of exchanges just like the ones you're facing. They're also excellent at pattern recognition, which means they can instantly flag the manipulation tactics you've been dealing with.

Here are some of the most common patterns they recognize:

- Emotional Manipulation
- Minimizing
- Gaslighting
- Blame Shifting
- Projection
- Guilt-Tripping
- Victimhood Playing
- Exaggeration (or, Catastrophizing)
- False Accusations
- Moving Goalposts
- Circular Arguments
- Deflection

- Stonewalling
- Triangulation
- Passive-Aggression
- Baiting and Provocation
- Boundary Testing
- Revisionist History
- Character Assassination
- Word Salad (Confusing Communication)

When you feed one of her high-conflict messages to an AI, here's what happens, it:

1. **Neutralizes Emotion:** Strips out the inflammatory language, emotional hooks, and bait, leaving only the core points.
2. **Clarifies Intent:** Distills "word salad" into a straightforward summary of the actual issue or request.
3. **Highlights Manipulation:** Flags tactics like guilt-tripping, gaslighting, or exaggeration so you can spot them instantly.
4. **Proposes Neutral Replies:** Suggests responses that stick to facts and logistics only, cutting off escalation before it starts.
5. **Maintains Boundaries:** Crafts replies that enforce your limits without giving her new ammo to twist.
6. **Documents for Evidence:** Creates a consistent, neutral record of communication, which is *gold* if you ever need to show a judge or mediator.

In short, AI strips away the chaos and hand you a clear, unemotional response strategy. They don't get angry. They don't get baited. They run on logic - 100% of the time.

The Bitter Ex-Wife Playbook

Over time, my ex-wife's responses became so predictable I could often guess her next move before she made it - with about ninety percent accuracy. That's because women like this all seem to pull from the same unwritten playbook.

The traits aren't unique to her. They're universal. Narcissistic behaviors like blame-shifting, gaslighting, or guilt-tripping show up again and again. And because they're so common, AI spots them instantly.

This predictability is a double-edged sword. On one hand, it gives you an edge. If you can anticipate her response, you're playing chess while she's stuck on checkers. You're already two moves ahead.

On the other hand, it means you'll also know exactly how she's going to punish you. If you have kids, that's where it gets painful. She knows you care about them, and that makes them prime targets for slow, deliberate alienation attempts. That's the darker side of this "playbook," and it's why you need to stay disciplined in how you respond.

Benefit 2: Super-Quick Data Processing Abilities

Another major advantage of AI is speed. I can feed it both the message from my ex and any relevant documents - my court order, parenting agreement, or parts of the child-specific legal framework - and it contextualizes everything instantly.

Here's a concrete example. I once pulled together thirteen official PDFs from the UK child maintenance framework. Each one was over a hundred pages long, and they were training manuals for the staff who calculate payments. No human could realistically read, cross-reference, and apply all of that in a useful timeframe.

The AI could. I uploaded those documents, and then asked it direct questions. Within seconds, it could cite the exact document name, page number, and paragraph that applied to my situation. It was like having an expert with years of experience sitting across the table, but available on demand.

That's the level of processing power we're talking about. It isn't just fast - it's thorough. And when you're dealing with a high-conflict ex and complex legal rules, that kind of speed and clarity is priceless.

Note: *I personally use a Pro ChatGPT package so my documents aren't pulled into future training data. That said, if you want total security, an offline model is your best option. The trade-off is that the quality depends heavily on the size of the model and the hardware you're running it on. Bigger models need serious power to deliver the same level of detail.*

Fine Tuning Your Responses - The "Yellow Rock" Approach

Coined by *Tina Swithin*, Yellow Rock is a communication style that favors balancing niceties with a business-like approach (i.e. sticking to the facts, keeping it short and sweet). The reason I strongly suggest you burn this approach into your mind (especially if you have kids) is that should you ever need to stand in front of a judge, then you can be confident that your responses will stand up to scrutiny.

Write For The Benefit of a Judge

Every reply you send should be written as if a judge is standing over your shoulder. That doesn't mean grovelling or overcompensating. It means professional, factual, and stripped of emotion. You don't respond to accusations unless they're so severe you have no choice. You never match her energy or fire back insults.

I never respond thinking my ex will listen or suddenly change. She won't, because she can't. That's not how she operates. Whenever I've tried to soften a boundary, she's shown zero appreciation. So I don't write for her. I write for the record, and for the benefit of the court if it ever comes to that.

"Duly Noted"

The length of your response should always match the type of message you've received. One of the most useful replies I've ever used, when I want to politely say "I don't give a shit," is a single word: *Noted*.

That's it. It shows you've read her message, but that you're not giving it any more energy. I've never once had her reply to that. But use it carefully. It only works when it's obvious that nothing more needs to be said. Overuse it, and you'll look dismissive in the eyes of a judge.

Here's an example from early 2025. My ex sent this:

> "Thank you for your message and informing me that your stance on encouraging the children to participate in enriching activities has changed. It is rather unfortunate that despite 12 months notice you are unwilling to support [our daughter] for this trip or any other as per your message. I can see the term "our children" only applies for certain aspects of their life and not all."
>
> — Steve From Accounting's Ex-wife

My AI-generated reply was simple:

> "While I don't share your view on this matter, your comments have been noted."
>
> — Steve From Accounting

It acknowledged that I'd read her message and understood her points, but made it clear I didn't agree. That's exactly the balance you want - professional, neutral, and free from escalation.

Of course, not every message should be answered this way. Use judgment. For more serious or logistical matters, a longer reply may be required. The key is to match your tone and length to the situation while keeping everything professional and neutral.

Here's another real-world example. She tried every trick in the book to get me to pay more than I was obligated to. My reply was short and precise:

"As per my previous OFW [OurFamilyWizard] message dated 4th March, my position remains unchanged. I'll continue adhering strictly to our parenting agreement, court order, and child maintenance commitments."

— Steve From Accounting

No defending myself. No accusations. No escalation. Just a calm, factual statement of where I stand. If a judge ever read it, I'd have nothing to worry about.

Pick Your Hills to Die On

When you're dealing with a high-conflict ex-wife, especially with kids involved, you need to know where your line in the sand is. Some battles are worth fighting, others aren't.

The first thing to understand is that you **will** be punished for pushing back. That punishment can take many forms - a missed video call, her refusing contact, baseless accusations, or some other bullshit. I've had all of those pulled on me (more than once).

The reality is simple: not every scenario is worth escalating tensions over. If you're in family court and you come across as uncooperative or unwilling to compromise for the sake of the kids, it will be used against you. That's why you have to choose carefully.

Don't be a pushover. But don't be a dick either. This dynamic is a constant test of your frame. Every decision you make has consequences - some good, some bad, and some you won't see coming.

Pick your battles wisely. Defend what matters most. Let go of what doesn't. That balance is what keeps you both effective and credible in the long run.

Don't Let AI Become a Crutch

AI is powerful for cutting through emotional bullshit, but it's not a silver bullet. Always, always, *always* read the AI-generated response carefully before you hit send.

Remember: AI runs on logic, not nuance. It doesn't know your full history with your ex. It doesn't grasp every detail of your parenting plan or your court order. At the end of the day, it's your name on the message, and it's your ass on the line if something blows back in court.

Trust the tool, but verify every word. Use AI as support, not as a substitute for your own judgment.

AI Doesn't Replace Self-Control

If you're leaning on AI because you can't control your own emotions, you've already lost. No tool can fix that. You need to keep your frame and stay in control of your reactions at all times. AI can help you structure calm, neutral replies, but it can't stop you from raging, snapping back, or letting her live rent-free in your head.

AI is a weapon for managing conflict, it's not therapy, and it's *definitely* not a replacement for discipline. Self-control is still very much on you.

Real-Life Prompts You Can Use

To make this practical, here are three prompts I've battle-tested. Copy, paste, and adapt them directly into your LLM of choice.

Prompt 1 – Neutral Boundary Setting:

"My ex-wife sent me the following message: [Paste her message here]. Using the Yellow Rock communication style, draft a brief, neutral, fact-based response that reinforces boundaries clearly, without any emotional or accusational language."

Prompt 2 – Neutral Acknowledgement (No Further Action Needed):

"Here's the message from my ex: [Paste her message here]. Craft a one-line reply using the Yellow Rock approach, politely acknowledging her message while clearly indicating no further action will be taken."

Prompt 3 – Logistics-Only Response:

"My ex-wife just messaged me this: [Paste her message here]. Please generate a brief, business-like reply that directly addresses only logistical details relevant to our children, using the Yellow Rock style. Ignore all emotional or manipulative language."

Quick Reality Check (Legal Disclaimer)

Let's be clear: *everything* I'm sharing here comes from my own experience. **It's not professional legal advice**. Using AI won't magically make your ex cooperative. It won't guarantee you a win in court. What it *will* do is help you manage the day-to-day bullshit: staying calm, replying in a judge-friendly way, and protecting your frame.

If things escalate beyond that - if she's making serious accusations, dragging you into new legal action, or pushing past what you can handle - get professional legal advice, **fast**. That's not optional.

What to Expect

AI-generated replies won't magically transform your ex into someone cooperative, logical, or fair. Her behavior won't suddenly change because you're responding differently. Expect the same patterns of bullshit to continue - and at times, to even escalate.

However, what AI *will* do is help protect you. It helps you strip the emotion out of her messages, spot the manipulation tactics immediately, and respond with calm, judge-friendly replies. That means fewer traps, less anxiety, and *far* more control over how you come across.

Think of it this way: AI won't fix her. But it will strengthen you by keeping your communication consistent, neutral, and strategic - even when her provocations are at their worst.

In Conclusion

Using AI to process your ex-wife's messages (alongside any court orders or parenting agreements), gives you an edge. It strips out the emotional bait, highlights manipulation tactics, and helps you draft responses that a judge would have no issue with. Just make sure you ask it to use the Yellow Rock style when you prompt it.

I still get plenty of bullshit from my ex. That hasn't changed. What has changed is me. I don't get worked up about it anymore. I let AI handle the emotional clutter, and I send back replies that are watertight, neutral, and impossible to twist.

If you're facing an ex-wife like mine, I *genuinely* wish you the best. Stay disciplined, use the right tools, and keep going. With time and the right approach, it does get easier. I promise.

The Cold, Hard Truth:

Never forget:

- **High-conflict ex-wives are predictable:** They all pull from the same playbook. Gaslighting, guilt-tripping, blame-shifting, and once you see it, you'll *always* see it coming. Predictability is your weapon.
- **AI strips emotion but isn't foolproof:** It can spot manipulation tactics and generate neutral, court-friendly replies. But it's still just a machine. Always review what it writes before you send it. Your ass is on the line, not the AI's.
- **You're still responsible for emotional control:** AI can help, but it's not a replacement for discipline. Staying calm and collected is always on you.
- **Respond like a judge is watching:** Yellow Rock (short, polite, factual), makes sure your replies stand up to scrutiny. Imagine every message is going straight into evidence, because one day it might.
- **Pick your battles wisely:** Some hills are worth dying on, most aren't. Defend your real boundaries, but be seen as cooperative when it comes to the smaller stuff. That balance is crucial if it ever reaches court.
- **Manage expectations:** AI won't make your ex reasonable or fair. What it *will* do is reduce your stress, block manipulation, and keep you consistent. That's the win.

17

How To: Navigate Your Life With Nuance

Look, unplugging with uncomfortable truths, building a solid frame, leveraging AI, all of that changes *everything* when you get it right. But Rich has seen far too many men screw it up by treating every principle like an unbreakable law, with rigid "if this, then that" thinking. Life doesn't work that way. Outside of programming, there are too many moving parts for binary rules to hold up.

Contexts shift, situations get messy, dynamics change. If you go full binary - always this, **never** that - you come across like a stiff robot who alienates everyone. Rich has watched men unplug hard, only to crash and burn because they couldn't adapt to the real complexity of their own lives.

Nuance is the answer. Done properly, it keeps your edge sharp while adjusting those principles to fit the moment. Think of it like tuning your bike's suspension; you hold onto the power, but you adapt to the terrain so you don't wipe out.

That said, it's absolutely *essential* that you first master the foundational concepts Rich teaches. You can't apply nuance with finesse if you don't even understand the basics of the framework.

Learning nuance means changing the way you think. It's the ability to take what you've learned, apply it to your own circumstances, and live life **your way** - unapologetically. Your passions, skills, and goals are yours to shape.

The trade-off is this: you have to work at it. Different dynamics demand different tools. You need to know when to pick the right tool for the job.

Eliminating "Black and White" Thinking

Nuance isn't about going soft or backing down. It's about learning how to adjust your core principles to match the messy reality in front of you - *without* selling out your frame. Too many men box themselves in with binary "all or nothing" thinking, which ignores how life *actually* plays out. That kind of rigidity turns wins into losses.

For men on the spectrum (Autism, ADD, etc.), this is even *more* important. Your brain processes the world differently, so you need to build ways to spot the gray areas and consciously apply them. If you don't, you'll miss subtle social cues, non-verbal signals, or emotional tells that make or break opportunities. That could mean losing out on a business deal - or failing to recognize when a woman truly has GBD for you.

Let's walk through a couple of examples.

Business Setting

You're a salesperson pitching CRM software to a small business owner, Mike, who's running a family auto repair shop. During the call, Mike opens up about his pain points - cash flow's tight because invoices pile up unpaid, inventory tracking is a mess eating hours, and he's stressed from juggling it all while dealing with his wife's recent health scare that's forced him to cut back on family time. He mentions how the chaos at work spills over, making him snap at his kids and feel like he's failing as a dad.

The "Black-and-White" Approach

You stick rigidly to using your "sell value, close hard" card - you hammer on software features like automated invoicing and inventory alerts, ignore his personal story, and push for an immediate sign-up with a discount ultimatum. The likely outcome? Mike feels unheard and pressured, like you're just chasing commission; he ghosts the follow-up, the deal dies, and there's no chance for referrals or up-sells later down the line.

The More Nuanced Approach

Dial in the empathy a little with some gentle probing, share a quick relatable story from your own early business days about how you found juggling family stress. Acknowledge his pain: "Sounds rough, Mike - I've been there with family pulling you in every direction while the shop grinds you down. This software's cut that chaos for guys like us by 30%, freeing up evenings for what matters. Let's tweak it to your setup - what if we start small with just invoicing?" The likely outcome? Mike feels seen and trusted, opens up more on needs, signs on the spot for a phased roll-out, and later refers two buddies while upgrading his plan twice in the first year.

Bottom line: The nuanced path builds real rapport through empathy, turning a one-off sale into loyal repeat business and a network boost – but if you push rigidly for the close, you'll kill trust, lose the deal, and burn future opportunities.

Family Setting

Your teenage son gets caught skipping class. The school calls you in, and you're staring him down in the kitchen that night.

The "Black-and-White" Approach

You slam the hammer down: grounding for a month, no Xbox, no hanging out with friends, end of story. The likely outcome? He resents you, hides things better next time, and learns to play the game behind your back. Lesson lost.

The More Nuanced Approach

You hold frame, but you probe deeper. You ask why he skipped- bullying? A teacher he hates? Just burned out? You listen, then lay down consequences that fit. Maybe it's two weeks grounded plus mandatory catch-up work. He learns accountability, but he also knows his dad listens and won't just nuke him for the sake of it.

Bottom line: While it's critical he understands where he messed up, nuance here builds trust and teaches responsibility; rigidity just drives rebellion and secrecy.

Learning to Read the Room

Part of mastering nuance is learning to read the room; picking up the unspoken energy in a situation. It's body language, tone, and undercurrents that often say more than words. This isn't some psychic trick. It's about sharpening awareness so you can adjust on the fly, lead effectively, and avoid missing signals everyone else sees but doesn't say out loud.

Ignore this, and even solid principles backfire because you're blind to the context. Nail it, and you can turn tension into opportunity - whether in business *or* relationships.

Business Setting

You're in a team meeting pitching a bold pivot for your company's marketing strategy. The room's tense - your boss is fidgeting with his pen, arms crossed, while a couple colleagues nod but avoid eye contact, and the new intern looks wide-eyed and overwhelmed. The air feels heavy, like pushback is brewing under the surface.

The "Black-and-White" Approach

You barrel through with rigid "lead with facts" unplugging - hammer your data points, ignore the vibes, and demand buy-in right then. The likely outcome? Your boss shuts you down defensively, colleagues resent the pressure, meeting derails into arguments, and your idea gets shelved while your reputation takes a hit for seeming tone-deaf.

The More Nuanced Approach

You read the room quickly - test the waters gently and weave in a relatable nod like "I see this pivot's a big shift; I've felt that with past changes too." Acknowledge the tension: "Looks like there's some hesitation here - let's break it down: what stands out as a win or worry?" The likely outcome? Your boss relaxes and shares their concerns, the team opens up collaboratively, you adjust the pitch on the spot, your idea gets greenlit with tweaks, and you build an alliance for future plays.

Tribe Setting

You're at a men's group meet-up. One guy's venting hard about his divorce. He's emotional, rambling, circling the same points.

The "Black-and-White" Approach

You shut him down cold with: "Man up, stop whining." The likely outcome? He feels dismissed, the room turns awkward, and other men stop sharing openly. The group fractures.

The More Nuanced Approach

You hold the frame but give space. Let him unload for five minutes while others lean in. Then you pivot: "Alright, brother, we hear you. Let's break down what you can control next week." Now the venting becomes action. The likely outcome? He feels heard, the group bonds tighter, and everyone leaves stronger.

Bottom line: Reading the room in male spaces builds trust and brotherhood; missing it fractures the tribe.

Learning to Sub-Communicate Better

Once you can read the room, the next step is sub-communication; the art of sending powerful signals without spelling them out. This is body language, posture, humor that lands, how you dress, how you carry yourself, even your physique. You're *always* broadcasting something, whether you realize it or not.

Women often complain that men need to "communicate better," but what they're really pointing at is this. They're hinting at this - somewhat ironically - through their own sub-communication.

Here's the reality: if you're overweight, dressed poorly, and slouched, you're sub-communicating that you don't care about yourself or your discipline. Fair or not, people assume you're also sloppy in other areas of life.

Flip it around: if you're in shape, well-dressed for the setting, wearing a clean watch, standing tall with a calm smile, you sub-communicate competence, pride, and self-respect. People respond to that before you ever open your mouth.

It's the same in public speaking. If you mumble, fill space with "umms," and avoid eye contact, you're broadcasting discomfort and lack of confidence. If you stand tall, pause when needed, look around the room, and speak slowly and clearly, you project authority. Whether you like it or not, people judge based on these signals.

Now imagine the extremes: a sloppy man fumbling through a talk versus a fit, sharp-dressed man who owns the room with pauses, presence, and eye contact. Both are saying something without words. One loses the room instantly, the other wins it before his content even lands.

Business Setting

You're negotiating a partnership with a potential investor at a networking event. The guy's guarded, arms folded, but mentions offhand his firm's struggling with scaling ops - he's testing if you're the real deal, eyeing your confidence and presence amid the crowd's buzz.

The "Black-and-White" Approach

You go overt by trying to "sell yourself" rigidly and launch into a scripted pitch reciting stats and credentials, ignoring the vibe, leaving no pauses for his reactions. The likely outcome? He tunes out, sees you as desperate or robotic, brushes you off with a polite no, and the deal evaporates along with any network ripple.

The More Nuanced Approach

Learn to stand tall with open posture, be comfortable enough to crack a quick, relatable joke about a relatable situation from your past (if you're competent enough to use situational humor), and learn how to hold eye contact *just* long enough to show your frame (without staring him down and making yourself look weird).

Acknowledge subtly: "Scaling's a beast; I've streamlined it for outfits like yours - let's walk through a quick demo if it fits." The likely outcome? He leans in, laughs, feels your edge without the hard sell, opens up on his hurdles, inks the partnership on the spot, and loops you into his circle for ongoing wins.

Relationship Setting

Your woman's just arrived at your place for the evening, fresh from a long day - she's smiling but tense, testing the energy as she steps in, her body language open but expectant, like she's gauging if you'll lead or fumble.

The "Black-and-White" Approach

Rigid "show desire" means you verbalize it all - blurt out how hot she looks, ask if she's okay, over-explain your plans. The likely outcome? She feels smothered by the wordiness, tension fizzles into awkward chat, desire cools, and the night drags without that spark.

The More Nuanced Approach

You read her vibe and you confidently pin her up against the wall with *just enough* firm grip (no struggle, showing her that you're in control of not only your strength, but of her as well), lock eyes with her a beat longer to build tension, hover close to her mouth with yours without *quite* kissing her, flash a her a smirk with light humor like "Rough day? Don't worry, I know how to get rid of that tension for you…"

It both simultaneously and subconsciously broadcasts to her about your competence, frame, and pull through physique and presence. The likely outcome? She melts into the tension, laughs breathlessly, feels that raw desire spike, pulls you in deeper, and the connection heats up fast, turning a routine night into something electric.

Bottom line: Sub-communication is frame made visible. You don't tell people who you are - you show it, and they respond accordingly. Show, don't tell.

Managing Non-Exclusive Relationships

Should you (as a man who's clearly demonstrated enough competence and created enough value in your life) wish to exercise your optionality when it comes to sleeping with multiple women, then it's *critical* to understand that there's more than one way you can approach such a dynamic. Also, the fact that this is the *very* last talking point in the book (which is intentional), should tell you that this really isn't for men who think it'll be some walk in the park (because - *at best* - it's a never-ending field of emotional landmines that you must learn how to navigate safely). However, it is **absolutely** possible and - when done with enough care and proper emotional management of all the women involved on your part - it can be a *very* rewarding and memorable experience for all involved.

While a woman with a solid 10/10 GBD for you will (more often than not) look the other way if you're not rubbing your "extracurricular activities" in her face, you'll often find that she'll be more inclined to join you as more women than ever are bi-curious (if they're not out-right bi-sexual). Let's take a closer look at some of these "Ethical Non-Monogamy" frameworks a bit more closely and then how not to approach it, and then better ways to see if this will work for everyone involved.

Spinning Plates

This is the classic casually dating multiple women at once approach and is usually the first path that men (who've worked hard) take once they note that they now have an abundance of female options available to them.

The "Black-and-White" Approach

You go full caveman: you tell your LTR she has no say in the matter, that you'll sleep with other women because "that's just what I'm going to do," and that she can either take it or leave it. You parade your side women openly, post about them on social media, and treat discretion as weakness. This is the blunt-force method - no tact, no calibration, just demand and decree.

The More Nuanced Approach

Spinning plates is about optionality - but that optionality requires constant management (i.e. to "keep those plates spinning"). If you're looking to date multiple women casually, then have the conviction and the balls to be crystal clear that you're non-exclusive from the start. Vagueness at the start only creates drama later on, when women assume you're committed to them. A simple, matter-of-fact statement early on in the dating phase "I don't do exclusivity right now, I'm focused on my business/career" sets the frame without the theatrics. Women with 9-10/10 GBD for you will at least consider the option seriously. The rest won't.

If you're in a LTR and still want to exercise options, then true discretion and discipline are non-negotiable. That means managing logistics cleanly, avoiding overlaps, keeping drama out of your home (e.g. stray hairs - stray hairs were the bane of my fucking life - not even joking, or them intentionally leaving their personal items around for other women to find), and **never** letting side women feel that they have leverage over your main relationship. Your LTR's safety and sense of respect have to remain intact, or the whole structure collapses.

The nuance is knowing where you stand in the sexual marketplace and what you can *actually manage*. High-value men can spin plates without breaking a sweat because they have the bandwidth, status, and demand to support it. Just remember, the more women you see at any one time, the more bullshit and drama you're risking. However, only you can decide where your "sweetspot" is when it comes to this.

Bi-Curious/Bi-Sexual Women

These days there's a much higher chance of finding a single woman that is at least *somewhat* curious to know what it would be like to be with a woman (however, as they're known as "unicorns," they're not easy to find). One way to get a feel for trying this approach with your LTR is to bring it up in the bedroom as a dream you had of watching her with another woman, and then calibrating how you proceed based on how she responds.

The "Black-and-White" Approach

You tell a woman that if she's not willing to sleep with another woman for you, then she's clearly frigid, that she's "not the one for you" and that you'll "go and find someone else who will."

The More Nuanced Approach

Unless she's hot-to-trot from the beginning, don't go dashing out the gate to find another woman like a bull in a china shop. Instead, you'll need to warm her up one stage at a time. I'd recommend taking her out to a casual social setting (I like taking my LTR out clubbing as we both love the music, we both love to dance, and her dancing with me attracts women like moths to a flame, but work with what setting you're both most comfortable with) and then dare her to kiss a woman in front of you.

If she's game, then you can - very slowly - take it to the next level either later on (e.g. watch her and the other women grope each other while they kiss), tell her how sexy she looks, and then stop (unless she's now all-in). You're now working with the ever-changing emotional state of **two** women at once (one of which will need you to make her feel *very* safe throughout as she'll be on high-alert for you negatively judging her). A lot of positive reinforcement helps and it's also just as important to make sure that *you* get to have the final say on who gets to join both of you - she should trust you to set the frame and the boundaries to keep your relationship safe.

Finally, women don't like to hurt the feeling of other women, so **you** need to be the one to lead this dynamic from start to finish - even if it means being the one to - gently - let a woman down who doesn't meet your high standards. How many steps you take to get it to the full-on Female-Male-Female (FMF) or Male-Female-Female (MFF) threesome depends on how unsure your LTR was at the start. Start slow and work your way up from there.

Swinging

The biggest issue with swinging is that you are - quite literally - inviting another man to fuck your girl and thus "poison the well" (which Rich made clear was a *very* bad idea earlier in this book). It's certainly not for me but, as Rich always says, we're not the penis police, so it's up to you whether or not you want to go down this road (just know it's one of the dynamics with the highest risks of things going horribly wrong).

The "Black-and-White" Approach

You don't hint, you don't warm her up, and you don't negotiate. You flat-out tell her you want to swing, that if she won't get on board then she's holding you back, and that you'll happily find a woman who will. You spring it on her like a command: "We're going out this weekend," only for her to realize you've marched her into a swinging club without warning. The message is clear: her only options are to play along, or be replaced.

The More Nuanced Approach

However, it absolutely **is** one way to sleep with other women and - for the women involved at least - it'll seem "fairer." It's also crucial to understand that, because women tend to bond to each man they sleep with, you're running the risk of your LTR developing some feelings for the other man, while also running the - very real - risk of her not feeling very safe or loved if she thinks you're wanting to hand her off to another man, just so you can fuck another woman.

However, if you're *still* dead set on trying this dynamic (which isn't new, especially in high-net worth circles - think masquerade balls in mansions), then you'll no doubt be able to find a "lifestyle" swinging club in a major city near you. My LTR's friend has gotten into this lifestyle via her boyfriend and (based on my LTR's friend's reports), let's just say that the quality of the women you'll find in the clubs will be "variable" (at best). The best looking women in that lifestyle are *far* more likely to be at the invite-only balls, but you'll likely need to bring your networking A-game out to get invited to such events if you're not in their trusted circle.

Bottom line: This is just a few of the options available to a man on the top shelf who want to sleep with multiple women. However, inviting other women into your life isn't a free ride. Whether your LTR's on board or you're playing discreetly, you own ***every*** consequence. The highs, the lows, the drama, the fallouts - it **all** belongs to you. If you can't lead your LTR safely through any of those emotional minefields, then don't even start."

In Conclusion

It all starts with mastering the basics Rich lays out. Those are non-negotiable. Without them, you've got no foundation to build on. But once you've absorbed those fundamentals, the next level is nuance; knowing when to bend, when to adjust, and how to fit the principle to the situation without losing your frame.

Ten years ago, I didn't have this skill. I lived like an unhappy man-child, clinging to rigid thinking and wondering why life wasn't working. Today, I live on my own terms. Not perfect, but a *hell* of a lot better; because I learned to apply Rich's concepts with subtle tweaks that fit my passions, goals, and circumstances.

I am my own mental point of origin. The good, the bad, the unforeseen consequences - they're mine, and I own them all. That's the final stage of unplugging: unapologetic living, built on strength, but guided by nuance. Ultimately: master the basics, then learn to dial them in. Rules alone will box you in. Nuance frees you to live as the man you choose to be.

The real prize isn't memorizing rules or parroting lines - it's mastering yourself. You've seen the foundations, you've tested them in business, relationships, and life. Now comes the highest tier: adapting with strength, leading with awareness, and owning **every** choice - without apology. That's nuance. That's freedom. And it's what separates the men still learning from the men who live as they choose. Go build your life on your own terms - and **never** look back.

The Cold, Hard Truth

Never forget:

- **Nuance adapts principles:** Core truths never change, but life is messy, dial them up or down to fit the moment. Rigidity kills opportunities; flexibility keeps you sharp.
- **Black-and-white thinking is a trap:** All-or-nothing logic boxes you in. For men on the spectrum especially, scanning the gray is non-negotiable. Miss it and you'll miss cues, deals, and desire.
- **Learn to read the room:** Energy, tone, body language, and silence carry more weight than words. Ignore them and you'll look blind. Tune in and you can turn tension into wins.
- **Sub-communicate with strength:** Your posture, presence, physique, humor, and pauses broadcast more than words ever will. Say less, signal more; your frame is felt, not explained.
- **Dials over switches:** Principles aren't on/off rules. They're adjustable settings. Learn when to turn them up, and when to back them down. Rules alone are brittle; dials let you bend without breaking.
- **Own the consequences:** Every choice, win or loss, belongs to you. No blaming, no excuses. Owning outcomes is what separates men who live by rules from men who lead with awareness.
- **Nuance is freedom:** Memorizing scripts keeps you trapped. Learning to adjust with strength frees you to lead your own life, your own way - without apology.

18

Acknowledgements

I've learned that a good book, that is also a useful book, is the collective efforts of many people.

My editor, "*Steve From Accounting*" who shall remain anonymous, was pivotal in the editing and marketing process of this and my prior book. Without his fastidious attention to detail in the editing process I would never have been able to produce any of this on my own. He was also invaluable in adding his own field reports in the 2nd Edition and full chapters in this book.

Chris Moffett (aka: Moff), and the men in my community who provided feedback on the early copy of this book, adding a final touch of refinement that ensured clarity and completeness. Appreciate the help brothers.

To my fans, who all encouraged me to continue to write and publish another book.

A **big** shout out to my haters, who if I'm being honest, are confused admirers. Nobody watches me harder, or talks about me more than the people who think they hate me. Without you constantly talking about me and my ideas, I would never have gotten amplified as much as I have.

Dr. Orion Taraban, who wrote a fantastic book called "The Value of Others" and publishes great videos on YouTube, has been pivotal in furthering my own unplugging.

I'd also like to acknowledge the following people for contributing to my own unplugging:

Dr. David Buss, Dr. Warren Farrell, Jack Donovan, Dr. Stephanie Coontz, Cindy Meston, Dr. Kevin Leman, Neil Strauss, Robert Glover, Christopher Ryan, Esther Perel, Robert Greene, Caleb Jones, Robin Baker, Tom Ingoglia, Cameron Harold, Dr. Shawn T. Smith, Andrew & Tristan Tate, Casey Jones, Alan Roger Currie, Philip McKernan, Steve Sims, Aaron Clarey, Rian Stone, and Rollo Tomassi.

www.ingramcontent.com/pod-product-compliance
Lightning Source LLC
Chambersburg PA
CBHW061725070526
44583CB00024B/3009